Praise For
SŬBMARINE-ĔR

After thirty years in the Navy, Jerry Pait—who calls himself "a brutally honest person"—tells it all. I've never read an autobiography quite like this, one that lets us feel what it is really like to serve as an enlisted man and officer in the Navy. At times adventurous and humorous, the author describes how he physically risked his life underwater and also discovered that a Soviet spy had moved right across the street from him. Want to know what caused the tragic explosion of the *Challenger* in 1986? Lieutenant Commander Pait reveals this as well as how it felt to almost die when an engine ignited. On occasion, he will even turn playful and pull the reader's leg. *Sŭbmarine-ĕr* is an inspiring, heart-warming, and heart-wrenching memoir by an authentic American hero.

– Professor John B. Rosenman
Norfolk State University
Author of *The Inspector of the Cross Series*

SŬBMARINE-ĔR, Lt. Cmdr. Jerry Pait semi-autobiographical history of his thirty years in and around the U.S. Navy's submarine fleet, shows us a side of naval operations rarely seen by outsiders, or indeed even many insiders. His highly entertaining anecdotal style kept me reading through his tales of events whether light-hearted or tragic (and there are both here). I highly recommend this book to anyone with even a passing interest in the subject matter, it's a great read!

– Alastair Mayer
Author of *The T-Space Series*

SŬBMARINE-ĔR is so interesting and brings back so many memories, I hate to put it down. At one time while I was in, there were five of us from Hamlet and Rockingham in the submarine service. The book looks great and I am so proud of you.

– Nelson Gainey
USS Nathan Hale (SSBN-623)
USS Sennet (SS-408)

Wow, what a life. You are one of the strongest men that I have ever met.

– Paul Kenard

I had many occurrences to work with you during my years at the Cape beginning as one of only two First-Class Missile Technicians at NOTU and eventually retiring as the Documentation Engineering Manager at Lockheed with twenty-two of my total of thirty-four years (NOTU, VITRO, SP205 and Lockheed). Never once did I ever hear anyone say a discouraging word about you. In fact, just the opposite. You were an officer and a gentleman—as well as a true professional. It was an absolute pleasure to know and work with you. I might also add, those individuals I know whom you mentioned in *SŬBMARINE-ĔR* were just as you described them.

– Bruce A. Campbell

Really enjoy your stories in *SŬBMARINE-ĔR*. A different perspective.

– Dan Jackson Jr.

Your stories in *SŬBMARINE-ĔR* are awesome. Some of the best I've ever read. I feel like I'm there when I read them.

– Séan Núnléy

Love your stories. Thanks.

– Everett J. Goff

Thank you for the great story. I enjoyed reading *SŬBMARINE-ĚR*.

– Richard R. Beauregard

SŬBMARINE-ĚR is excellent writing. I could envision the whole story. Amazing! Thanks for beautiful memories of the early 80s.

– Teri Jean

Great story telling! *SŬBMARINE-ĚR* brought back many memories of so long ago. Thanks for sharing, Brother!

– Ron Griffith

Wow! Sounds very stressful. *Bravo Zulu*, Sir!!!

– Glenn E. Oaks

Outstanding story. Me, I could barely get through quals. You are a credit to America, Sir.

– Barry Corkery

Thank you my brother for your wonderful stories in *SŬBMARINE-ĚR*. Sharing the committed love you have for Dee says more than anyone can imagine in this world. You sure have been given a life time of trials and tribulations in the chapters of your life.

– Steve Aumen Sr.

After all the joy you've brought us through *SŬBMARINE-ĚR*, I am in your debt for the reality you presented us. Now, after reading the last chapter, you are in our prayers.

– Bob Dobbe

SŬBMARINE-ĔR

30 Years of Hijinks & Keeping the Fleet Afloat

SŬBMARINE-ĔR

30 Years of Hijinks & Keeping the Fleet Afloat

JERRY PAIT
Lieutenant Commander, USN (Ret.)

Compiled by Robert G. Williscroft
Author of the Bestselling *Mac McDowell* Missions

Fresh Ink Group
Guntersville

SŬBMARINE-ËR:
30 Years of Hijinks & Keeping the Fleet Afloat

Fresh Ink Group
An Imprint of:
The Fresh Ink Group, LLC
1021 Blount Avenue #931
Guntersville, AL 35976
Email: info@FreshInkGroup.com
FreshInkGroup.com

Edition 1.0 2022

Compiled by Robert G. Williscroft
Cover by Stephen Geez / FIG
Artwork by Jerry Pait & Robert G. Williscroft
Book design by Amit Dey / FIG
Associate Publisher Lauren A. Smith / FIG

BISAC Subject Headings:
BIO008000 BIOGRAPHY & AUTOBIOGRAPHY/ Military
BIO026000 BIOGRAPHY & AUTOBIOGRAPHY/Personal Memoirs
BIO034000 BIOGRAPHY & AUTOBIOGRAPHY/Aviation & Nautical

LCCN: 2022911530

ISBN-13: 978-1-947893-55-9 Papercover
ISBN-13: 978-1-947893-56-6 Hardcover
ISBN-13: 978-1-947893-57-3 Ebook

Table of Contents

About the Title

The term *submariner,* as used in the U.S. Navy, is pronounced *submarine-er,* meaning someone who rides submarines. The British pronunciation is *sub-mariner.* In the U.S., this pronunciation designates a below-par mariner. In a submarine bar, to call a submarine sailor a sub-mariner is to invite an immediate honor challenge.

Primus Inter Pares
—First Among Equals

Strange, the things you remember. The people, the places, the moments in time burned into your heart forever, while others fade in the mist. I've always known I've lived a life different from other men. And when I was a lad, I saw no path before me. I took a step and then another. Ever forward, ever onward. Rushing towards someplace, I know not where. And one day, I turned around, and looked back, and saw that each step I'd taken was a choice. To go left, to go right, to go forward, or even not go at all. Every day, every man has a choice, between right and wrong, between love and hate. Sometimes, between life and death. And the sum of those choices becomes your life. The day I realized that, I became a man.

The voice of *The Outlander*
James Alexander Malcolm Mackenzie Fraser,
by Diana Gabaldon

There are no roses on a sailor's grave,
No lilies on an ocean wave.
The only tribute is the seagulls' sweeps,
And the teardrops that a sweetheart weeps.

Unknown World War II Poet

Dedication

To my wife, who served twenty-six of my thirty years with me.
She raised four magnificent, successful sons.

Foreword

by
Captain George W. Jackson USN (Ret.)
aka G. William Weatherly

Jerry Pait has added a unique autobiography to the world of literature. First and foremost, he presents some of the finest traditions, opportunities, and experiences that the United States Navy Submarine Force is noted for. Most submarine biographies are written about officers, and few, if any, document the lives and experiences of the *Chiefs* and *Petty Officers* that are the backbone of the service. His leadership style and pushing authority to the lowest levels in the organizations he ran are worthy of emulation. Similarly, he never ducks the responsibilities of his assignments and endeavors to protect his people whenever possible. There are lessons here for every aspiring naval officer.

In every command, Jerry displayed the excellence of character and performance that marked him for promotion and increasingly important assignments. Neither of us realized it at the time, but our paths crossed several times. First, when I was a midshipman first-class on summer cruise on the *USS Bang,* alongside the *USS Hunley* for refit, and later, on many of my trips to Cape Canaveral and the wonderful people at the Naval Ordnance Test Unit (NOTU) that made every trip a delight. I have great memories of the *Green House* that he mentions as a place for lunches. For attack submarine crews on port visits or doing torpedo load-outs, it was a welcome site for a cold beer or other beverage.

His language and usage reflect Navy culture and may require some readers to do Google searches of the euphemisms that are common within the military and add to the authenticity of his writing style—and be sure to check the Glossary. As he explains, he is brutally honest in his appraisal of how the Navy has changed over his thirty years of service. But that is a function of how far removed from the operating forces any command is, and once he returned to NOTU, even in the age of political correctness and congressional oversight, the emphasis on doing well without favor or bias was again evident. Having lived through the early retirement boards, there is no doubt in my mind that he would have been selected for Commander (O-5) and been recognized for outstanding performance if only his detailer had sent him the orders to the White House a week earlier.

Fate dealt him and his wife cruel blows after he retired, but he has met them with the same fortitude and perseverance that his career epitomized.

G. William Weatherly is the pen name Captain Jackson uses to write his alternative history novels of WWII naval thrillers. Sheppard of the Argonne *and* Sheppard and the French Rescue *are available through his website: www.gwmweatherly.com and Amazon.com.*

Disclaimer

*Everything in this book is true
except for the parts I made up.*

PART ONE
Diesel Boat

My Submarine School section. I am on the far left, kneeling.

CHAPTER ONE

You're in the Navy Now!

HOLY CRAPOLA!

In the beginning, God created heaven and hell. Hell includes, among other things, a fifteen-foot-long steel tube, seven feet in diameter. Inside are two rows of benches for the chamber victims to sit facing each other. Aside from valve wheels, gauges, and thick glass small portholes, there is one instructor and one diving medicine Navy Corpsman. The operators controlling the high-pressure air are on the outside. The diving medicine corpsman is there to assist you if you have a seizure. The instructor is in there to assist the corpsman if you freak out.

I was eighteen. I joined a group of fellow submarine hopefuls inside the chamber, filling all the available seats. Was I scared? Not really, but I certainly was apprehensive.

"Once the HP air flows, swallow if you feel pressure on your ears," the instructor said. "If that doesn't clear your ears, squeeze your nose and blow 'til you feel your ears pop—we call this the Valsalva maneuver. If your ears still don't clear, raise your hand. We'll bring you back to the surface." He looked at each of us sternly. "Try to stay ahead of the pressure."

HP air began flowing into the chamber with a deafening roar. The air got hot and clammy, my heart raced, and all my senses came to immediate high alert. I swallowed and swallowed, my ears popping each time. Then it started to get ahead of me. My ears began to ache, especially my right one. I squeezed my nose and blew hard: Pop! Pop! And then the pressure increased again. Squeeze—blow—pop! Squeeze—blow—pop! I heard screaming, and it wasn't me. Squeeze—blow—pop!

The HP roar stopped, and I could feel the pressure dropping as snot flowed out my nostrils. After a minute or so, the pressure equalized, the door opened, and the problem child was removed for evaluation. The rest of us got to start over.

Once again, the HP roar and the heat... Squeeze—blow—pop! Squeeze—blow—pop! Squeeze—blow—pop! Finally, we reached thirty-three feet, and the roar stopped. Cool air entered the chamber, removing some of the heat. I started to ask a question, but my voice sounded funny. The instructor scowled at me.

"Everyone sit quietly and don't talk," the instructor ordered. "We're gonna be here for five minutes." His voice sounded funny, too.

The corpsman constantly scanned both rows to detect anyone about to convulse. I felt fine. The five minutes seemed to last forever. Finally, the vent valve opened, and the chamber pressure began to drop. The air got cold, and fog filled the chamber.

"It's okay, people," the instructor said. "This is normal."

Now, the fun part began. The next level of hell was a steel blister on the side of the Escape Tower, fifty feet from the top. It had no seats, unlike the chamber, and we were packed in like sardines.

"Listen up, people," the instructor said. There was no corpsman this time. "We're pressing down to fifty feet, but we're doing it wet. Water will fill from the bottom while HP air pressurizes the top."

Before they stuffed us into that blister, our instructor thoroughly briefed us on what would happen and what we would do. I had been SCUBA diving since I was fifteen, so I was looking forward to it—mostly.

HP air roared into the blister, and water began rising around my ankles. Swallow—swallow—equalize that pressure! The water rose as the pressure increased rapidly. Squeeze—blow—pop! Squeeze—blow—no-pop! Again—no-pop! I raised my hand.

They backed up a foot. Squeeze—blow—pop! I gave the instructor a thumbs-up, and we continued down. One of the other guys held up his hand at forty feet. He cleared his ears in a few seconds, and shortly thereafter, we reached fifty feet.

"Okay, people, inflate your life vests," the instructor told us. His voice was even more distorted than in the chamber at thirty-three feet.

By this time, the water was up to my chest and had covered the top of the watertight door into the main escape tank. Someone opened the door to the main tank. All of us started moving toward the door, staying as close as possible to the person in front. When I reached the door, I took a deep breath and ducked underwater to pass through the door. Still holding my breath, I stood on the platform outside the door. The water was crystal clear. Even though I was not wearing a facemask, I could clearly see the bottom seventy feet below and the surface fifty feet above. Two SCUBA divers held me down. When I gave them the OK sign, they released me. As instructed, I started blowing as hard as I could while rising toward the surface.

Another diver with a SCUBA tank rode up with me to ensure I exhaled all the way to the surface. If I had stopped exhaling, the rider would have hit me in the stomach to force me to exhale continuously. No need to breathe in, of course. As I rose, the compressed air in my lungs expanded rapidly. If I had not continuously exhaled, I would have embolized or even ruptured my lungs and not be any good to anyone.

The trip to the surface seemed to last forever but was less than ten seconds. Both I and my rider popped through the surface almost to our waists. I gave the okay sign, a circle with my thumb and forefinger, the other fingers pointed up. If I had forgotten to do so, I would have really upset many people. They would have dragged me out of the water in a heartbeat to make sure I was okay. I swam to the edge, climbed out, and stood at parade rest along with the others so we could be observed for any possible after-effects.

So, now that I got your attention, let me take you back to the beginning.

THE BEGINNING

I graduated from Hamlet High School in Hamlet, NC, in 1964. Upon graduation, I had four options: college, work, wait to be drafted, or join the military.

Bill Maples, a longtime friend, and I decided to join the Navy on the Buddy Plan and volunteer for submarines. There were several others from Hamlet on subs at the time. Nelson Gainey was the closest to our age, and we knew him well. He served on the *USS Nathan Hale* (SSBN-623), the *USS Sennet* (SS-408), and was a navy diver.

September 1964 was our month to enlist. We were given a choice, Great Lakes or San Diego. Not wanting to freeze, we chose San Diego. Bill qualified for the Nuclear Power Program, and due to my extraordinary hearing ability, I was designated to enter the Submarine Sonar Program.

SONAR SCHOOL & SUB SCHOOL

After boot camp, Bill went to Mare Island, and I went to Sonar School across the street from boot camp. It was a very technical school involving oceanography, all kinds of math, Trig, Logarithms, and whatever was required to determine how sound traveled underwater. The class did not include any troubleshooting of sonar equipment. My sonar class began with twenty-two students. Nine weeks later, only eleven graduated, and everyone headed to Submarine School in Groton, Connecticut.

Before beginning Sub School, we were subjected to physiology testing and interviews, pressure chambers and submarine underwater escape training, and a submarine physical. Many did not make it through those. If you passed, next was the dentist. If you had wisdom teeth, they were removed to avoid possible later problems at sea. Mine did not go willingly.

Next, Submarine School. All my fellow Sonar School graduates passed Sub School. Keep in mind, I was still an eighteen-year-old boy from little ole Hamlet. Talk about naive, wet behind the years, and not wise to the ways of the world—that was me. I was about to make some major changes and grow in all areas.

Near graduation, we received orders for our first submarine. A Sub School class contains all ratings. Those who were nuclear trained went to nuclear powered boats. The rest of the class could go to any sub out there. A fellow sonarman, Paul Rompel, and I received orders to WWII diesel boats. These WWII pig boats, as they were called, were brought back to active service after being overhauled and given upgraded equipment. I was not very happy with my orders.

After graduation, I walked down to the lower base and reported to my first submarine, the *USS Entemedor* (SS-340).

My first submarine, the USS Entemedor..

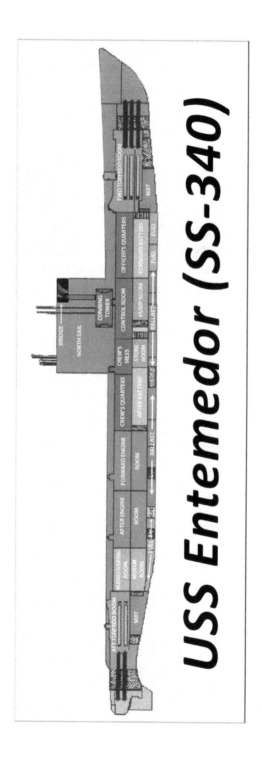

USS Entemedor (SS-340)

My first time underway. I was in the Seamen Gang. I was mess cooking, for 90 days, washing dishes and cleaning in the galley. Then back to Seamen Gang. I loved being on the bridge and went up every chance I could. There would come a time, however, when I did not like being on the bridge.

CHAPTER TWO

Submarining Basics

RELIGION, POLITICS & RACE

There are three subjects you never talk about in the submarine service: Religion, politics, and race. After thirty years, I only know the religion of two of my crewmates because we attended the same church in Charleston. Race was never an issue either.

In every boat I served on, the crew looked like the United Nations. Not as diverse as the Brooklyn Tabernacle Choir, but close. Every man got along with everyone, and we are cherished friends to this day. I never heard an unkind word regarding anyone's ethnicity. We, like the *Band of Brothers*, were and always will be submarine brothers. When we have reunions, they are joyous and sad occasions. We rejoice with old shipmates and are saddened by those on Eternal Patrol. Yes, I have a few tears in my eyes. We are that close.

QUALS

As a new member of the crew, and especially as a non-qualified puke, your sole function in life is to get qualified. Submarine qualification goes back to the days when Moby Dick was a minnow. When you report aboard, the Chief-of-the-Boat (COB), who is almost God, will get you settled in. He assigns you a bunk; he shows you how to flush the toilet without sinking the boat. He tells you where you will stand watch in port and at sea, and most importantly, he introduces you to the qualification program.

It is your responsibility to learn every system aboard the boat—electrical, high and low-pressure air, hydraulics, water, sanitary, and ventilation. You must know how to operate every piece of equipment, line up and start the diesels, shoot a torpedo, and on and on. Learning systems means drawing the entire system on a piece of paper from memory showing all valves and switches, and how to isolate each part, and all masts and antennas, and their function. Until you are qualified, you do not watch movies, play cards, or do anything other than your job and qualify at your watch station.

Even if you report aboard from another boat, you have to requalify on the new one. It is much easier, however, to requalify the second time.

Qualification is the most critical job in your life. Everyone onboard depends on everyone else. Suppose there is flooding or an electrical fire in a compartment that you may be passing through. In that case, you have to take action immediately. There is none of this standing around and yelling fire or flooding, hoping someone will show up who knows what to do.

From the day you report aboard, you have one year to complete this process. You will turn in your card weekly, or you die. At specific points in the process, you must get a *group* signature. In addition to getting signed off on every system, you sit down with a qualified person. He asks you all manner of questions about four to eight systems in a group to make sure you know those systems.

At the end of the qualification process, you do a compartment walk-through with a person who works in that compartment. For example, the Forward Torpedo Room walk-through would be a senior torpedoman who owns that space and knows more about it than most on the boat. After all the compartment signatures are obtained, you have a walk-through with an officer, and he asks you all kinds of things you never heard before. Any question you cannot answer, you write it down, look it up and return to him with your answer.

The final step is a sit-down board with at least four senior crew members, and they ask you questions about everything on board and what you would do in different situations. There are many system drawings. If you pass, the board forwards your qual card to the Executive Officer (XO) and then to the Commanding Officer (CO). Then and only then are you presented with your Enlisted Submarine Dolphins. It usually is done topside with all hands present to witness. Everyone pats you on the back, shakes your hand, and then throws you over the side, summer or winter.

I believe the day an individual qualifies for the first time is the most important day in their life. Now they are officially part of the crew.

If you do not complete submarine qualifications in one year, you are transferred out of the submarine service. Everyone is given one month grace on quals, but there are NO do-overs, extensions, or participation trophies. When I turned in my qual card, I was one month ahead, which is good.

I was very fortunate; the first dolphins I earned are the same dolphins I wore for thirty years. I never lost them, and they are in my retirement shadow box.

Don't worry; I will get to the good stuff shortly.

Submarine Escape Tower at Submarine Base New London in Groton, Connecticut. It was used between 1930 and 1994 when it was razed. I trained there.

View from inside the tank at the new Momsen Hall Submarine Escape Trainer at Submarine Base New London in Groton, Connecticut. It was inaugurated in 2007.

CHAPTER THREE

Submarine Escape Training

THE TOWER

I thought I might add a bit of nostalgia—submarine escape training. Both Sub Base New London and Sub Base Pearl Harbor had escape training tanks. They were 120 feet deep and thirty feet wide, and they were heated.

On the outside of the tank were *blisters* at various depths. Escape training was conducted at fifty feet. The blister was large enough to hold ten men. They crammed sixteen men inside, closed the outside hatch, and began flooding and pressurizing the blister.

Inside, you are holding your nose and popping your ears as fast as you can. Heat is building as air is pressurized, water is rising, and it is very loud. If you have a scintilla of claustrophobia, you totally become a raving maniac. You want out, and you want out NOW!

Claustrophobia is not something you can attend classes for and work it out. You have to live with it, but not on board a submarine. We didn't have any fancy one-piece suits, Momsen lungs, or Steinke hoods. We did it the old-fashioned way—with an inflatable life jacket and no face covering, called blow and go.

None of this was designed to help you survive if your sub sank. The depths where we normally operated were way too deep for survival. Maybe if your boat sank in the channel, you could use this. I believe it was mostly for mothers and wives—to satisfy them. Perhaps the main purpose was to weed out any individual who had a tiny bit of claustrophobia or one who did not know he was claustrophobic.

Submarine Base New London now has a new escape training facility. Basically, it is a large, thirty-seven-foot-deep, twenty-foot-wide pool with simulated escape pods at the bottom. Mostly, the Navy conducts training using a one-piece suit that doubles as an environmental protection rig on the surface. These suits can be used to 600 feet deep. That would have to be some experience, escaping from *that* depth!

My first underway on USS Entemedor.

CHAPTER FOUR

My First Underway

LOOKOUT WATCH

I was still eighteen, my first time underway. We got underway in Long Island Sound. I had no idea what lay ahead, but waterboarding the Officer-of-the-Deck (OOD) and Lookouts would be part of the drill.

When the *Entemedor* operated in the North Atlantic, the weather was, at best, totally unpredictable. There were no satellites to help the weather guessers make an erroneous forecast. Today, they have many satellites and still can't get it right. I digress.

No matter how accurate or inaccurate the forecast, as a diesel submarine, we would have to stay on the surface during rough weather—unlike nuke wimps. They go deeper when they feel the boat rock. Don't want to upset their delicate tranquility as they quietly glide along at comfortable temperature, humidity, and all gases finely tuned to keep everyone a happy camper.

I can't imagine ever seeing anyone on a nuke boat puking in a clear plastic bag for everyone to see while standing watch, or wearing a #10 can around his neck to barf in without leaving his watch station.

When the weather raised its ugly head in the North Atlantic, we stayed on the surface. The OOD and two lookouts, dressed (hopefully) for the worst possible conditions, climbed the ladders toward the light, and prayed they did not drown while on watch. The third lookout stayed in the Conning Tower, on the helm. Lookouts and the helmsman rotated watch stations. The poor OOD was stuck up there to be a sacrificial anode. He was lucky to be able to talk after four hours on the roof. Yet, here the three of us were, shaking like a dog trying to pass a peach kernel and expected to be the eyes of the ship and keep everyone below safe.

If you saw the movie *The Perfect Storm* (*Twilight Zone* music playing in the background), imagine the storm in that film represented a typical North Atlantic day. Which class diesel boat you were aboard determined how quickly you would drown as a lookout or OOD. Many boats had a Step Sail, God rest their souls, and others had a North Sail. The only real difference between the two was the North Sail placed the lookouts and OOD twice as high above the waterline. In the North Atlantic, I am positive the waterline no longer existed.

There is a specific place for taking drafts—determining how deep a surfaced sub sits in the water, but that was the furthest thing from our minds. Staying alive was the number one thought. Everyone was dressed in the following: super heavy socks, your regular dungaree pants, and blue long sleeve shirt, a heavy sweater, winter insulated boots, long bib winter overalls, a long winter parka with hood, and on top of that, full waterproof rain gear. God forbid you had to go to the head (bathroom).

Oh, joy of joys. It started to get rough. The bow climbed and climbed up the face of an oncoming wave. I was sure miscellaneous debris below decks left the Forward Torpedo Room and stopped all the way aft in the After Torpedo Room. That would also include people. Those in their bunks would be lying flat one second, standing on their head the next, and then standing on another guy's head, all while sleeping.

Back to the bridge. We finally crested this wave, and there was another massive wall of water waiting its turn at drowning the lookouts. Down we went on the wave we just climbed. We knew what was coming. There was no way we could climb the oncoming wall of water, so the OOD moved as far forward as possible for protection under a plexiglass half bubble, squatted down, and hugged the steel gyro stand. I and the other lookout grabbed our rain gear hood and pulled it down over our faces as far as we could, and prepared to hold our breaths for as long as possible. This is no exaggeration. This is how it was—serious business. Hundreds can verify this is a no-Sh***r.

When the bow hit the bottom of the oncoming wave, the amount of stress placed on the boat caused the submarine to shake like a sailfish trying to throw a hook. Half the boat was still coming down the wave we went over. Talk about stress placed on the hull. I am sure the numbers were off the chart if there was one. I took a quick peek to see when I needed to suck in all the air I could, and at the last second, I yelled to the OOD and other lookout, *Hang on!* and then filled my lungs. You haven't lived until you are on the surface of the ocean but thirty to thirty-five feet underwater.

Because of the fiberglass and steel structure around us, we were spared the full force of the water going by the boat, but it *was* underwater, and the pucker factor was real. Slowly, and I mean slowly, the boat finally rose and broke through the wave, and we could breathe again.

Then I heard the understatement of the year. "Control, Bridge, it is starting to get a little rough; send up three safety harnesses."

I love an OOD with a sense of humor.

"Bridge, Control, aye!" came back.

The OOD looked at us, and we all laughed out loud like crazed pirates walking the plank for funzies.

Of course, the ocean did not stop for us to get better prepared; we continued to repeat and repeat the same thing over and over. Control had already called up and asked us to notify them when it would be safe to open the upper Conning Tower hatch and bring up the harnesses.

He told them he would, but it was too dangerous for anyone to come up; he'd have a lookout come down and wait at the top of the hatch. Then, he looked at me. If I had known that this selection would be the number one curse/blessing on me for my entire thirty-year career, I would have jumped overboard.

I looked like the Michelin Tire cartoon man in all my clothes. As soon as we broke through the next wave, I moved as fast as possible, forced my way out of my lookout position, and got down the ladders as quickly as possible without killing myself. Those metal ladders were incredibly slick when wet. By now, the boat was in a nosedive. The OOD called down on the squawk box screaming, "Open the hatch!" and a split second later, I arrived; the hatch was opening, and as soon as the bag of harnesses came up, I grabbed it and started climbing for my life. I went through the next wave, crouched down next to the OOD, with both of us hugging the gyro mounting. I wasn't that much of a religious man then as I later became, but even though I was raised in the church, I was not thrilled with these baptism forms. Not to go preaching, but that experience in the North Atlantic helped me see the light.

Everyone was wearing a safety harness and chained into place. We still had to hold our breath, rotate the watch without getting killed, and on and on. Then, if you can believe it, the weather started getting worse. I will not say what the OOD exclaimed to us loudly, but he called below and asked permission to shift the watch from the bridge to Conn. I'm pretty sure he had had enough fun for one watch. The Captain came back and told him to make it happen.

First of all, you don't abandon the bridge. You have to rig the bridge for dive, I mean, as if you were diving the boat; what we were going through was not considered a dive. Now things got hairy. Both lookouts, who were standing on top of the sail, unhooked and climbed down to help the OOD rig the bridge and hang on simultaneously. The wind was howling by this time. I imagine those poor nukes had to go deeper again.

Finally, we were ready to make our move. The three of us trying to get down and through the hatch had to be among the most exceptional Chinese fire drills I have ever witnessed. I was first through the hatch and forgot to use the ladder and bounced off the back of the helmsman, and almost fell through the next hatch down into Control. Maybe *forgot* is not the correct word to use. I had two guys on my tail and an open hatch. I was in a hurry and got with the program. I did not want anyone to be held up by me or have millions of gallons of water come pouring through the hatch. Fortunately, with all the padding I was wearing, I didn't even get a bruise.

CONTROL

Control had arranged for a couple of guys to man the scopes while we removed many clothing layers and got those huge life-saving boots off. I cannot imagine being up there with wet feet. After grabbing a cup of black coffee, we headed back up into the Conn. We profusely thanked the guys who filled in for us and stood lookout on the periscopes.

As I look back on this experience, which happened more than once, the weather ended up getting a lot worse. We may not have had an opportunity to safely get below if the OOD had not become upset and called down to shift the watch. Many diesel boats and nukes have had officers and enlisted crew washed over the side in rough weather. In a few instances, the safety harness was the only thing that saved them from certain death.

We were in the Conn, dry, not holding our breaths, nor chained to the sail. We were running on the surface with the snorkel mast raised and the head valve cycling—God, what great memories. The only way you can experience what we went through as volunteers is by waterboarding. How the hell is that torture? We did it standing our watches!

MY ORDEAL ON THE *ENTEMEDOR*

This is where the tears part comes in. I didn't shed any, but my life on board *Entemedor* was about as miserable as it could be.

I reported aboard the same day I graduated from Sub School. At the time, the sonar gang had a Sonar Technician Submarine First-Class (STS1) and two Second-Class (STS2s). According to the COB, they were fully manned, so I was put into the Seamen Gang. When it was my time, I left the Seamen Gang and did my ninety days mess cooking. Then I went back to the Seamen Gang. I stood planes and lookout watches.

Every chance I got while underway, I went to Sonar to spend some time on the gear. We were given one month's grace on turning our qual card in. When I turned mine in, I was already one month ahead on submarine qualifications. I made seaman, and then I made STS3.

I was moved to the sonar gang. I spent one month in Sonar as we traveled to Philly Yards on the surface. Shortly after arrival, all the sonarmen were transferred. Then the boat started sending me back to Groton for schools, including diver's school. I stayed at the Sub Base for several months, going from one school to the next.

All the schools were once over lightly. Similar to an introduction to the equipment and how it worked. No electronics or troubleshooting. I finally returned to the boat about two months before the end of the yard period. Not another sonarman in sight. I was a Leading Petty Officer (LPO) of one.

Our Navigator also had control of Sonar. For some reason, he expected me to know as much as an STS1. He asked me one day if all the field changes had been made. I didn't know what a field change was. He went berserk. In fact, I didn't even know where the sonar gear was in the shipyard. I finally found it by asking around.

I asked one of the shipyard techs what a field change was. He looked at me like I was crazy. I told him I was the only STS on board with zero experience. Thankfully, the techs helped me do field changes on the auxiliary sonar gear, such as the BQC-1 and all the other equipment Sonar was responsible for.

I would ask the XO if and when I could expect other sonarmen to show up. He would always reply, they are ordered in but are in school now. That answer lasted one year. In the meantime, we left the yards, and I had the load. The Navigator almost broke me. Anytime he was on watch and the BQH card needed changing, he had someone wake me to change the card in Control. If the Bearing Time Recorder (BTR) on the Conn jumped, he'd have someone wake me to fix it. I had no clue how to troubleshoot sonar equipment. When we were in port at the

Sub Base, I walked up and down the piers with a tech manual under my arm, knocking on submarine doors, looking for a Chief or STS1 who would help me. Most of the time, I was out of luck and on my own. I finally found a Chief STS who was in total disbelief that I was a sonar gang of one.

I do not remember his name or the boat he was on, but he saved my life and career. Every day, he would come to the *Entemedor*, and we commenced a power training period like I had never seen. I was living on about two hours of sleep a day. The Chief started asking me questions, and all I could say was, "I do not know."

He asked me about the ESL log. I had no clue, again. We started looking around Sonar and finally found it. Every problem that occurred in Sonar was logged in the ESL (Equipment Status Log) along with the solution to repair it. This was back in the tube days. He taught me how to zero synchros and servos. Those items were never mentioned in A-school. Also, how to take resistance readings on each winding to determine if it was bad.

I cannot emphasize enough, the Chief saved my life. Slowly but surely, I began to recognize problems and fix them. When at sea, I finally got some sleep. One of the biggest problems on diesel boats was that the BTR on the Conn would fall behind the master and start going into convulsions trying to catch up. I finally figured out the problem—one cheap 5814-A tube in a cabinet located in the torpedo room. I replaced it and re-zeroed all the synchros.

The next time we went to sea, the squadron Commander rode the boat. He would stand in the Conn and watch the BTR and made several remarks to the CO that we had the only boat in the squadron with a working BTR. The next thing I knew, he wanted to meet me. He shook my hand and congratulated me on a job well done. Before we returned to port, the CO called me to his stateroom. He said the Commodore wanted me to go to every boat in his squadron and fix their BTRs. Holy Crap…like I didn't have enough to do!

I was also in the process of setting up the brand-new Planned Maintenance System (PMS) for Sonar. What a pain that was. We had to do paperwork on dailies in addition to weeklies, monthlies, and quarterlies. Talk about flying blind. That was me.

So, in all my spare time, I was going from boat to boat helping all those guys who would not help me a few months before, fixing their jumping BTRs. I was still an STS3 helping STS1s or STSCs.

About a year out of the yards, I took the STS2 exam and passed. Shortly after I was advanced to STS2, two first-class and two second-class sonarmen reported aboard. Ain't that a bitch.

USS HUNLEY (AS-31)

Sixteen years later, after I was commissioned, we took the sub tender USS *Hunley* to Holy Loch to relieve the *USS Holland* (AS-32). Our track and time of year were almost identical to where we were during my first underway. Compared to a diesel boat, a tender is a huge ship. Your feet on the bridge are eighty-five feet above the water. I would have killed at one time to be eighty-five feet above the ocean. The weather was horrible. All the weather decks were closed; everything that was not bolted or welded to the deck had to be secured. A chain fall on rollers had been missed in the machine shop, and it took a wild goose ride across the machine shop. It ran crazy loose, slinging chain all around, and there was hell to pay to catch and secure it. We had several injured people in sickbay over this thing.

I was Junior-Officer-of-the-Deck (JOOD) on the bridge and telling a few folks about coming through here on a diesel boat. They were having a hard time believing my story. We stood eighty-five feet above the water, and green water was hitting the bridge windows like we were in a small Chris Craft. All of the bridge windows were dogged down tight. On the bridge marine band radio, we heard distress calls one after the other. Ships more substantial than the tender were in trouble and needed help. Every call was plotted. They were too far from us. In my mind, a sub tender with one screw and no thrusters would only add to the disaster. It is hard to believe as old as the *Hunley* was, she weathered the storm just fine.

Seal on the bow of USS Entemedor.

CHAPTER FIVE

Sally

ATLANTIC OFF HALIFAX, NOVA SCOTIA

Late summer '65, we were off Halifax, Nova Scotia, providing target services for tin cans (destroyers) and P-3 type aircraft. During the nights, we'd *lie to* (not moving) on the surface and charge batteries. We would move if a group of fishing trawlers headed our way, usually at one-third speed, just enough forward motion to get out of their way. Fortunately, the weather was good at that time of the year, and the seas were calm. The Gulf Steam comes up through there and moderates the air temp. We were to submerge at sunrise, proceed to a certain depth and play all day.

I had reported aboard my first sub, an updated WWII diesel boat, in May of that year. Everyone in my sub school graduating class had received orders to a nuke fast attack or a missile boat except two of us. I went to the *USS Entemedor*, and my friend Paul Rompel went to the *USS Bang* (SS-385). We had a North Sail, which meant the OOD and lookouts were right at thirty feet above the waterline. It came in handy when operating way up north in thirty-foot-plus seas. Even though I was an STSSA (Submarine Sonar Technician, Seaman Apprentice), I was mess cooking for ninety days, then on to the Seamen Gang. At the time, I wondered what I had done wrong to deserve an assignment to a submarine service relic. After all, my boat had made war patrols in the Pacific. Later, I realized I was a very fortunate submariner; few served on diesel boats before everything went totally nuke. It turned out to be the best years of my submarine career. We worked hard, but we sure as hell played hard on the beach.

As daylight was barely making an appearance, the OOD and lookouts started cleaning up the bridge of coffee cups and foul weather gear. The off lookout climbed up and down with all the equipment. A complete picture (range and bearing) of all contacts was passed below to the quartermaster (QM), so when submerged, we had an idea of where everyone was. Radar hadn't picked up any of the destroyers, but it was still early.

It wouldn't be long before we'd drop below, shut the conning tower hatch, open the vents, and dive to periscope depth before continuing to our ordered depth. Just before we left the bridge, the port lookout spoke up, reporting to the OOD that he thought something was up near the bow but couldn't figure out what it was. Both lookouts and the OOD tried to find it.

"Are you sure?" the OOD asked.

"Yes, sir, I can barely see it. It blends in well."

The OOD called down to Control and told the Chief-of-the-Watch (COW) to send up a battle lantern (large bright light).

About fifteen seconds later, the off lookout came up with the lantern, and the OOD shined it up toward the bow. Almost in unison, all four of us said, "Damn, it's a seal!"

We still had one coffee cup on the bridge. The OOD threw it at the seal to scare it off the boat. The cup missed but shattered and should have frightened it away. The seal did not move.

"Chief-of-the-Watch, ask the Captain to come to the bridge," The OOD ordered.

Shortly, the Captain came up, and the off lookout went below.

"What do you have?" the Captain asked the OOD.

The OOD turned on the lantern and lighted up the seal.

The Captain said the same thing the rest of us had. "How the hell did a seal get on board?"

The OOD said we did not know it was there until the sun started to come up. We had heard nothing during our watch. The Captain leaned over to the comms box and told the COW to get the Chief-of-the-Boat (COB) and a couple of seamen topside through the torpedo room hatch to check out a seal about ten feet forward of the hatch.

The Captain watched the sunrise and his watch. Finally, the Torpedo Room hatch clanked open. Up came the COB and two seamen with flashlights. They moved forward and lighted up the seal. The COB turned around and yelled to the bridge, "It's a seal!"

All of us yelled back, "No sh*t, Sherlock!"

"Is it dead or alive?" the Captain asked.

The COB said he thought it was alive.

"Put it in a blanket, get it below, and have the Doc look at it," the Captain ordered.

As soon as they were below and the torpedo hatch was shut and dogged, the Captain said to the OOD, "I'm going below. As soon as you are ready, submerge the boat."

It takes about three to four seconds to slide down two ladders and a little hop, and then you're inside the conning tower (Conn).

About one minute after the Captain's order, the OOD yelled, "Clear the bridge!" He sounded two blasts on the diving alarm and on the 1MC announced, "Dive! Dive!"

Both lookouts dropped through the Bridge hatch and down as fast as possible, the main vents opened, and the air was being displaced by water as the boat slowly started to sink. The OOD had to be down with the Bridge hatch shut in a hurry. After the OOD dropped through the conning tower hatch, the quartermaster dogged it down tight. If everything didn't work like a Swiss watch, the ocean would start pouring into the *people tank*.

The two lookouts dropped one more level to the Control Room, where they operated the bow and stern planes. The OOD remained in the Conn and raised the #1 periscope. The helmsman was in the very forward part of the Conn and received his course orders from the OOD, who is now the Conning Officer. The lookouts manned the stern planes and bow planes. They made sure they were rigged out and tested. The Diving Officer, who could be an officer, chief, or senior first-class petty officer, stepped into place to monitor the planesmen and relay depth and angle orders from the Conning Officer. It is like *Destination Tokyo* with Cary Grant all over again.

While all this happened, the COB and two seamen took the seal back to the crew's mess and laid it on one of the tables. The Doc checked it out the best he could, took its temp, listened to the heart and lungs, and pressed all around, looking for any broken bones or touchy spots. Finding nothing obvious, he came to the Control Room and briefed the CO and XO on what he found. The Captain thanked him, and the Doc returned to the mess decks.

The rest of the day, we continued playing anti-submarine warfare (ASW) games. We had to make noise; we had to broach, make bubbles, etc., to be found—same old games for the next fifteen years.

It is tempting to stop this story right here, but you probably want to know what happened to the seal.

The CO directed the XO to contact Halifax Port Operations and tell them about the seal. Also, to ask if they could have a marine animal group pick up the seal when we docked the next day. Halifax Port Operations responded that they would look into it and let us know.

From watching movies and WWII footage, you'd think the crew of a submarine would be a bunch of cold, heartless sailors only interested in wine, women, and song. Then you'd be incorrect. We are a strange breed, but what I just related is true; sometimes, we have hearts and can be downright charitable—our other side.

After the Doc said he could not find anything wrong, the cook thought maybe the seal was hungry, so he entered the freezer, opened a case of frozen fish fillets, and brought some back to the galley and thawed them in warm water. The seal and blanket were moved to one side of the mess hall so they would not be in the way. One of the crew suggested we name the seal. Someone suggested Mortimer. Another crew member pointed out it was a female. One of the more devious crew suggested we call it Sally, after the COB's wife. The COB was there at the time, and he would never indicate he disapproved. Once you let a submarine sailor know how they can get to you, you are dead.

We had ourselves, Sally, the seal.

The fish fillets were thawed, and the cook placed them on a plate on the deck near the seal's nose. It wasn't long before the seal picked up one of the fillets and ate it. Everyone cheered. To us, it was a significant event, and word quickly spread throughout the boat.

Now, we needed a place to keep the seal until the boat moored in Halifax.

The most unused spaces on a diesel boat are the two showers. Two men volunteered to remove the trash stored in one shower and get it cleaned and ready. It would be perfect. The tile deck, stainless steel door, and water could be turned on for the seal and to clean the shower deck.

By now, Sally had eaten all the fillets and had even made a few barking sounds. There was no shortage of volunteers who offered to look after the seal until we reached port. Our cooks worked out a routine to keep fillets thawed and ready overnight. When we pulled into Halifax, two men from the Canadian Wildlife division with a special truck with cages were there to take the seal.

Everyone not on watch was topside to see Sally off. As they drove off with Sally, I am sure I saw a few wave bye.

Aerial view of Bermuda

CHAPTER SIX

Kicked out of Bermuda

SHORTY LONG

Our first port visit to Bermuda didn't last long. The sky was very stormy. Our stay was cut short due to a hurricane headed straight for Bermuda. We got underway and out to sea. Sometime after we departed, the storm changed course, missed Bermuda, and ran right over us. Being a diesel boat, we had to ride it out on the surface. Very rough ride but nothing like storms in the North Atlantic; those were majestic.

Our second port visit to Bermuda was for one week. Why, I have no clue. It is the last place I'd go on vacation or pull into for a port visit. *Mucho dinero*, if you know what I mean. The Captain's wife flew in. They had reservations at some fancy resort, and had planned to spend the week together.

Not so fast there, *Gonzo*. At that time, our head cook was *Shorty Long*. Go figure. Shorty was what you would call *a cheap drunk*. He didn't need but a few beers, and he was smashed. Shorty went on the beach and started giving some local beat cops, Bobbies, a hard time about their Bermuda shorts. He had only had one beer, so he wasn't falling-down drunk yet. Shorty was also a fast runner. So here he went running from the Bobbies and jumping over garden walls. He eventually evaded capture.

About an hour after he had been on liberty, a cab came down the pier, and Shorty climbed out, yelling, "Corpsman!"

He had already paid the cab off, and there he stood screaming for the Doc. He was soaking wet, his uniform was shredded, and he was cut and scratched pretty much over ninety percent of his body. The last garden wall he jumped over wasn't a garden wall, it was next to the ocean, and Shorty tumbled and slid down the coral until he hit the partially submerged rocks at the cliff's base.

No way to climb back up, so he had to walk/wade/swim around the edge until he finally got to a beach and could get out. While doing so, he was getting pounded by the waves and getting more cuts. Between all the other boats' topside watches calling down on the 1MC and announcing, "You need to come topside and see this," there must have been seventy-five people topside. Everyone laughed and laughed at Shorty. It was a topic of sea stories for years to come. When Doc finished with him, he looked like the Mummy.

Ah, the good times.

CLUB 40 THIEVES

Continuing with our port visit to Bermuda, some of the guys found the *Club 40 Thieves*. As word spread around the boat, on Wednesday night, just about everyone on *Entemedor* who was not on watch ended up there. The XO, Eng, Weps, etc., right on down. The place was popular with the locals. That particular night, the Governor of Bermuda, his wife, and one daughter were there. You all know how much diesel boat sailors respected authority, and that night was no different.

Most of the crew was well underway. Many guys danced with the Governor's daughter but not with his wife. She was butt ugly. We were having a great time until the Eng told the Governor his wife's face reminded him of an elephant's knee cap.

Well, that was it. The Governor ordered all the sailors out of the club. Of course, no one paid any attention to him. Who the hell did he think he was, anyway?

So, then the Bobbies came, and things got serious. The XO intervened and dissuaded the gendarmes from locking up most of our guys. He asked us for one favor before we left; he wanted us to sing the Governor and his wife a song. Don't ask me why. Perhaps he was in his cups as well.

Hell, we all knew the song, so, as best we could, we lined up in a choir-type formation, and as loud as we could, we sang them the well-known submarine *hymn—Him, him, f*ck him!* As a result, we got thrown out of the club.

The next morning, when the CO returned from being with his wife in their hotel, he was fuming because the Governor had ordered *Entemedor* to leave Bermuda.

What a great day to be a submarine sailor! The CO was upset for a long time because he had to leave his wife behind. Even today, it was worth it. First time I was ever thrown out of a country.

Seven diesel boats outboard the tender. Three boats and the ASR behind the photo. New San Juan is in the background.

CHAPTER SEVEN

The Caribbean

NEW LONDON & BOSTON

After we returned from our little trip up north, the boat settled into a more normal diesel boat routine. We did one week as a sub-school boat, conducting daily ops in the Long Island Sound. One of the significant differences between diesel boats and nukes, if we had 100 feet of water, we submerged. With students on board, it was dive, surface, dive, surface all day, making sure everyone had an opportunity to take a turn on the helm and planes.

We made a run to Boston via the Cape Cod Canal for a week of submarine reserve training. I stayed ashore almost every day and took in as much history as possible. I went to the Old North Church, where the Rector took me up into the tower—where the *one if by land, two if*

30

by sea lanterns were shown. It was closed to the public then; I do not know if they ever opened it. What a view from up there.

I went aboard the *USS Constitution*. I would have been miserable on that thing. Every deck below the main deck was built for sailors under five feet five inches tall. At six feet four inches, I had enough problems bobbing and weaving on *my* boat. The *Constitution* would have broken my back. That had to be a rough life on those early warships.

SAN JUAN AND PORTS SOUTH

Typically, a diesel boat was away from homeport for at least 300 days a year. As soon as September rolled around, along with other boats, we headed south for an ASW exercise called *Fallboard*. Sometimes, we'd stop in Bermuda on the way down or returning. Then on to San Juan. It was weekly ops, and almost every weekend, we'd be in a different port. St. Thomas, St. Croix, Ocho Rios, and many others. It all depended on whether we were operating with P-3s or destroyers.

The funny thing about Ocho Rios was that the Jamaican employees were not allowed to touch money. When we went to a resort, we had to exchange our money for small, yellow, plastic bananas on a stem. Each stem was $10.00. A Planter's Punch was so many bananas (65 cents), and that is what you gave the waiter. (If I started digging around here, I might find one or two bananas stuck away.)

The place we did not care for was *Rosie Roads* (Roosevelt Roads). You couldn't walk to the beach—too far. You couldn't walk to the exchange—too far. The EM Club was up on a hill with a cliff on the side we were closest to, so you had to follow the road up and around. Some of the guys had no problem coming down the cliff after a gallon or two of drinks.

We also worked with UDT/SEALs for a week or two. They would tell us we were out of our minds for riding subs. I have never understood that, considering what they do.

Today, the port of San Juan looks nothing like it did when we were pulling in there. Back then, a sub tender would moor at an Army pier. Subs tied up outboard her. Just aft of the tender, any extra boats and a submarine rescue ship (ASR) would moor there. Old San Juan was a significant den of sin. After Havana was closed to U.S. vessels, Old San Juan was the next best thing. Some of the older guys had made runs to Havana. They had a hard time explaining just how wonderful it was.

We always returned to Groton around December 15 and left again for the Caribbean in January. One time, we and the *USS Hardhead* (SS-365) made a four-day visit to Miami. OMG. No one could do anything wrong. Jackie Gleason had his TV show out of there. He invited enough guys to fill up the front two rows. Before the show, he had a big cookout at his place, and all those hard-body June Taylor dancers were there. Several more took a ride on the Goodyear Blimp, and we went up and down the beach areas. You would not believe the number of sharks we could see just beyond the breakers. There was a considerable number gathered near the main ship channel as well.

Each day, one of the boats had an open house, and there were lines of people to tour. Great liberty port. Police would bring guys back instead of arresting them.

SOME OF MY FAVORITE PLACES

Aside from St. Thomas, Jamaica, and Puerto Rico, one of my favorite places was Frederiksted, St. Croix. A sub could stay submerged until about 300 feet from the end of the pier. We'd surface, pull next to the pier, and moor. The water was crystal clear and about sixty feet deep. You could read the label on a beer can on the bottom without a problem. No matter when we came in, one of the local ladies was there with her pickup. The truck bed was filled with ice and beer. She was a big old girl. Sometimes we thought she owned the pier. Whatever she said was law.

On *Entemedor*, liberty was ALWAYS put down before mooring. As soon as the brow was over and you completed all your duties, if you didn't have the duty, "Get the hell off my submarine," the Captain used to say. Usually, I was the first one off if I didn't have the duty.

It wasn't until I was in Diego Garcia many years later that I saw water better than St. Croix. The old lady selling the beer loved submarine sailors. Her prices were very reasonable, and she would laugh and carry on with the best of us. The only other larger town on St. Croix was Christiansted. It was on the opposite side of the island from us. That was the main tourist area, primarily due to Buck Island Underwater National Park. A great place to snorkel. I do not remember how many times we pulled into St. Croix, but I never went to Christiansted.

One evening as I was walking around Frederiksted, I found a place—*Your Mother's Tongue*. It was an old two-story home with a porch across the second floor. The new owners converted it into a B&B. It was surrounded by an old stone wall, its garden filled with tropical plants. Around a giant banyan tree, they had built a bar. Hidden among the tropical vegetation were speakers and a great sound system—for the 60s, that is. All they played was classical music, but not to blow your eardrums out. Every night I had liberty, that is where you could find me. To me, the tropical breeze, the fragrant flowers, and bright colors of Bird of Paradise, along with many flowering vines, were about as far away from a submarine as you could get. One evening, the full score of Bolero played, and I was in seventh heaven. That is a memory permanently burned into my little brain. It was a magical place. Besides, a magnificent Planter's Punch was only 65 cents, and a Rum and Coke 50 cents. Not any of the assembly line cruise ship swill.

I was never much of a drinker. My father was an alcoholic, and I had no desire to follow in his footsteps. It would have been easy to fall in line with most of the crew and get plastered in every foreign port; I couldn't see it.

A bottle of rum was $1.50. Coca-Cola was more expensive. Chivas Regal Scotch was $4.95. Crew members bought gallons and gallons of all kinds of booze. Of course, none of it went through customs when we returned. I heard that a Commanding Officer of another diesel boat always brought a keg of rum back. He stored it inside a torpedo tube.

Submarine Tender USS Fulton *at State Pier, New London, with three diesel submarines berthed alongside. Notice the deck guns on the* Fulton.

CHAPTER EIGHT

How Cold is It?

STATE PIER NEW LONDON

January 1966 was probably the coldest in memory for me. *Entemedor* was tied up in Connecticut on the Thames River at State Pier, New London, outboard the submarine tender, *USS Fulton* (AS-11). I had not yet qualified in submarines, so I was standing topside watches. At that time, there was only one person on watch topside. When the longer ballistic missile subs came into being, two people stood watch topside, one forward and one aft.

Standing topside offered zero protection from the elements. Very similar in all branches of the service when you are on guard duty outside. If you were fortunate, your guard post had a small watch shack to stand in—no such luxuries on a diesel boat. You dressed for the weather, and you had best pay attention to the weather before you assumed the watch.

34

Entemedor had spent four months that Fall in the Caribbean operating with surface ships, aircraft, UDT/SEAL teams, and other subs. Each weekend, we'd pull into a different port. It was interesting, bouncing around from island to island. On our way back to New London, the cooks discovered we had a freezer problem. On a diesel boat, the route to the freezer was through the chill box or refrigerator. Access to the chill box was through a thick, insulated hatch in the mess hall deck. The hatch was located in the passageway through the mess deck, so safety chains had to be snapped into place before opening the hatch to keep crew members from falling into the hole.

When we arrived in New London, two army field food storage units were placed topside aft of the sail, one freezer, and one chill box. Upon arrival, the onboard contents were transferred to the units topside while our freezer was repaired. After these trips down south and especially around the holidays, maximum leave was granted for several weeks. Each day, only the duty section was present on board.

Winters can be brutal in Connecticut, with winds howling down the river, heavy snow, and waves sending freezing spray into the air. A topside watch's primary purpose was to check mooring lines, ship's draft, and security, with security at the top of the list. No one could come on board the boat without proper identification. You had to be on an access list and have the required identification.

Access to the boat was via an accommodation ladder. On the tender side, it would swivel. On the submarine end, it had a roller to allow for movement. The accommodation ladder was set in place with a crane. Depending on how much the boat moved, the accommodation ladder would move slightly toward the boat's edge. We were the only boat outboard, and anytime the accommodation ladder got close to the edge, I would get under it, and using my back and legs, I'd lift it and walk it back into place. I couldn't see rousting out the crane crew for something like that. Pretty soon, I would be called topside to reset the accommodation ladder no matter what duty section had the boat.

The weather was as miserable as it could be. I was assigned the 0400-0800 watch, the coldest part of the day. You relieved the watch at 0345, and you were relieved at 0745. The below decks watch woke me at 0300. He informed me it was fifteen degrees topside with a ten-knot wind and to dress accordingly. This meant I wore heavy socks, Arctic boots, my working uniform, heavy full-length winter bib-overalls, a very large full-length parka with a fur-lined hood, and winter gloves from the foul weather locker. When fully dressed, I looked like I had gotten carried away and put on too much.

I informed the below decks watch I was heading topside. Of course, the forward hatch was closed to keep heat inside the boat. I climbed up the ladder, opened the hatch, and climbed out onto the deck. Immediately, I knew I was going to freeze to death. I shut the hatch and turned to locate the poor soul who had stood the mid-watch, 0000-0400. I found him standing on the east side of the army chill box, using it to shield himself from the wind. He was shivering and said everything was okay and quiet. He had not seen anyone since he came on watch. We hurried through the watch turnover requirements. He signed out in the watch log, and I signed in, which officially meant I had the watch. He could not get below fast enough.

I made my first series of rounds, checking mooring lines, drafts, and the overall condition topside. If it snowed, I had a broom to keep the walking deck clear as best I could. At the end of my first round, I returned to the chill box area and made a log entry concerning my round. Then began the deep freeze effect as cold slowly penetrated the layers of clothing one by one. Even sheltered from the direct wind, the subzero wind chill swirled around the chill box, and there was nothing I could do to avoid it. I tried walking around, jumping around, jogging around, slapping my arms around my body, anything to generate some heat but not enough to sweat. Sweating is a ticket to certain death from hypothermia. I figured this would be the worst possible watch in my entire navy career.

I made my second set of rounds topside and said to myself, *This is stupid.* I don't know why, but I opened the chill box door, and right there was a thermometer indicating forty degrees. *You have got to be kidding me*, I thought. *It is warmer inside the refrigerator than it is outside.*

I quickly figured out how I was going to survive my watch. I moved a few things around inside the chill box, put a wood crate of cabbage on end, and sat down. There, with the chill box door cracked, I could see the after deck and the accommodation ladder. Essentially, I had the same view I had when standing outside. I hadn't been inside the chill box very long, and I started to get hot. I flipped the fur-lined hood off, unzipped my parka, and took my gloves off. Now you were talking. I was comfortable, sitting my watch, and reached over, pulled an apple out of another crate, and started eating.

When it was time to make rounds, I zipped up, put my hood back up, put my gloves on, and braved the elements. What began as an experiment in freezing a human turned out to be a very comfortable watch and one of my favorite stories. All it took was a little ingenuity and bending the rules just a wee bit. You know it is cold when you stand a watch inside a refrigerator to stay warm.

Camden, Maine.

CHAPTER NINE

Camden, Maine

CAMDEN, MAINE

When we returned from the Caribbean after participating in an extensive ASW exercise known as *Fallboard*, we underwent repairs. After repairs, we headed back to the Caribbean in mid-January for *Springboard*. We carried a little over 250,000 gallons of diesel fuel. Running up and down the east coast was not a problem.

Our first port of call was Bermuda again. We had a new Navigator. As before, all the wives, kids, and girlfriends gathered on the pier to wave goodbye. All participating submarines backed out into the Thames River, headed downriver, under the bridge, past Race Rock, and turned to port. After we cleared Montauk Point, we turned in a southeasterly direction.

Some of the boats headed to different ports along the east coast—marvelous places like Norfolk or Charleston. Just where a submarine sailor wants to go, a port filled with sailors.

Soon after I reported aboard, my first port of call was beautiful Camden, Maine. I know, strange place to go. The way this works, a city or town located on a navigable waterway sends a request to the Pentagon or a senator from the state and requests a military vessel visit them for Armed Forces Day, Memorial Day, or another holiday. Show the flag, bring in tourists, make more money.

On the Hamlet level, this would be similar to bringing one of the giant steam locomotives down from Strasburg, Pennsylvania, for the Seaboard Festival. The difference, Hamlet would have to pay all expenses. For Camden, Uncle picked up the tab. The annual *Fleet Week* in NYC is a perfect example.

Entemedor was the first submarine to visit Camden and the first Navy vessel to visit since WWII.

Of course, the waterway has to be able to accommodate the vessel. These requests have to be submitted at least a year in advance. *Entemedor* had received orders to visit the picturesque port of Camden.

The harbor was not deep enough for us to moor next to a pier. Besides, they didn't have a pier. We arrived at low tide and crept into the harbor until we scraped the bottom. Backing slowly, we dropped anchor and continued to lay chain on the bottom. It was a sheltered harbor, and a mountain stream flowed into the harbor at the end, so those who made these decisions were not worried about swinging on the anchor and grounding the boat. Not that it would have been a problem. During WWII, diesel boats often ran aground on purpose to pick up Coastwatchers, missionaries, and army or marine troops. There is a big difference in a Captain's career between running aground or intentionally grounding the boat. The hull of a diesel boat is designed to sit on the bottom and hide. So, running it aground on purpose was easy. None of this applies to nuclear submarines.

Camden, Maine, is where that *sinful* movie, *Peyton Place*, was filmed. Many of us remember all the talk about that movie. Today, it would be on the Disney Channel.

My 19th birthday was in Camden. OMG, did I get my eyes opened! This beautiful New England town was not a Puritan stronghold. Women came out of the woodwork, especially single schoolteachers, and were all over the submarine twenty-four hours a day. I will not go into details, but several lasting marriages[1] came out of that port visit. For the town's Armed Forces Day parade, the boat put together a gaggle of semi-sober crew members to march in the parade. I use the word *march*, loosely. Sub sailors do not march. They had a lot of fun, and the townspeople loved them. Your basic marine would have had a heart attack.

My cousin, Tom Smith, and his wife are frequent visitors to Camden and that area. He asked me one time if he should look for people who resembled me. I said, not a chance. This little Southern boy was in awe, and that was it.

BERMUDA, AGAIN

We were heading to Bermuda on the surface, making around twenty knots. Every day the weather was becoming warmer and more wonderful. Whenever I had a chance, I would climb up to the bridge and take in the scenery. What scenery, you ask? The blue water ocean is a magnificent marvel: sea turtles, different types of dolphins, an octopus here and there, sea birds, and if you are in the right place at the right time of year, millions of migrating birds. Several times, I saw the boat entirely covered in birds, taking a brief rest before continuing their journey. At night, there is no place on earth like being at sea. The heavens are open from horizon to horizon.

If you know anything about stars, planets, or constellations, you know God was not messing around when He created the heavens. He also placed Polaris (North Star) and the Southern Cross (points south)

[1] A sub sailor lucked out if he fell in love, not lust, and married a teacher or nurse. Enlisted pay was so low, if you wanted a family, you needed a second income. Dee and I sold blood many times over the years to buy food. We qualified for food stamps until January 1978. We never took the food stamps. While we lived in Charleston, my mother would bring a car trunk full of vegetables that many of my friends' parents grew and gave to her for us. Mr. W.B. Wright sent a trunk full of silver queen corn once.

for future navigators. They are perfectly positioned so that you never lose sight of one before the other rises above the horizon. Additionally, there are many other navigational aids. The sun and moon are also used by navigators.

Speaking of Navigators, after about one week, the boat came to *all stop*. According to our new Navigator, we were sitting high and dry in Bermuda. Scanning the horizon, it appeared Bermuda had moved. The CO had the radar operator shift the range to the maximum. There it was, eighty miles SW of our position. After the XO went over the Navigator's calculations, he discovered the Navigator did not allow for the offset caused by the Gulf Stream. The surface area of the Gulf Stream is moving north at 3 to 3.4 knots. If you do not allow for this, you will miss Bermuda. Underwater in the Gulf Stream is a different animal. Depending upon your location, the Gulf Stream will push you south.

After we entered port, the Navigator was relieved and replaced with another officer.

Diving School section. I am the squared-away-looking guy in the middle of the front row. Three men in this photo, taken on Monday of the last week, did not graduate.

CHAPTER TEN

SCUBA Diving & Other Matters

PHILADEPHIA NAVAL SHIPYARD

May 1966, I was qualified and the only sonarman on *Entemedor*. I made Third-Class Sonarman and was assigned to the sonar gang. There was a First-Class and two Second-Class. My experience in Sonar was a surface transit from Groton to Philadelphia. We did not submerge, and no maintenance was performed on any equipment. Within three months of entering the shipyard, all three sonarmen were transferred.

Entemedor went to Philadelphia Naval Shipyard to change both batteries. Each battery has 126 cells. One cell is five feet tall and holds thirty-three gallons of sulfuric acid electrolyte. We also had a complete overhaul of our three GMV-16 diesels (same as the railroad used), two air compressors, the Prairie Masker, and upgraded sonar and radio equipment. Some of the old WWII electronic gear was still 100 percent tubes. Many sections were removed and replaced with solid-state components. Our upgrade version was archaic compared to solid-state today. High-power diodes were huge.

The Prairie Masker was installed on a small number of *Guppy Class* diesel boats (post-WWII). The installation required the removal of one diesel engine. Most diesel boats had four engines. A *Guppy IIIA* (us) had three. The installation included a super high-pressure blower, pressure regulators, many isolation valves, and several hull penetrations. A brass strip was attached flush to the hull. It was similar to a pipe cut in half but less, so it would not generate any noise as water flowed across. The strips had tiny pinholes to allow small bubbles to come out. As they flowed aft, they created a curtain of air over three-quarters of the submarine to mask all machinery noise. It also provided air to the trailing edge of each propeller blade. The system could only be used while the snorkel was raised.

In our standard mode of operation at periscope depth, we could raise the snorkel and charge our batteries with three main engines. A submarine running diesels at periscope depth generates a massive noise signature. When we ran the Prairie Masker, we disappeared. Sound will not travel through water, hit the air, and continue. It hits a bubble and dies. The Masker provided air to each propeller blade to minimize cavitation. Cavitation is generated when a propeller turns at depth. At the trailing edge of each blade, a low-pressure area forms, causing bubbles to form. As they leave the low-pressure area, they collapse and make a distinct squeaky sound associated with all submarines.

The boat completed our overhaul in early December, and we headed south in January for Springboard and returned early April. Those who could went on leave, and the rest of us worked on the boat. By then, I was an STS2 (SS) (DV)—sonar gang of one.

I attended many schools while the boat was in overhaul, including Navy Dive School. Our class started with fifty and graduated nine.

We learned SCUBA and hard hat. Nelson Gainey, a friend from Hamlet, had a similar experience when he attended dive school in Charleston.

When I graduated from Hamlet High School, I was six feet four inches and 190 pounds. After boot camp, I was still at 190. I entered dive school at 195. I graduated from dive school at 210. The military has schools and programs that awaken the beast inside. I am sure many other Hamlet boys had similar experiences. What you thought was a good run before joining went out the window in the service. In dive school, we ran with thirty-five-pound sandbags across our neck and shoulders. Our top was soaking wet, and sand filtered down and began to sand our nipples off. It was an *awesome* experience to jump into saltwater each day.

On one occasion, when I was back in Philly for a week or two, my crazy friend, QM3 Joe Petrello, came to me and said, "Hey, I know a place out in town that is full of beautiful women we can dance with."

I told him it sounded good to me. Then Joe said, "It's a gay and lesbian bar, so we'll have to hold hands to get in, but it will be worth it."

I responded, "Sounds like something a couple of submarine sailors would do. Let's go!"

Joe had a car, and we zipped on out there. Sure enough, there were two big bouncers at the door, and Joe put on his feminine act. He put his arm around my back, and we tee-heed and giggled through the entrance without a challenge. Yes, all you ordinary people, this is the type of thing we submarine sailors do to break the monotony and generate hate and discontent. Wow! Joe was correct. That place was full of fruitcakes, female NFL linebackers, and a gaggle of beautiful young ladies.

Not being afeared of anything, Joe and I began to ask some of the young lovelies to dance. To our surprise, all of them said yes, to the chagrin of their 250-pound Dykes. After each dance, we'd return them to their respective partners who had steam coming out of their ears. Then we'd move on to another set of lovelies. We treated them like the beautiful, misguided ladies they were.

I believe we lasted thirty minutes before two larger bouncers were unchained in a back room and told to remove us from the premises. Joe and I laughed so hard on the way to the yards. We stopped at a submarine bar, where mainly sub-sailors hung out. For hours, we told how we infiltrated a gay and lesbian bar. Everyone laughed and laughed. I would imagine some of them tried the same thing on other nights, just for S&G.

In the sub-bar were sailors from WWII and all the boats in the yards with us.

THE ZOO

The *USS Tripoli* (LPH-10) was being outfitted just down from our boat's dry dock. Every day the Gunny would march his Marines up and down, back and forth. Every time they came close to where the duty section had built a makeshift home away from the barracks, the Gunny would threaten to kill any of his marines who even looked our way. He would scream at his Marines, "These people are not part of the military!"

When the Gunny was finished for the day, he'd always come by our hobo encampment, that was constructed almost exclusively with merchandise acquired through midnight acquisition. He'd sit around having a beer and laughing at all the stories and how we had *appropriated* all our materials. Two Navy guys with a clipboard, some papers, and a pickup truck would go into an office and tell the occupants that they were getting a new refrigerator and that they were there to pick up the old one first. Not one person ever bothered to look at the bogus papers or call anyone until it was too late. A truckload of 2x4s and several large pieces of canvas for our roof showed up. Some plywood for the door, and we were walking in tall cotton. The outside of the door was painted green, and in bright yellow, we stenciled the word *Zoo* on it.

The duty section was always filthy from working on the boat in dry dock. Someone took it upon himself to tap into a water supply and set up a shower. There was a 55-gallon drum outside in the sun for hot/warm water. It was always nice to get all the asbestos off us; that stuff itched.

The Gunny was told where the sub-bar was, and he had a standing invitation. The day the *Tripoli* was commissioned, he stopped by and wished us all good luck. He said we were the most fantastic group of sailors he had ever met. As he shook hands, I am sure he had a tear or two. He had seen us make do with what little we had and was impressed. It may have been the deal we made with the shipyard fire department. We let them borrow some of our checked-out movies, and they gave us a fire permit to build a barbecue to cook hot dogs, steaks, hamburgers, etc. They ensured we had a hood and exhaust pipe properly mounted through the canvas. For the most part, they came down and built it for us.

On the day *Tripoli* was commissioned, with so many VIPs in attendance, we were notified not to leave the Zoo. After they got underway, it got mighty quiet down our way.

Eventually, it was time to dismantle our makeshift duty section quarters and move back onboard the boat. The non-duty section crew remained in the barracks and came down every morning to get their spaces ready to leave the yards.

SCUBA

I bought my first SCUBA outfit when I was fifteen. There used to be a Dive Shop on the way to Rockingham, North Carolina, on the left side. It was in the low area right before Highway 1. I dove at Boyd's Lake, Crawford's Lake, and later at Richmond County Golf Course (RCC), recovering golf balls from their lake. The Golf Pro would pay me five cents a ball, no matter the condition. He would pick out the usable ones and make shag bags to sell back to those who had lost them. They would use them for practice. The first dive had been the only dive since RCC was founded. Many of the balls were in very, very, bad shape. There was also a large amount that ranged from Pristine Titleist to substitute balls with a cut. Not everyone played by the rules. After my first collection, the condition of all the balls increased dramatically. The Golf Pro and I made a lot of money off of local citizens. I tried to go out every three months.

Once, the lake was frozen over, and I wore a full wet suit. I had been under about thirty minutes, and my mouthpiece came out when I exhaled. I grabbed it and used my gloved hand to hold it in place. In a full wet suit, a thin area around your mouth is exposed to the cold water. The cold had penetrated deep enough to allow my jaws to release the mouthpiece. I immediately began swimming to shore under the ice. When I got out, I could tell hypothermia was setting in. For southern diving, a one-quarter-inch thick wet suit is perfect. Not so much on that day. My navy dive suit was three-eighths of an inch, but I had a dry suit to wear over it if it was really cold. I will not be going into the joys experienced when you pee in your wet suit.

I saw Ray Perry out there every time. We were in the same HHS class. Before joining the Navy, I turned my golf ball job over to Ed Davis, another HHS grad. Tommy Tew took my drummer spot with the *Shantellas*, which was a good thing. He was a much better percussionist than me. We formed this group my senior year. They went on to play all over North and South Carolina.

TORPEDOES

After returning from Springboard, *Entemedor* went out into Long Island Sound for a week or two and shot and recovered exercise torpedoes.

I had to be in the water in a wetsuit to bring exercise MK-37 torpedoes alongside so they could be hoisted on deck and lowered into the Forward Torpedo Room. The torpedomen would service the torpedo for re-use. I had a big concern when swimming out around 100 feet from the boat, attaching a line to the torpedo, and helping bring it alongside. Each type of torpedo had a noisemaker that started at the end of the run, so we could obtain a sonar bearing, surface, and head in that direction. The noisemaker also attracted sharks. I would be on the bow and wait for the CO to signal me to go. There was a sailor on top of the sail with a rifle. I don't know who was in the most danger, me or the shark.

WAY UP NORTH

Back in port, the word was put out that we were leaving for at least two months. No one ever said where. One day, truck after truck showed up with supplies. They did not stop. Our dry stores areas were filled to the deck hatch. Case after case continued to come down the hatch. We stuffed every nook and cranny, and the deck in berthing was covered in cases of #10 cans. Needless to say, *WTF* was often used.

Then the foul weather gear started coming down. We loaded winter clothing similar to that worn in the movie *Ice Station Zebra*, not really, but it was super heavy-duty cold-weather clothing. That's when we realized we were going north, way north up to where you never are invited to go.

After a short briefing, we learned our departure date and time and were to keep our mouths shut. The day arrived. After a few non-designated Seamen reported aboard, and with little to no fanfare, we backed out into the river and headed toward Long Island Sound. When we passed Race Rock, instead of turning left, we turned right and went out across the sound to a relatively isolated area. The boat stopped, and the word was passed for the Seamen Gang to lay topside. What most of us didn't see until months later, they were up there spraying a camouflaged paint job. When I finally saw it, at best, it looked like dog crap. It did, however, blend in nicely with ice floes.

When they finally finished, we headed north without wasting time. We spent the first week on the surface, running full or flank speed (19-21 knots). When my non-designated seaman arrived in sonar, I introduced myself as the entire Sonar Division. You could have stuffed a full twenty-gallon garbage bag into his mouth, his jaw dropped so far. The next week, we submerged during the day and ran on the surface at night. We were gone for over two months. I wore the same clothes the entire time. We could only wash our hands, faces, and brush our teeth. Everyone was issued a bowl, cup, and silverware. Only one hot meal a day, and everything else was cold. Eventually, water started freezing in the bilges. Our breath would fog inside the boat because the heaters were set on low and could not keep up.

It was a pretty hair-raising mission, and we did well. When we finally got back far enough south, all the garbage in the showers was compacted and flushed out the Trash Disposal Unit (TDU). Then we could finally take showers—only one gallon per man; it was magnificent.

I threw the clothes and yellow underwear in the trash. Finally, a night's sleep between clean sheets after months of sleeping fully dressed on top of the flash cover. When I was called for my watch, I felt like I had been skinned alive. My fingertips hurt so badly, I could not button my shirt. I had to get one of the guys to help dress me. All the others who had taken a shower had the same problem; newly exposed skin hurts. It was a temporary problem, but we all suffered through it. I don't know how many more years before I can tell the entire story.

Large female Great White Shark
Length about 20 feet, weight about 5,000 pounds

CHAPTER ELEVEN

Denizen of the Deep

TRANSITING THE VIRGIN PASSAGE

Recently, I was reading about the *USS Samuel B. Roberts* (DE-413). It had a stellar career during WWII, fighting in the Pacific Theater, where it eventually was sunk. In the early days after being released from the shipyard, however, she got off to a bad start. During training and certification, she hit a whale and damaged one screw bad enough to reenter the yards for repairs. After repairs were made, she left for the Pacific via the Panama Canal.

Her story reminded me of one night on the *Entemedor* in the 60s. We were surfaced, transiting the Virgin Passage at twenty knots. Back in those days, navigation was not as sure-footed as today. There were many hazards to be aware of as you made the transit.

I was in my bunk semi-asleep when all of a sudden, the boat literally shook and appeared to move to port. The OOD on the bridge sounded the collision alarm, and we immediately started slowing. Everyone was up and headed to their stations. The OOD asked Control for damage reports. Of course, the CO, XO, and other officers were up also, and the CO wanted to know what had happened, what we had hit. I imagine the CO, Nav, and OOD could see their navy careers dissolving. A collision at sea can ruin your entire day, along with other things.

The OOD called down to Control to inform the CO that they never saw a thing. Control was receiving reports from all compartments. No flooding, no damage. As the boat slowed, Sonar had no close contacts. Of course, at speed on the surface, you couldn't hear much anyway. Radar did not hold any close contacts either.

I am sure everyone agreed that either we hit something or something huge hit us.

The CO headed to the bridge to talk to the OOD and two lookouts. They all said they never saw anything. They were as surprised as everyone else.

After the excitement, everything returned to normal. We increased speed and continued our transit to St. Thomas. I climbed back in my rack and soon nodded off.

The next day, we pulled into St. Thomas Harbor and moored starboard side to the old UDT pier away from downtown. I had been briefed by the CO, XO, Weps, and anyone else who thought of things to check. The CO and XO were primarily interested in damage. Weps was concerned about torpedo tube outer doors. The Engineer wanted me to check the screws.

As the only ship's diver, I was doing this underwater but in full view of anyone who wanted to watch. I did not go inside any of the ballast tanks, so they didn't have to worry about me disappearing. I walked forward and jumped over the side. I came to the surface and adjusted everything, and began my inspection. There was no damage on the bow, but there was a long line of what appeared to be pointed, very sharp teeth marks down to bare metal about 3 inches apart, and all marks went down about six inches long. I do not remember how many teeth marks there were—more than twelve and less than twenty. It appears some denizen of the deep launched an underwater attack on us. I'm sure we did not taste very good. I continued on my way and inspected the rest of the boat and screws. Everything was like it should be.

I made my lackluster report. Everyone who read it was perplexed. These types of sea creature encounters were few and far between since Moby Dick was harpooned.

My guess: A really large great white shark like the photo at the top of this chapter.

USS Wasp, *the aircraft carrier that*
Entemedor *tracked while following in her wake.*

CHAPTER TWELVE

Needle in a Wet Haystack

CANASILEX

Sometime in 1967, a large group of diesel boats participated in CANASILEX—Canadian American Submarine *something* Exercise. A can of worms was more like it. The East Coast was divided into operating areas that were very long and narrow, from the Keys to above Halifax. Every anti-submarine warfare (ASW) unit on the East Coast was organized to search each corridor. *Entemedor* was up north in the Halifax zone of operations. Each boat was to sneak inside a specified mile marker from the coast without being detected. This damn exercise went on and on. As subs were detected, some on purpose, they would enter their assigned exercise port and party. Not us; we took this exercise seriously, and eventually, we were the last boat undetected.

The powers-that-be decided to send as many ASW assets that could fit into our area of the ocean to track us down. You never heard so much active sonar in your life. The CO and XO were excellent, and we drove the ASW units nuts. Slowly we continued to approach the mile marker, and I believe they must have thought we were lost, as in sunk.

Nighttime was snorkel time with the Prairie Masker running. One night, we penetrated the destroyer screen around *USS Wasp* (CV-18), got in her prop wash to hide from radar, raised the snorkel mast, and charged batteries half the night. When we were ready to go back down and hide, the last thing we did was fire a red flare indicating a torpedo had hit the *Wasp*. We slowly snuck away and managed to upset everyone wearing gold. OMG, after that, I'm surprised they didn't try to kill us out of spite. On the last day, we purposely broached parallel to our line during the last hour, and those *fantastic* ASW guys got us dead to rights. The operation was a 100 percent success—anything to ease the conscience of Skimmers and Airdales.

Darn, they got us, and we entered Halifax for many days of great liberty because all the other earlier detected boats had to leave. We had the entire place to ourselves. That is what I call excellent planning. The Canadians and especially the Australians, always treat the American military well.

Many years later, after 9-11, all inbound U.S. flights were grounded. The townspeople of Gander, Newfoundland, drove *en masse* to the international airport, rounded up 9,700 stranded passengers, and took them home until flights resumed. They slept, ate, and bathed with each family. It did not matter race or gender; everyone was welcome. Not one person was asked to pay for anything. That is what I call hospitality.

That was my last trip to Halifax.

REPAIRING A RADIO ANTENNA

Back in the old days, my old days, we were not subject to as many restrictions. Along came nuclear power, and the requirements, procedures, and getting permission to do almost anything invaded the submarine world.

Entemedor was outboard the *Fulton* at State Pier. One evening I had the duty, and a radioman came to me and asked if I'd ride the snorkel mast up and throw a line over an antenna they could not get to lower. It was mounted on the starboard side of the sail and was raised and lowered from inside Radio. The lower half was streamlined, and above that was a whip antenna. Anyhow, I said sure, I'll do it. So, the duty officer and duty chief helped me put on a safety harness. Before I headed up, I made sure the three electrodes on the head valve were turned off. They were set 120 degrees apart. When saltwater hits them, the head valve automatically shuts. I didn't want to fry my butt.

Before I climbed to the top of the sail, I picked up a heaving line. On top of the sail, I walked down the center to the snorkel mast. I asked Control to raise it about three feet, so I could sit on it, which they did. I sat down and found a place to attach my safety line and told them to raise it all the way. So, here we go, bumping along, headed straight up. About seventy feet above the waterline. By then, I had a crowd of tender sailors on their main deck, taking all this in. When we reached the fully raised position, I lowered one end of the line down to the Radiomen. I coiled enough of the remaining heaving line to throw over the whip antenna and extend down far enough for them to grab it. They informed the duty officer they had the antenna. As they pulled it down, the snorkel mast began to lower. I stopped them at three feet, detached my harness, walked back across the sail, and dropped down into the Control Room. No big deal, I was not shot at sunrise, the Radiomen were able to repair their antenna, and all was well in the world—just another day on a diesel boat.

A heaving line has a *monkey fist* knot on the throwing end. We made them onboard. Usually, to provide more weight for distance, a small piece of lead was inside the monkey fist. When I was in the Seamen Gang, due to my arm length, I could make that thing sail. Whoever caught the line would begin to pull over the mooring line that was attached.

There was no way to throw a mooring line. Surface navy uses pneumatic line-throwing guns. It serves the same purpose as a heaving line but can travel much further. The line they send over is attached to a larger line, and that line is attached to a huge mooring hawser, sometimes wire rope. When it comes to line handling and seamanship, there is so much to learn, or you die. A two-inch nylon mooring line under massive stress can part, sounding like a stick of dynamite. It will cut you in half if you are standing in the wrong area. Many officers and enlisted have died over the years due to this. Once a mooring line starts vibrating on its own, you best be moving fast out of the danger zone.

The flight deck of a carrier is the most dangerous place to be in the world. If you let your concentration lapse for one second, you can be sucked into a jet engine, walk into a turning propeller, get blown off the flight deck 100 feet down to the water, or have an arresting gear cable snap and cut you to pieces. Catching King Crab in the Bering Sea is a piece of cake by comparison.

I much prefer the safety of a submarine at test depth.

Jerry and his love, Dee

CHAPTER THIRTEEN

How I Met My Wife

WHAT I TELL NEW ARRIVALS ON MID-WATCH

L ining Bank Street in New London in the 60s were mostly submarine bars; some were for locals only. When I went to Bank Street, I'd visit Whitey's, a seedy place. In New London, we never had to worry about surface sailors invading our space, unlike Norfolk.

We called surface sailors *skimmers*, and they, in turn, called us *sewer pipe sailors*. In the submarine force, we would say, "There are only two types of ships in the Navy, submarines and targets." The only other Navy guys we shared bars with were UDT/SEALS. We spent many days at sea transporting them around, and under cover of darkness, they would disappear in a rubber raft or swim to some far-off island, usually about thirty to thirty-five miles offshore. They would sneak in undetected, visit a nunnery or a hospital for orphans. They were all such sweet, kind boys, very well-mannered. Any mother would have been proud to have one for a son—NOT!

As prearranged, we'd surface, pick them up, and get the hell out of Dodge. Talk about closed mouth; until the day I retired, I never heard one SEAL ever talk about where they had been or what they had done. I'm sure their non-disclosure agreement included killing not only them and their family but all their relatives on both sides of the tree.

I drifted off again with a commercial. Anyway, I decided to go by Whitey's to see what was going on and if anyone I knew was there. I walked in, and lying on the floor passed out was a female hippy type. The bottoms of her feet looked like a K-Mart parking lot. I asked the bartender what her story was. He said she came in once in a while, drank too much, and fell off her bar stool.

I said, "WHAT?"

He said, "Yes, we leave her there, and she eventually wakes up and moves on."

Talk about dirty; she was a mess. She had blonde hair, so matted that it looked like she hadn't washed or combed it since the Woodstock concert. I got down and looked her over and said, "I bet she will clean up prettier than a bucket of fresh hog liver."

I told the bartender I would take her home and see what was under all that mess.

"Knock yourself out," he replied.

Five of us on the boat had decided to pool our money and rent a house out in the country. Back then, they were called *snake ranches*. I brought my car around the front, picked her up, and put her in my car.

I had participated in killing and scalding a few hogs before joining the Navy, so I figured it could not be much worse than that. She never moved nor made a sound from the bar floor to my car and during the drive out to our place.

We had lucked out and rented a large two-story farmhouse with an apple orchard. I had a nice place in the basement with a good-sized bathroom. I stopped at my door, went in, and filled the tub with warm water. Then I brought her in. She was out like a light. Yes, ladies, I undressed her and gingerly lowered her into the tub. She finally made a moan, which assured me she was alive. My mother raised me to be a Southern Gentleman, and this lady had nothing to worry about.

After that, I realized I should have taken some photos to show the guys on the boat. They were never going to believe me.

Before I started scrubbing and cleaning, a very dangerous-looking scum rose to the surface. I drained the tub, rinsed her and the scum down the drain, and refilled the tub.

The more layers I washed off, the better she began to look. I had to use a wire brush on the bottoms of her feet. I managed to get her hair washed and rinsed without drowning her.

She actually scrubbed up pretty good. I stood back, taking it all in, and decided to keep her. Of course, I would need to find out if she wanted to be saved and pampered for the rest of her life.

I got her out, dried, and dressed in one of the other housemate's clothes. Mine was way too big. I put her on my bed, placed a light cover over her, and sat down in a chair. As I watched a TV program, she began to stir and finally opened her eyes, and I thought I might have a mad bobcat jump on me, but she looked around and asked me what was going on and where she was.

I told her the story of how I had rescued her from a bunch of drunk sailors, brought her out to my place, and cleaned her up. Then she took a look at her clean self. Then her eyes became wide.

"You did all this?" she asked

I said, "Yes, ma'am, you were very dirty." Ever since that day, this has been my favorite song, sung by Willie Nelson.

Angel Flying Too Close to the Ground

If you had not have fallen,
Then I would not have found you,
Angel flying too close to the ground.
And I patched up your broken wing,
And hung around a while,
Tryin' to keep your spirits up,
And your fever down.
I knew someday that you would fly away,
For love's the greatest healer to be found.
So leave me if you need to, I will still remember,
Angel flying too close to the ground.
Fly on, fly on past the speed of sound,
I'd rather see you up than see you down.
So leave me if you need to, I will still remember,
My angel flying too close to the ground.
Leave me if you need to, I will still remember,
My angel flying too close to the ground.

It is a wonderful love song and still brings up a bit of emotion after fifty-four years.

Then I asked her if she liked apples, and she said yes. I said, "So, do I. Would you like to get married?"

Boy, did that shock her. She said, "I'll have to get a divorce first."

Okay…I made this up. I thought it was time to pull your leg a bit. Ole Road Hog was just funnin' ya. Feel free to kill me later.

WHAT REALLY HAPPENED

This is the truth; however, there are a few similarities to my first fairy tale. Also, *Angel Flying Too Close to the Ground* is my favorite song.

Four of us on the sub did rent an old farmhouse twelve miles out of New London. It had an apple orchard and a lake. We were not responsible for either.

One evening, one of the guys (Mike) asked me to come out with him that night. He was meeting his girlfriend, and she was bringing a friend. I agreed.

There was a club under a hotel out at the beach in New London. I had never been there. It was a blind date, plus Mike had never seen the *other* girl. In my mind, I was expecting 300 pounds with a mustache.

We entered the club, and Mike saw his girlfriend. As we headed over, I saw her friend. I was smitten immediately. I could not believe it. We talked for a few minutes, and I knew she was the girl I would marry for life. I think we danced every dance that night and talked and talked. I had no idea if Mike and his girlfriend were still alive.

If there was ever a match made in heaven, this was it. She was a Christian and, to me, the most beautiful woman in the world. I still remember what she was wearing that night.

I have an eye for details. At our last class of 64 reunion, Vicki Blanton and her husband were there. Vicki was my first ever date. In the eighth grade, I invited her to go with me to the HHS Band Banquet at the VFW. I told her at the reunion what she wore that night, and she was blown away. Her husband promptly moved her to another table.

Unfortunately, this was on Thursday, and Dee had to fly to DC Friday to visit her brother and his wife over Labor Day weekend. We made a date for the following Tuesday.

After I returned home, I called my mother and told her I had met the girl I was going to marry. My mother replied, "Oh, good."

I knew she was thinking, *You ain't going to marry anyone until I meet her and approve.* Southern Mothers are closer to God than preachers.

It took Tuesday a long time to arrive. Dee was an office manager in a large building across from the Court House. Her friend, who turned out to be the Coast Guard Commandant's daughter, worked across the hall.

I didn't have the duty, so I went to her office early. As soon as she saw me, she started shaking. I'm telling you, it is hard to beat that Southern Charm. Later, she told me she never expected to see me again. Not a chance— I was sucked in hook, line, feathers, and sinker.

We went out for dinner and more talking. I never tried anything. Hang on—I did find out she was married. Her parents had sheltered her so much as she grew up that when she went to University of Connecticut, majoring in math, she met a guy and fell in love. Six months after they were married, he tried to commit suicide. She found him, and he told her he was gay. She called his father and told him to come and get his son. Back in those days, it was not uncommon for gay men to hide in marriage.

Being a submarine sailor, I almost burst out laughing when she told me about him. I maintained full control, however, and told her I was so sorry—*heh, heh, heh. Want a piece of candy, little girl?*

We spent every night together (not all night) unless I had the duty. My boat was leaving on that CANASILEX exercise I described in Chapter 12. So, after being together for four days, I went to sea for about one month. When we finally pulled into Halifax, I had a ton of letters. Some from my mother that I placed aside for later, and the rest from Dee. I sorted them out by postmark and started reading. I never realized why mail call was such a big deal in war movies. Now I understood completely. I read every Dee letter twice; then I read my mother's letters.

I went up on the pier with a pocket full of change and called Dee. She answered, and we talked. Then we listened to each other breathing for a while. You know exactly what I am talking about. I told her when we were scheduled to return to the Sub Base. It was a wonderful evening in Halifax.

When we pulled alongside our pier, she was one of many waiting. I was one very happy camper. I kissed her and ran a fathom of tongue down her throat. When she needed air, she tapped me on my shoulder. That was the first time I had kissed her.

The rest of the year, the boat was out a week, in a week, and back out a week.

I do not remember the date, but at some point, I asked her if she would marry me when her divorce was finalized.

She said, "Well, I may need to examine all my options." NOT!

She said yes. I had already bought her a ring. I put it on, and she said there would be times she would have to remove it, like divorce court and that kind of stuff.

We drove all night to Hamlet between Christmas and New Years. I needed approval from a higher authority. As I expected, my mother loved her. Actually, my mother pushed me aside over the years, and Dee and the boys took stage center.

As usual, my boat left for the Caribbean in January. I left my 1967 Camaro SS convertible with Dee while I was away. On our last night in San Juan, the boat threw a big party for me. They took over an entire bar and whore house and ran everyone else out. (Yes, I was a good boy.)

We returned in April. Dee was there, and she told me about all the cars she had been racing with my car. I found out years later that she always wanted to be a NASCAR driver. I was about to marry a crazy woman.

Dee made all the arrangements for our rehearsal dinner and wedding. I had a trainload of relatives come from Hamlet. It was a wonderful time. None of the Southerners tried to restart the war with all those Yankees. My father was killed in a train wreck in 1966, so no one was drunk, starting fights, or making a fool of themselves.

So, on May 25, 1968, I married Priscilla F. Hardisty for life. She was born in Syracuse, NY, raised in Port Washington, NY, on Long Island, graduated from Paul D. Schreiber High School, moved to Connecticut, and then off to UCONN as a math major. She ended up with a MRS. Degree, and one heck of a ride.

While on our honeymoon, Dee told me she knew there was more to marriage than taking walks and holding hands.

I left the *Entemedor* for Key West in July, 1968. Dee and I packed our meager belongings, headed south to North Carolina, and then on to Key West.

In 1975, I started dabbling into genealogy. As the years went by, I found out that my wife is a direct descendant of five passengers on the first voyage of the *Mayflower*. Her mother knew this and had all kinds of family information passed down through the centuries. No one bothered to tell me. Dee could be a member of the D.A.R., Mayflower Society, and several other groups. She had no interest in doing so. That was fine with me. Some of those outfits cost money.

I swear or affirm, all the information above is true.

Me

St. Thomas Harbor

CHAPTER FOURTEEN

One of Many Port Visits to St. Thomas

PIRATES VS PIRATES

Every January, the *Entemedor* and other Groton and Norfolk submarines would cast off and head to Springboard, the winter/spring ASW operations in most of the Caribbean. As SubLant sent at least fifteen boats, SurfLant provided at least fifteen to twenty destroyer escorts and destroyers and a communications ship—I specifically remember the *USS Wright* (CC-2); it looked like an aircraft carrier covered in antennae. SurfLant also sent various other vessels and all types of ASW aircraft. This was a critical exercise every spring and every fall.

We visited so many Caribbean islands I can't remember them all. Old San Juan was a young sailor's paradise. St. Thomas and St. Croix were two different atmospheres. In Puerto Rico, Roosevelt Roads Pier was ten miles from the front gate; however, the EM Club was across the street and up the hill. *Rosie Roads* was our least favorite place. When in Jamaica, as I reported earlier, at the resort we frequented, you had to change your money into strips of plastic bananas.

We visited different ports down and back—Bermuda, Miami, and Key West (or *Key Waste*, as we called it).

Key Waste had the *USS Gilmore* that had attached itself to the bottom of the basin. The T-boats (training boats), *Mackerel*, and *Marlin*, the K-boat (ASW), *Barracuda*, and the diesel boats *Harder*, *Darter*, *Trigger*, and *Trout* that were *always in and never out*. The *USS Grenadier* (SS-525) was known as Building 525. I would imagine any former crew members would argue about that.

In St. Thomas, we consistently sailed past the good piers and went down to the old UDT barracks and wooden pier. I was mess cooking on my first trip down, but I remember the pier was still in good condition. The following year, when we visited, the end of the pier was in the water.

All port visits to St. Thomas were excellent. One particular trip sticks out, however. The *Entemedor* and two other diesel boats were in port for the weekend. One boat was alongside the pier, and the *Entemedor* and another boat were on the other side with the *Entemedor* pier side. Nuke boats are so delicate they have to use fenders between each boat. For diesel boats, we didn't use any stinking fenders or camels. We didn't have any streamlined ballast tank covers on the bottom either. I could go over the side, swim down, and come up inside a ballast tank if I needed to look for something rattling.

It was around 2200 to 2300, and most people were in their racks. Other than snapping shrimp, it was pretty quiet. Then off in the distance, I heard a motorboat propeller coming our way. The sound was getting louder and louder and closing fast. Then, all of a sudden, all kinds of racket broke loose when the motorboat went between us and the outboard boat—jumping the ballast tanks and continuing on the other side and opening. Like I said, diesel boats seldom used camels between each other for separation; it was usually tank to tank.

Then the sound changed to closing, and they came again. As I got out of my rack, others were doing the same. It was a WTF moment, and we all went topside, barefoot, in dungaree pants and a T-shirt. And, there they came again. Two of our crew members were in a stolen boat.

They came through again, made the ballast tank jump, and left laughing. Our OOD and the other boat's OOD told everyone to toss and lower heavy lines, and when they came through again, we'd lift them out of the water, and a few guys would jump in the boat and take over.

The plan worked like a charm. Our pirates overpowered their pirates and brought an end to the shenanigans.

It turned out, these two had swum out to an anchored big-bucks sailboat in the harbor and had gotten underway. After sailing around for a while, they got bored, pulled the dingy up, jumped in, got the motor running, and cast off from the free sailing sailboat. We let the motorboat idle out into the bay and got those two below.

The next day, truckloads of fecal matter were dumped all over the pier, but no one knew anything about the sailboat or the runabout. Mum's the word.

I don't know if they found the sailboat, but they did find the motorboat on the rocks of one of the outer St. Thomas Harbor islands.

Pilgrim Airlines—De Havilland DHC-6-100 Twin Otter

CHAPTER FIFTEEN

Pilgrim Airlines

THE DE HAVILLAND TWIN OTTER

Growing up in Hamlet, I had two uncles, JB and Vester, who made sure the kids did not miss any new inventions. It wasn't unusual to ride to Charlotte and visit the new Sears and Roebuck store. All we did was ride the escalators for hours. We made an annual trip to Ft. Bragg for Armed Forces Day to watch parachuting, and climb on tanks and other equipment. We even went to Charlotte's Douglas Airport to watch the first Boeing 707 land. We waited all day to watch it take off. At some point, the new McDonald's fast-food place opened by Ovens Auditorium. We made trips to Ovens to see the Harlem Globetrotters. I especially enjoyed Meadowlark Lemon; he was born in Wilmington. Also, the Barnum & Bailey Circus. JB got us special seating at ground level. We had the best seats in the house.

At McDonald's, hamburgers were fifteen cents, fries, ten cents; I do not remember the Coke or Pepsi price. $1.00 was enough to fill me. Then, out of nowhere, the modern age descended upon us.

There was one airport in the New London/Groton area. If you never had the pleasure of flying Pilgrim Airlines in the early years, you do not know what you missed. Home-based in Groton, flights to LaGuardia, only. Someplace over toward Hartford was a larger airport, but it was too far away.

The original airline carried one pilot and five passengers. Essentially a giant station wagon. Airfare from Groton to LaGuardia, $14, and change one-way. Round trip, the fare doubled, no discount. Usually, a one-way flight made a believer out of you, and you took the train from then on.

At the time, the *high* price for a ticket was worth it in my tiny little mind. By the time you paid for a cab from the base to New London's train station, then $1.26 for a one-way train ticket to Grand Central in NYC, plus the ticket price for the express bus from Grand Central to LaGuardia, well, it was much easier to fly and didn't cost that much more. By the way, there is no such thing as an *express* anything in NYC. That only meant it didn't stop anywhere along the way, but it was slow going.

Back then, there was no reason to rush to the airport, so you had plenty of time to go to the ticket counter, check in, and check your bags at the same time. You didn't have to take your shoes off, none of the requirements of today. You could have a suitcase full of C-4, and no one cared—no dogs sniffing around back then either.

On the other hand, if you lived on the submarine and had leave, you could sit on the boat or sit in the airport terminal. The word terminal is not precisely what it was; there was a building where you waited for the ticket agent and baggage checker to arrive. Oh, that would be the pilot of the incoming flight. So, you decide to go to the airport early; otherwise, you could get caught up in a drill on the boat or even an actual casualty.

Pretty soon, the inbound flight lands. All passengers, five of them, head straight to the bar. Pretty soon, the pilot comes in, weighs your bag and tags it, sells you a ticket, and you go back and sit down. After all five passengers are checked in, the pilot says, "I'll be back to get you after I load the bags." So, we sit again. Meanwhile, the pilot, also known as the ground crew, is washing windows, checking the oil, and picking feathers out of the intake. The pilot loads the bags, and then conducts a general once-over of the aircraft to ensure nothing of importance fell off on the last trip.

When the pilot returns and asks us to follow him to the aircraft, I also notice most of the last five passengers are leaving the bar.

What an experience this was. Eventually, we were all seated by weight to make sure the De Havilland Twin Otter was balanced as closely as possible. No flight attendant, no bathroom. Two engines, two wings, one pilot, five passengers, and baggage. And off we went into the wild blue yonder. As we reached a cruising altitude of 2,000 feet, we got the standard welcome aboard, thanks for flying, pilot speech. In case of an emergency, hang on. That was about it.

It was nice to fly at lower altitudes; you got a much better look at seagulls, hawks, and other predators gliding by. If you sat on the left side, the view was of Long Island gradually getting closer. If you were on the right side, you could look into people's backyards. Not being a flyer at such a low altitude that frequently, there was always a little more turbulence than I anticipated. After all, the pilot could have turned around; essentially, we were in a high-altitude station wagon. He announced that the turbulence was normal, and we should be on the ground in about twenty minutes.

I would have preferred he had said we would be landing in about twenty minutes. Being on the ground leaves many possibilities wide open. Sure enough, despite all the ducks and geese migrating south, we landed safely at what used to be a very nice airport.

As we peeled ourselves loose from our seats and gradually got our legs working, we climbed out of the De Havilland Twin Otter plane and then climbed up the terminal stairs. At the time, I didn't drink, but I followed everyone else to the next bar. I was brave and ordered a screwdriver. Do they still make those? Everyone else was into double martinis. I believe Pilgrim had an agreement with TWA for a gate and baggage claim.

I got my bag and headed over to Eastern Air Lines to check in and give them my bag. They had a long counter full of people selling tickets and taking bags, and none of them were pilots. All checked in, I headed to my *real* departing gate in a *real* waiting area with lots of glass, and sitting right there in front of me was MY gleaming airliner—a four-engine Lockheed Electra. These planes were known in the Navy as P-3 ASW aircraft. It was magnificent.

So far, every airline I mentioned is no longer with us. I looked around at all the female employees. All of them looked like they had just walked off a beauty pageant stage, unlike today, when most are retired middle school teachers with a sprinkling of grays. Then the call to board came; so organized, so efficient, such beautiful, charming flight attendants. As I entered the aircraft, I could hear the Hallelujah Chorus playing in the background. A real live airplane with large seats, large bathrooms, enough overhead storage to put a toddler. I had a window seat and fully intended to use it. We flew non-stop to Raleigh from NYC, and I never saw one bird. What a great flight.

Now, you have to realize one little detail. I lived aboard a diesel boat; my uniforms stayed on the diesel boat. No matter how long you kept them in the plastic bag from the cleaners, they smelled like a diesel boat as soon as you put them on. No matter where you went, you were a walking, talking engine room. The unfortunate passengers on Pilgrim were stuck with me. On the Eastern flight, the lady in the middle seat next to me politely excused herself and never returned. I'm sure it must have been the half a can of Old Spice underarm spray I used.

Those were the good old days of *Trains, Planes, and Automobiles.*

Over the years, I have talked to many sub sailors stationed in Groton. When I mentioned Pilgrim Airlines, every one of them who had flown let out a groan. Like me, all of them flew only one-way one time. After landing an aircraft on the George Washington Bridge, Pilgrim filed for bankruptcy, and eventually, their routes were taken by another company. I couldn't care less; I only need to see God's face once in a while.

Navy Sonar School, Key West, Florida

CHAPTER SIXTEEN

Sonar B-School

KEY WEST

I began Advanced Electronic School in Key West for one year. The material was new, but I didn't have a problem passing.

Dee enjoyed our time at Key West. My wife passed Senior Life Saving and then passed the Water Safety Instructor course. She worked at several military pools in Key West. I would dive almost every afternoon after school and bring home spiny lobster, also known locally as crawfish, bugs, or langosta, grouper, and snapper.

I believe I was halfway through Advanced Electronic School when some of my Hamlet friends made a trip to Marathon Key. Joe Gregson, Larry Hendrick, Nelson Gainey, and someone I cannot remember. He might have been Joe's oldest son.

Because of school, I could not spend the entire time with them, but I did go for their last two days. They had rented a boat and I showed them how to catch lobsters. There is a limit per person, but if you are snorkeling, your limit is higher. On one dive down, I was trying to get a lobster out of a hole on the bottom. My hand touched something slimy that had a fin along its side. I just knew it was a moray eel, and it was going to sink all his sharp teeth in my wrist, and I was either going to drown or use my knife to cut my arm off below my elbow. Your mind works extremely fast when you are scared out of your wits. I removed my arm in a hurry and surfaced. As my heart slowed from 250 bpm to normal, I remembered whatever I had touched, made a thump-thump sound. I had heard that before; it was a grouper. Back down I go, had my arm in the hole beyond my elbow, grabbed it by the gills and pulled it out. A very nice grouper indeed. The others were amazed. That evening, we dined like kings. I enjoyed their visit and wished we could have spent more time together.

While I was in Key West, I resumed the semiannual muster with a group of strangers taking the E-6 (first-class) exam. For some off-the-wall reason, up until E-5 (second-class), we were STS or STG; the latter is a surface craft sonarman (two different schools). An E-6 (first-class) was an ST, no S or G.

In the submarine world, your chances of going to a non-submarine job are slim to none unless you are medically disqualified from sub duty, and especially if you are in a critical rate. My first-class test was roughly 80 percent surface and 20 percent submarine. Trying to learn all that gear and its capabilities was extremely difficult.

The submarine portion of the test was a piece of cake. I left Key West and reported aboard the USS Von Steuben (SSBN-632) (B) (B is for Blue Crew. The other crew is G for Gold Crew.). She was close to finishing overhaul at Electric Boat (EB). I got there about two weeks before the first sea trials. Sea trials is when a sub or ship goes to sea and tests every system, conducts drills and in the submarine world, dives, shallow at first but gradually deeper and deeper until you reach test depth. It can be a bit frightening since over the past year or so, massive holes were cut into the pressure hull and finally welded back in place. Submarine hulls are made from special HY-80 steel. As the years progressed, pressure hulls became thicker, and new steel was developed that allow newer classes to go even deeper. For example, on my WWII diesel boat, our pressure hull was one inch thick. During peace time we were restricted to no deeper than 412 feet. I will not talk about follow-on submarine hulls or depths or speeds. I will not even get into some of the experimental subs. Their crews should have been paid a lot more in submarine pay.

On my first night, I went to Sonar to check out the place. As I begin looking things over, I discovered all kinds of problems. These were problems the yard techs should have taken care of before the boat went to sea. I filled an entire page of a yellow legal pad. Both crews had one chief, four first-class, me and another second-class, and a gaggle of thirds. The next morning, I turned in my discrepancy list to the LPO, and he about freaked. He showed it to the Division Officer, Lt. j.g. Robert Williscroft, a former submarine sonarman who was commissioned through the Navy Enlisted Scientific Education Program (NESEP). He was really beside himself. It was like the shipyard was giving them a bag of worms before the first sea trials. I made an excellent first impression. My list was passed to the shipyard, and they were butt holes and elbows for a week fixing everything.

Sea trials went well, and we headed to Cape Canaveral for our Demonstration and Shakedown Operation (DASO) missile launch. We successfully finished that and turned the boat over to the Gold Crew. We flew back to beautiful Quonset Point in January. We were in whites, and it was snowing sideways.

After the Gold Crew finished their DASO, they loaded armed missiles in Charleston and went on patrol. The rest of us moved to Charleston. Most of us settled in Goose Creek. At that time, the boat was making patrols out of Holy Loch, Scotland. When it came our time to take over, we climbed aboard a chartered jet airliner at Charleston Air Force Base and flew to Prestwick, Scotland. This pattern continued until I transferred to San Diego Antisubmarine Warfare Training Center in 1975 to be an instructor.

I took the E-6 exam five times before I made first-class. Very frustrating. There was nothing that could happen to the sonar gear I could not fix in a hurry. At first, a ballistic missile sub (SSBN) made ninety-day patrols. Later, they were extended to 105 days. Fast attack subs (SSNs) operated in a different world. They went to sea for much longer periods, but they did make port visits. SSNs conducted all the sneaky missions gathering intelligence, among other things. On many of their missions, they were under control of the President and CIA. If my career had taken me to them, I would not be able to document anything. There is only one crew on SSNs. Their slogan was: "Big and black and we never come back."

PART TWO
Nuke

USS Von Steuben

CHAPTER SEVENTEEN

Hijinks on the High Seas

USS VON STEUBEN

In Chapter 16 about Advanced Electronics School in Key West, I talked about the struggle I had passing the Sonar test to advance to First-Class. While on the *Von Steuben*, I passed and was promoted to Petty Officer First-Class, STS1 (SS) (DV).

I had been aboard the boat for three years when STS1 (SS) Ernest Bergstrom reported aboard to be the Leading Petty Officer (LPO) of Sonar. Bergy was a very knowledgeable sonar tech. He had the experience, knew all our equipment very well, and I have no problems saying he was better than me. Not by much. I did learn many things from Bergy. I never learned anything from the other STS 1 LPO. Bergy was married, had several children, and to say he was a character would be an understatement. Like my wife, Bergy and I were a sonarmen match made in heaven. We had the crew in turmoil between the two of us, and no one ever knew we were the culprits. One patrol, we stole the XO's door and hid it. The XO was livid. I'd be on watch in Sonar, the door would suddenly fly open, and the XO would look around and ask if we knew where his door was. Of course, we knew nothing. Bergy and I had executed the plan so well, we were the only two who knew the location.

For privacy, the XO had a double navy blanket put up over his door opening. What we did, was not that unusual for the submarine world. Every boat had one or two pranksters who discreetly went about their sinister tasks. Over the years, based upon the training I had from my diesel boat crew, especially the men who had made war patrols, this type of innocent child's play was a submarine tradition. Some of the things we did, if we were aboard a real live Navy surface warship, we could have been court martialed. Those people did not have a sense of humor. Stuck underwater for months, however, the crew needed a little excitement.

One of my other talents, I became a professional rumor monger. There were several days during the refit period when there were all-hands working parties to load supplies in port. During these types of working parties, where crew members were strung out in lines passing cases of food or other items, I began my rumors. All I had to say to one of the guys in front or behind me was, "Hey, did you hear about......?"

I'd put out some BS, and before you knew, it had traveled all through the boat and even topside. One of my rumors involved one person on the sub who would be selected to go home for Christmas and didn't have to make the patrol. In less than a week, the CO's wife called him from Charleston to Holy Loch, Scotland, to get the details about this event. One of the crew had called his wife and told her what was going to happen. She contacted the other wives, and they contacted the wives on their call tree. When the CO and XO wives were contacted, they were upset because neither husband had bothered to inform them. Of course, the CO and XO did not know what the CO's wife was talking about. All this in a matter of four days.

When other crew members called, their wives would ask them, and they would confirm the story. You have no idea how hard it is to remove information from a wife's mind. The XO got on the 1MC, demanding to know about this trip home for Christmas. Everyone knew about it, but I didn't go out and say, "XO forgive me, I have sinned."

Not on your life. I broke so many hearts. We have laughed about that for decades. I didn't spill the beans until one of our reunions. Several of the wives still did not see any humor in my rumor.

One thing we all look forward to on patrol is Halfway Night. Halfway through the patrol, there is a special meal, skits, guys playing guitars, and singing; it was always a good thing to break the monotony of poking holes in the ocean. During Halfway Night, we reinstalled the XO's door and stole the CO's door. That didn't go over well at all. We were not concerned. We knew the CO and XO went back to nuke land when they would have drills for the nukes only. We waited, and one day, when they went back, we put the CO's door back up. The entire time, we hid the doors over the CO's stateroom. The boat had been searched high and low, but no one looked up there.

Another one we did, about an hour before a junior officer was to get off watch, was to go to his stateroom, take his pillow, remove it from the case, wet it all over, and put it in the freezer. Right before he was relieved, the frozen pillow went back into the case and placed back where it belonged. When he finally was ready to climb in his rack, his head would go clunk. You could hear this guy screaming bloody murder. In his case, pretty much all the officers senior to him had the same thing pulled on them as a junior officer. He received no sympathy. I have so many stories regarding stupid stuff. Spools of pipe thread, cans of steam, keel wheel grease, mail buoy watches, a can of compression, relative bearing grease, and so forth. On those subjects alone, volumes could be written.

I will post a few more adventures with Tweedledee and Tweedledum. One, in particular, will kill you.

As juvenile as what I described above was, it served mainly to boost the crew's morale and give them something to talk about. Before I left the boat, I had a sit-down with the XO and confessed. He thanked me and said he was glad we did those things; they kept the crew entertained, and the patrol goes by faster. He also said, "The Captain and I had narrowed the door thing down to you and Bergstrom, but that was fine."

Basically, the CO and XO played along with our schemes.

The XO did ask one question, "Who started that damn Christmas rumor?" I claimed full responsibility. He responded, "Outstanding!" He also asked me about who stole all the cups on board (see Chapter 23, The Great Cup Caper). I never confessed to that until years later. I checked out that day, and my family moved to San Diego. My XO later made Two-Star Admiral. He deserved it. He was a great submarine sailor.

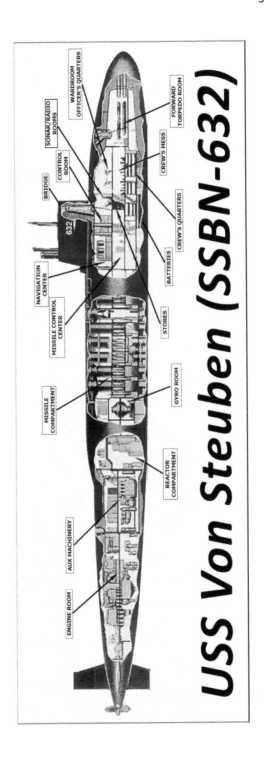

WARDROOM
OFFICER'S QUARTERS

SONAR/RADIO
ROOMS

FORWARD
TORPEDO ROOM

BRIDGE

CONTROL
ROOM

CREW'S MESS

CREW'S QUARTERS

632

BATTERIES

NAVIGATION
CENTER

STORES

MISSILE CONTROL
CENTER

MISSILE
COMPARTMENT

GYRO ROOM

REACTOR
COMPARTMENT

AUX MACHINERY

ENGINE ROOM

USS Von Steuben (SSBN-632)

Extracting out sick Nav ET by chopper

CHAPTER EIGHTEEN

Head for Bermuda, and Make it Fast

CHOPPER EXTRACTION

We had been on patrol for about one month above the Arctic Circle when one of our Navigation Electronic Technicians (Nav ET) became ill. Years before, Ballistic Missile Submarines carried a full-fledged MD, plus a corpsman. Over the years of keeping records of crew member illness while on patrol, MDs were deemed unnecessary. Specially trained corpsmen were the only medical help onboard while on patrol for two and one-half months.

It didn't matter. In all the years I made patrols, this Nav Electronics Technician (ET) was the only person ever to become sick. Well, we did have a man die, but we put him in the freezer. While submerged, we made our air and water. Moreover, as part of the ship's ventilation system, machines called scrubbers and burners continuously cleaned the air. At the end of each patrol, we would surface and open the hatch. Fresh air stinks. Very few ever got sick on patrol, but we all got a sore throat or a slight head cold after being exposed to fresh air again.

The Nav ET had appendicitis, and we were nowhere close to a NATO military base to offload him. Our area had been crawling with Soviet warships. The Doc (Corpsman) hooked up an IV and loaded him up with antibiotics and something to put him out and slow his systems down.

A message was written and put into the radio computer explaining the situation and asking for guidance. After a thorough search with sonar of the area, we slowly came to periscope depth (PD). The computer transmitted the message in a microsecond, and down we went. When a msg is transmitted, there are no dots and dashes. A low-powered encrypted signal is emitted, which sounds like you spit out a watermelon seed. An overhead satellite picks it up and sends it on its way. Standard operating procedure dictates this is something a ballistic missile submarine never does while on patrol unless it is an emergency.

It wasn't long before we received a reply. We do not have to stick an antenna out of the water to receive msg traffic. The radio waves will penetrate water down to a certain depth. Due to the number of Soviet operations in our area, we were directed to come off patrol; in other words, our alert status changed. Our orders were, go to a specified depth (deep), and a corridor would be cleared for us to make flank speed for Bermuda. Bermuda? We were nowhere close to Bermuda, but those were our instructions. We were to surface at a specific place and time, and a helicopter would be waiting on us.

We did a thirty-degree down angle, slowly increasing speed, hit the ordered depth, and cranked on the turns. We had a tube in the ocean just for us.

Any non-US sub would have to get out of the way. Underwater, our class sub was blind at any speed over eight knots. We passed eight knots in a hurry. We were poking holes in the ocean at high speed.

Over fifty years ago, our government secretly placed very sensitive long sonar arrays in various deep-water areas worldwide. This classified program was called SOSUS. You can search the internet for details about SOSUS. If you were a submarine or surface ship in the Atlantic and certain parts of the Pacific, we knew where you were and what you were. It was a Top Secret program until John Walker spilled the beans to the Soviets. So, they knew, but it did not stop the system from performing its purpose. It was a great help for us to know in advance where their ships and submarines were.

On the same note, you did not want to receive a message that SOSUS had picked you up. There is no doubt in my mind, as soon as we cranked on the turns, SOSUS had us. Of course, they received the same message as we and were watching to make sure there was not going to be a close encounter with another country's submarine. Not only Russian, but UK and France were out there.

We had a Top Secret plotting contact board onboard the sub, which showed our position and exactly where all the bad guys were. Only a few people on board know where we were in the world. Where we went on patrol was not general knowledge to most of the crew. They performed their jobs every day on patrol like it was a walk in the park. I believe the wives knew more about what and where we were than most of the crew. Navy wives are strange critters.

Our transit to Bermuda was long but fast. When we surfaced, the helo was ready to take our sick crew member to Bermuda's naval hospital. He was taken topside in a stokes stretcher, hooked to the helo cable, hauled up, and departed. We submerged and stayed at periscope depth. It wasn't long, and we received a message stating surgery was successful, and a full recovery was expected.

TARGET PRACTICE

Instead of immediately returning to patrol depth and continuing on our merry way, the powers-that-be in Norfolk gave us to the anti-submarine warfare (ASW) aviation squadron stationed in Bermuda to use as a real target for them to get some practice for twenty-four hours. What that meant, we go to a specific area, specified by the ASW Commander, are given a no-deeper-than depth restriction order. They try to find us using all their equipment. I don't know how long we had been putting around in this box when I came on watch in Sonar. They had the ocean full of sonobuoys echo ranging up a storm.

The buoys are dropped from the P-3 aircraft, after hitting the water, a small transducer on a cable drops down to a certain depth and starts pinging away. Each buoy is monitored by equipment onboard the aircraft. We had a piece of equipment in Sonar that told us exactly where the buoy was relative to us. We could turn and go away from it as long as we stayed in our box. It just so happened that at the max depth we were allowed to operate, we were just above a layer or thermocline.

If we were allowed to drop below the thermocline, they would have never found us. We could have held a square dance on board and never been detected. As I sat at my equipment, however, I noticed something below the thermocline headed our way but slowly drew to the right. Thinking it may be a large school of biologics (fish), I pointed it out to the OOD and asked him to put the bow right on the layer. Our main sonar is located in and around the bow. By placing a small down angle on the boat, we can keep our engineering noise above the layer but listen with our sonar below the layer.

The Diving Officer gradually changed to a down angle and eased the bow into the layer, and there it was loud and clear. A Soviet diesel boat on the battery, trying its best to get out of Dodge. Not realizing we were there, he thought all the sonar buoys pinging up a storm were meant for him. It was a prize of all prizes for us because diesel boats are tough to detect. I remembered, two weeks before, a Soviet *Type III Foxtrot* was headed for the Med but disappeared. He sneaked over to Bermuda to do a little photo/electronic spying.

I informed the OOD what we had, locked all our sonar gear on him, and the boat quietly manned battle stations torpedo. The Captain immediately came in Sonar and asked if I was sure. I said "Yes, Sir," and let him listen. I pointed out several discreet frequencies we were picking up, that are only found on that class boat. The fire control party plotted all the data. The fire control computer figured out a solution. In a matter of a few minutes, we had this guy dead to rights. He had no clue we were there.

The CO came back to Sonar and told us we would go to periscope depth to pass the info to the aviation squadron. We would slowly move out of the area to make sure we were not detected. We gradually came to PD. All information was passed in code, and shortly after, everything flying and dropping sonar buoys changed direction. Their buoys were reset to go lower below the layer. Those guys had a ball. With our help, they had a real-live bad guy to harass. We gave them his course, speed, depth, and all they had to do was keep the buoys dropping in front of him. I am sure they were happy campers.

We slowly disengaged from that operation and headed back to parts unknown. The next day, way off in the distance, we could hear the *Foxtrot* running his diesels, charging batteries. I bet he had P-3s all over him taking pictures. Later, we received a message from the ASW Command, giving us an Atta-Boy for all the help.

Of course, we got no acknowledgment or award for doing what we did. Our Nav ET made a full recovery and met us back in Charleston when we flew back from Scotland. He was sorry he missed the encounter. By the time we returned, the sea stories were getting outlandish, most of them are anyway.

After the collapse of the USSR, if you had the money, you could buy a *Foxtrot*. Just about every one constructed has been scrapped or is sitting somewhere rusting. The Soviets had many of their submarines decommissioned. They have had a hard problem getting a new class of subs to last longer than four to five years. My first Fleet Ballistic Missile Submarine (FBM) was commissioned in 1964 and decommissioned in 1994. Our subs are made to last.

U.S. Submarine Base Holy Loch, Scotland

CHAPTER NINETEEN

How to Do a 30-Day Refit in 14 Days

THE YOM KIPPUR WAR

On October 6, 1973, hoping to win back territory lost to Israel during the third Arab-Israeli war in 1967, Egyptian and Syrian forces launched a coordinated attack against Israel on Yom Kippur, the holiest day of the Jewish calendar. Taking the Israeli Defense Forces by surprise, Egyptian troops swept deep into the Sinai Peninsula while Syria struggled to throw occupying Israeli forces out of the Golan Heights. Israel counterattacked and recaptured the Golan Heights. A cease-fire went into effect on October 25, 1973.

Moored alongside the tender near beautiful downtown Dunoon, the *Von Steuben* Blue Crew, with not a care in the world, was two weeks into a twenty-five-day refit (maintenance period). I can only speak for Sonar because we were doing our own thing to prepare for patrol. I had disassembled the BQR-2 BTR right down to shafts and gears. I was in the progress of replacing bad/worn small and large gears so everything would mesh properly and not jiggle and jump around as the one and ten-speed synchros tried to line up. The boat was pretty much in disarray as major maintenance was in high gear.

Suddenly, the Captain came over the 1MC. "This is the Captain speaking. As of this moment, put everything back together that you can and prepare to be underway in twenty-four hours or less. All supplies, food, and spare parts from the tender must be aboard and stowed for sea. Due to the war between Israel and Egypt, our THREATCON level has been raised, and we must be at sea ASAP."

The entire sub-site turned into a gigantic beehive. Cranes started swinging pallet loads of everything you could think of over the side—some for our boat, some for other boats. Torpedoes were going here and there, everyone working like crazy to suck as much stuff down a hatch as possible. Working parties galore. I was up in the machine shop on the tender with my BTR housing. I had a bag of shafts and gears, and as fast as I could get a gear in the correct place, a Machinery Repairman (MR) would drill a perfect hole in the stainless shaft, and I'd drive in a roll pin. Then we'd move on to the next shaft and set of gears. With this MR2's help, we finished the job in record time. I still had to put this bucket of bolts back in place, attach a few dozen wires to all kinds of synchros and servos on the backside, and do an electrical signal alignment. Until it was completed, that was my sole purpose in life. In Engineering, several pieces of machinery could not be restored to operating status in time.

When the clock hit twenty-four hours later, the only thing left in Holy Loch was a dry dock, living barge, and boat crews. There was no machinery noise echoing between the mountains, no announcements of any kind, total quiet. Everything and everyone, for the most part, was either at sea or on its way. The tender, at full speed, downhill with a tailwind, might hit eleven knots. Having been at sea maybe once or twice in five years, they had no rig-ship-for-heavy-seas concept.

As best as I can remember, the old *Von Steuben* was in good shape. Our assignment was to go out and play with another boomer for a week or so. When allowed, we came back up the Firth of Clyde and rendezvoused with a Tug to take on fresh vegetables, milk, and mail. The Tug departed, and we made a U-turn and headed back to sea to begin our patrol. By the time someone opened the mail bags and commenced sorting, we realized the post office had mislabeled the bags. We had mail for another sub. Much of the letters were IRS income tax refund checks. Oh, well. Their checks went on patrol with us. There are very few things that will delay an FBM from going on patrol and alert status.

Typical shock mount. The Von Steuben *had such mounts on all rotating and vibrating equipment, and additionally, the decks were isolated from the hull with shock mounts and Teflon.*

CHAPTER TWENTY

We Were so Quiet that We Never Showed Up

BERGY

In Chapter 17, I told you that Ernest Bergstrom reported aboard to be the new Sonar LPO. I also evaluated his experience and ability to be better than mine, but not by much. Aside from all our tomfoolery, Bergy had a more concentrated sonar experience due to his assignments. Unlike me, who had been beaten down by the Bureau of Naval Personnel's mistakes, Bergy previously served on submarines in a Submarine Development Group (SUBDEVGRU). Unlike other SSN or SSBN squadrons or groups, these SSNs were experimental platforms. These boats were the first to receive and test almost everything before approval for fleet use. I can't discuss what they did, mainly because no one knows outside DEVGRU. Don't bother searching the internet for SUBDEV sonar projects. The only thing you will find is about deep diving subs.

Almost the first thing Bergy asked me was, "Do we have a sound signature of the boat?"

I told him no. That was the first time I heard of a sound signature. Beginning with Sonar A school, including all the additional sonar, oceanographic and related training, never a word was mentioned about a submarine sound signature.

Let the training begin. Bergy took sound silencing exceptionally seriously. Sonar had one piece of equipment with hydrophones mounted throughout the superstructure from bow to stern. It allowed us to monitor our own ship's noise. It allowed us to listen to individual hydrophones or all of them at once. Bergy demonstrated that listening to them was not good enough. We needed to see what our electronic monitoring equipment heard. As sonar system technology became more sensitive, many external contacts never heard by a human ear could now be identified with 100 percent accuracy long before the old Mark-1 ear could detect them. A comparison would be bird watching without binoculars or a scope. Magnified images, whether sound or visual, require something extra.

Here is an example of classifying a contact with your ears. Everyone can tell when an old VW Bug starts and runs. If you are old enough, you remember the horrible sound a Chrysler product made when the starter was engaged. A person did not have to see them to know what they were. A semi going by is entirely different from a Cadillac. It is the same with all types of ships and submarines. This is why sonarmen have to have excellent hearing across the human ear's acoustic spectrum. I had and still do. There are no secrets in my house. In a restaurant, I can block out all other noise and concentrate on a conversation two tables over. It drives my wife nuts.

On the other hand, other than the VW Bug, you have no idea what engine was in the Chrysler you heard start. You do not know how many cylinders the semi's engine has. You can't tell the reduction ratio for engine speed vs. tire rotation. With electronic listening, you can obtain that info and much more. I just covered many years of training in a few sentences.

Our first time at sea together, with our onboard mounted hydrophones patched into several pieces of electronic ears, we worked with the electricians. Often, the CO or Engineer Officer would come in and observe. Both were extremely interested in what they saw, especially the Engineer. We had them start and stop ventilation fans, pumps, and other equipment throughout the boat, and we cataloged sound frequencies and level readings to determine which equipment was the quietest. The quietest equipment was placed on the engineering run list for ultra-quiet. We knew the exact frequency all shipboard equipment emitted into the water, and if we saw an increase in frequency level, we'd let the appropriate division know, and they would check it to see what caused the increase. Usually, it was a bearing starting to wear. It was not audible, but electronically, we could see it. When rigged for ultra-quiet, one man went to an electrical distribution panel and turned switches so that only the quietest equipment still ran.

All US vessels use 60 hertz power. All Russian vessels use 50 hertz. If any of our electronic ears began showing a line at 50 hertz, we had a Russki. Each class of Russian sub had its own set of discrete frequencies. This made our job of classifying a type of sub much easier.

During ultra-quiet running, most equipment was turned off, and only essential equipment ran, and then only the quietest. It is hard to explain how far a discrete frequency can travel underwater. On a perfect submarine, no sounds would reach the water. Rubber shock and vibration mounts and entire submarine decks sat on Teflon pads to isolate sounds. Even nuclear-powered boats had one diesel. A little larger than a greyhound bus's engine. If your reactor scrammed and couldn't be back online soon enough, you lived off the battery, half the size of my diesel boat's. Your only alternative was to go to periscope depth, raise the snorkel, and start the diesel. It had an electrical generator on one end, which would produce more than enough amps to restart the reactor.

No, there is no reactor start key and a starter button. You need to run cooling water pumps, raise and lower rod shields, and a few more things. If you cannot restart your reactor, you would be in a world of super deep crap and have to head for home at three knots. This is not a good thing. You would be like a piece of raw, bloody meat thrown in a river filled with piranha. Russian subs would be all around you in no time.

BACK TO THE YOM KIPPUR WAR

During our quick departure from Holy Loch, we operated with another FBM, conducting sub vs. sub exercises to see who could detect the other first. Both boats received a transmitted message with all operation details—the two boats were to rendezvous at a designated latitude and longitude at a specified time. A delineated depth separation ensured there would be no trading of paint. One boat crossed through the lat/lon and proceeded on a specified course and speed. The other boat was to lay off that lat/lon, wait for the sub to come by, and then trail behind and remain undetected. At the end of the first run, the two boats would trade places and begin the exercise again. The goal, when you were designated the trailing submarine, was to remain undetected. However, the lead boat was rigged for patrol quiet, and at some point, after it crossed the lat/lon dot, they could shift to ultra-quiet.

For our exercise, we were the first boat. As we approached the start point, we picked up the other sub, which was supposed to remain undetected. We started a plotting party and manned the torpedo fire control system. Before we crossed the spot and changed to the specified course, we had him nailed and could have blown him away. As we changed course, we could still pick him up in our baffles. He was supposed to be the aggressor and remain quiet. I'm not sure what they were doing, but we had no problems locating him.

Halfway to the end, we rigged for ultra-quiet and slowed to two knots. In just a few minutes, we picked up the other sub coming from directly under us, then pulling out front. If it hadn't been so sad, it would have been hysterical. We remained at ultra-quiet and continued the exercise. They never did find us again, but we were there. We were both Fleet Ballistic Missile subs—same size, same class, but his sound silencing program was non-existent. I would not have been surprised if, during our exercise, there wasn't a fast attack out there tracking both of us...or at least him. The other boat was so concerned after we disappeared; they sent a message saying we failed to show up for the exercise.

The real kick in the pants for them, after both boats eventually returned to port, was that we exchanged sonar tape recordings so each could listen to how their boat sounded. A copy was sent to the Squadron Commander also. I am sure their Commanding Officer was on the receiving end of a significant one-way conversation from the Commodore. As with all branches of the service, fecal matter flows downhill, and by the time it got to their Sonar Division, it was moving at light speed. For a submarine that failed to show up for the exercise, according to them, we had several hours of sonar recordings, plot charts, and fire control solutions of them.

We all received an Atta-Boy from the Captain. His confidence in our sound silencing work was bolstered. I enjoyed listening to their recordings of what they thought was us but were unsure. I was incredibly amazed at how we literally disappeared acoustically and electronically when we rigged for ultra-quiet.

That explained how we could have a top Soviet fast attack class make a circle around us while clearing their baffles and never detect us. We were close enough to hear them talking inside their hull. FBM submarines are not supposed to get that close. Our mission was to be ready at all times to launch if directed, and ALWAYS to remain undetected.

Our missile compartment held more destructive power than what was used by all parties in all previous wars. We were only one FBM, and there were many more on patrol.

A few years after I transferred, I found out they did a similar op with one of our top-of-the-line SSNs. They also reported we failed to show up. Bummer, *Von Steuben* had tapes of them.

I will take a leap of faith here and state that I do not believe our Captain, Executive Officer, or Operations Officer had any knowledge of the sound silencing program. Bergy really showed me the light, and I never forgot it. It is these little things that go in your record that get promotion boards' attention. When they look at your record in DC and see something that catches their eye, you have an assured seat at the table.

Bergy also showed me many technical adjustments for our gear, which vastly improved our ability to pick up contacts and track them. Again, none of these techniques were taught in any school. If you are a computer gamer, you know there are sites you can visit that give you all the cheat codes. Those are the types of technology Bergy brought from DEVGRU. He wasn't cheating, just making us better; fine-tuning, if you will. A few years later, when I was teaching Sonar A-school, I made sure every class knew everything there was to know about sound silencing. Later, I was asked to write a new school curriculum. I would have loved to see the senior sonarman's face when the kid from A-school asked about the boat's sound signature.

PROMOTION

Bergy made Chief his first time up, and as much as I struggled to make First-Class, I made Chief my first time. I don't think I would receive too much push back from those who served in other branches when I say a Chief Petty Officer (E-7) in the Navy carried so much prestige. All senior Marines we dealt with loved the Chief's quarters, and many attended a Chief's initiation. Not a pleasant affair, but it was a rite of passage. My initiation was videoed, and I burned it. There was no way I wanted my wife or kids to see it. It was much worse than the Shellback Initiation when crossing the Equator. Women making Chief went through the same thing along with the men. Many of us were in tears when it was over, we were so proud of our accomplishment.

I know some of you will see this as childishness, but a tradition that goes back to the early days of the British Navy's sailing warships is not something to be taken lightly. The purpose is to celebrate your accomplishment and humbly break you so you can handle all the garbage coming down from above. You are the only thing standing between your people and higher authority. After Chief, then comes Senior Chief and finally Master Chief Petty Officer. These old crusty sea dogs are not to be messed with. Unless you'd like to be thrown overboard or sent to Tierra del Fuego as a Lighthouse Keeper.

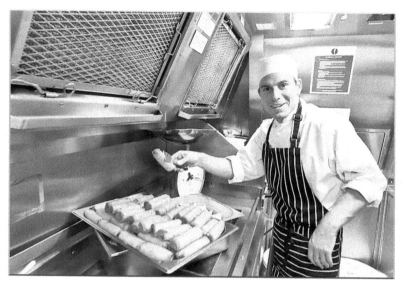

Fresh rolls baked in the Von Steuben *galley.*
(The cook in this image is not Petty Officer Wild.)

CHAPTER TWENTY-ONE

Cornelius Wild MS 2 (SS)

COOKS AHOY!

In the 70s, there was a critical shortage of cooks on submarines. It was crucial. A fleet message went out, asking specifically for Cooks (MS) to volunteer for submarines. The only requirement was to pass the physical. No sub-school required. Sub-school would have been too technical for many.

So, one day out of the blue, we received fleet MS3 Cornelius Wild reporting aboard. Wild came to us from a seagoing fleet tug. Seagoing tugs are over twice as large as a regular harbor tug. Wild had never seen the inside of a sub. Once we flew to Scotland and took over the boat, he was an outstanding night baker. He made great bread and magnificent cinnamon buns.

I quickly learned I could get to Wild easily. Keep in mind, as a sub sailor, you never get on the Yeoman's or cook's bad side. A Yeoman was the ship's secretary, so to speak. Every chance they had, they came to Sonar. Everyone on the boat loved Sonar. They would stop by and listen to whales and other critters outside making sounds. Snapping shrimp was a significant source of background noise. If we had a merchant ship they could listen to, it was really exciting. We'd tell them, yes, that is a merchant ship, with one four-bladed propeller, steam turbine propulsion with a reduction ratio of 20 to 1. It is making 125 revolutions and, on a course, whatever. If gigantic diesels powered the merchant, we could tell them the number of diesels running and how many cylinders were in each diesel. These types of propulsion systems were always diesel-electric. A merchant diesel engine is about the size of an entire CSX locomotive, maybe larger. They are large enough to allow maintenance engineers to take a cover off and walk inside the engine.

None of the merchant ships had a power plant as compact and powerful as our nuclear subs. No matter what we were doing, we could never come close to the maximum power our reactor could generate. There are plans in place to bring in nuke subs to provide electricity to cities where a disaster had knocked out the power grid. There is one catch, however; you have to have a port for the sub to enter.

It is so easy for me to get sidetracked. Consider these distractions as commercials.

Back to the Yeoman and cooks. They automatically have you by the short hairs on day one. Yeomen typed all required reports and also maintained each crew member's personnel file. In the Navy's Yeoman world, a submarine Yeoman is the cream of the crop. Same as our Corpsmen. Both submarine Yeomen and Corpsmen automatically advanced every time. They certainly deserved it. When I was on *Entemedor*, our Yeomen was John Colhoff, a full-blooded Sioux. He was a full-grown man with an even disposition. I guess he went back to the Dakotas after his time was up. As you can see, the submarine service does not discriminate. Now that it is fully opened to everything Washington can throw at it, I'm so glad I am retired.

To say Wild was not the brightest bulb in the palace chandelier would be an understatement. He was a good ol' country boy from Texas, but he had pride in being on a submarine. You had to admire him for his love of the community, and even though he enjoyed the fleet tug, he just beamed with pride in being part of a sub crew.

All Wild did was volunteer and pass a physical. I used to talk to him in a serious manner to see how he was holding up and if there was anything I could do to help him qualify, etc. I have always had a soft spot for those who may struggle, and it was all part of my survival plan if he ever decided to chase me with a cleaver.

He made MS2, and we all made a huge deal out of it. He smiled and enjoyed the fanfare. He had an MS1 and an MSCS over him, but I was never quite sure they had his best interest at heart. I got the impression they felt he could do less damage as night baker and breakfast cook. They were not remotely interested in training him for positions of higher responsibilities. My method was to train my relief.

One day we changed from family-style meals to a line, and as you passed the galley window, you ordered from the menu. Of course, seconds were not a problem. I would go through. If Wild was there, I'd order everything but the carrots (they were not on the menu). Invariably, Wild would come out and look at the posted menu and inform me there were no carrots on the menu. I'd tell him I didn't want any anyway. He would go back in the galley, grumbling. That was the extent I would mess with him.

Later on, Wild decided he would disassemble the ice cream machine and make it squeaky clean. After he reinstalled everything, he forgot to screw in the little drain plug. There stood Wild pouring ice cream mix into the top of the machine, and it came out the drain hole, hitting him in the chest. He started screaming for help, and no one moved. He continued to pour, and the ice cream mix was still hitting him in the chest. Everyone was laughing their butts off. I finally got up, grabbed a tray, and put it under the drain spout. I told Wild to get the drain plug and screw it back in place. The mess decks were a mess, and he was a mess. He finished pouring the mix into the machine, and he and the mess cooks cleaned up the mess on the deck.

One of the Machinist Mate (MM) auxiliary gang Chiefs had buttered up to Wild and asked him to make one straight load of vanilla ice cream instead of another flavor. So Wild made a perfect batch of vanilla just for the Chief. As soon as Wild went back into the galley, one of the guys dumped a bottle of lemon extract into the top of the machine. When the machine had run for the required amount of time, Wild went to the Goat Locker (Chief's quarters) and told the MMC the ice cream was ready. The Chief came out, got a big bowl of vanilla ice cream, took one taste, and spit it all over the place. He threw the bowl and spoon down and yelled obscenities as he returned to the Chief's Quarters. Wild got a cone and took a taste, and for the life of him, he never could figure out how his vanilla ice cream turned into lemon ice cream.

I was on his qual board, along with the COB and others. It became very apparent there was no way Wild could qualify on Subs like everyone else. The COB met with the XO and devised an individual qual plan just for Wild. All he had to know was his compartment. I wasn't sure if that was too much. It was eventually narrowed down to the mess decks and galley and did not include berthing and the heads.

A little note here: Wild did manage to open the sanitary flushing valve when the sanitary tank was being blown to sea. A three-inch-wide solid stream came out with force, covered Wild, the bulkheads, and everything. Standard policy, no matter who does this, they clean it up. Everyone knew if tiny bubbles were coming up through the toilet water, do not pull that handle!

Another side note: We never allowed air to go over outside the boat. When pumping tanks or blowing sanitaries, you always stop before the tank is empty. Under normal conditions, the air we began a patrol with returned with us. When sanitary tanks were vented back into the boat, it didn't sound delightful. The air vented back inside the boat through a large charcoal filter. We only used the best charcoal in the world. It was made from coconut shells. Finely ground and placed in porous, sewn shut bags. Sanitary vent bags were replaced before each patrol. No nasty smells ever survived a trip through them.

We made oxygen from distilled seawater. Our O2 level was maintained at all times. Two systems attached to the ventilation system, called scrubbers and burners, removed other contaminants. Many items were prohibited during patrol—shoe polish, any type of spray can, paint, and several others. If you wore a watch with glow-in-the-dark features, the nukes had to check it for radiation. Above a certain level, it was tagged and placed in a lead-lined safe.

I know, I know, some of you are bitching already. Get over it!

Finally, the day came when Wild completed his severely altered submarine qualifications and got his dolphins. I have never seen anyone so proud to be qualified in my entire career. He was beaming from ear to ear, and everyone on the boat was patting him on the back, shaking his hand. He was bursting with pride. No one ever mentioned to him that he received a pass.

When we flew back to Charleston, his parents were there from Texas to meet him. Wild was dressed in his blues with his new dolphins. As I went by, he asked me to meet his parents. I went on about how fortunate we were to have such a great cook and baker on board. They just ate it up. Hey, WTF, over? What else should I have done? They were proud of their son, and so was I.

The next time we went to Scotland, the two MSs who were senior to Wild put him in charge of the store's load-out. The freezer on a boomer is gigantic. The first thing he put in the far recesses of the freezer was butter, which cooks used every day. It got worse from there, but he got it all in, and everything put away. Every single day during patrol, middle-level ops was knee-deep in frozen stuff as he looked for things.

Thanksgiving underway, Wild was the night baker, and he could not find pecans for pecan pie, the Captain's favorite. So, he improvised and made Thanksgiving pecan pie with peanuts. You could hear the Captain screaming at least one mile away. When you take a nice piece of pecan pie on the end of your fork and stuff it into your mouth, and you bite down on peanuts, it ranks right up there with a sh*t sandwich (sorry). OMG, the CO almost killed the Supply Officer. I ran into the Supply Officer years later. He had changed from Supply to Weapons.

Eventually, I received so much satisfaction when I was COB. The first-class cook and now the Master Chief got busted for stealing a truckload of food they had marked for disposal but never made it to Norfolk to be turned in for disposal. All I could think of was that it was sweet justice for how they treated Wild. Wild was out of the Navy by then and back in Texas, where he started a restaurant business. It was a small local place frequented by his hometown friends. He was very happy.

Years later, I read his obituary. The article talked about his serving onboard a submarine. The townspeople loved his submarine picture signed by many crew members which showed his framed dolphins. He was much admired, and many veterans were regular customers. His specialty was soft serve lemon flavor ice cream (I'm kidding).

He died young, too young. In the submarine world, we keep tabs on as many of our former shipmates as possible.

Glasgow, Scotland.

CHAPTER TWENTY-TWO

Fine Dining in Glasgow

CROSSED EYES & HONEST TIPS

Unfortunately, my time on *Von Steuben* was coming to an end. I enjoyed going to sea with Bergy. If you have to go on patrols, it is much better to enjoy the company of those around you. With Bergy, there was always something in the works. I haven't mentioned this before, but our crew missed five Thanksgivings and Christmases in a row. We were home for all the biggies—Ground Hog Day and Flag Day.

During my last refit in Holy Loch, Bergy and I had an opportunity to go on liberty together—hit the beach, as we called it. We decided we'd catch the train to Glasgow. We didn't have any plans but to walk around. I had never been there except to change stations and catch another train to Edinburgh or London. I loved going to Edinburgh, a magnificent city overlooked by a foreboding castle. The ferry and train schedules are coordinated, unlike in the USA. They took public transportation seriously, and everything worked perfectly. It was a thirty-five-minute ride to Glasgow. We left the station and headed out to visit this grungy industrial city. We did a lot of window shopping and stopped at several appealing pubs for a pint.

Soon, I told Bergy I was hungry and asked if we could find a place to eat something besides fish and chips. Eventually, we saw this unusual restaurant. It had two stories, and your food choice determined which floor and which side you entered. If one person wanted seafood and another steak, they were in two different parts of the place. We settled on the meat side. Compared to the one Chinese restaurant in Dunoon, this was a nice place. We asked for a table for two and were escorted to our table. Shortly, our charming, young, cross-eyed waitress arrived with menus. Having consumed several pints, it was all we could do to maintain a proper demeanor. Both of us were dying on the inside.

After all, we were submarine sailors, and this was funny. She gave each of us an excellent padded menu and said she would be back shortly with warm bread and butter. After she left, we had to let out some pressure but made sure she was far enough away not to hear us. There is a big difference between being mean and being cruel. Years before, on the *Entemedor*, I graduated from Doc Hardy's couth school in the After Torpedo Room. That is why sonarmen are so *savous* and *deeboner*. That course was not offered to A-Gangers or Torpedomen; everyone knew they were beyond repair.

We hadn't yet made our selections when she returned with a basket filled with fancy hot rolls and butter. Instead of setting it on the table, she placed the butter in the middle of the table and then looked at me but offered Bergy rolls. Then looked at him and stuck the basket my way. I swear to God, this is a true story. It is much funnier if I am there to demonstrate her movements. Then she placed the rolls down next to the two dishes of butter. There was only one but being cross-eyed, she saw two.

"Are you ready to order?" she asked.

Again, she looked at Bergy and asked me for my selection and then looked at me and asked Bergy for his. We asked for a wine list—big mistake.

Shortly she returned with the wine list, and Bergy told me to pick something. I ordered a burgundy. She thanked us and departed. Soon she returned with the wine and two glasses.

Let the games begin.

She placed the glasses touching side by side on the table, pulled the cork, looked at Bergy, and handed me the cork. I smelled it like I knew what I was doing. It is all spoiled grape juice anyway. Bergy and I were kicking each other under the table like two little kids.

Okay, pay close attention. Bergy and I were already about to die. She had two wine glasses sitting on the table, touching each other. Keep in mind that she saw four glasses. She moved the opened end of the bottle over the top of the glasses and very slowly started to pour—I'm talking molasses in winter slow. Bummer! The first drop hit the tablecloth. She moved the bottle over a bit, filled one glass, and then filled the one beside it. She didn't say a word, and her congeniality toward us remained constant. I about wet my pants. We enjoyed her performance so much that halfway through the meal, we ordered another bottle—the same routine as before. We were silent as she poured the second bottle. The same thing happened as before, one drop on the table, move the bottle, and began filling both glasses.

It was a delicious meal, and she was so wonderful. We left her a $20 tip, which was large for 1975. Today, I would add $100. Bergy and I laughed and laughed about that all the way back to the boat and then told our story so many times.

PCS TO THE LEFT COAST

Before we left Charleston for Holy Loch, I filled out my request for orders to shore duty. It was known as a *dream sheet*. While on my last patrol, the boat received a message with my orders. I was to be transferred to San Diego to be an Instructor at Sonar A-school—the place where I began. I had asked to stay in Charleston. We were happy there, owned our first home, and there was a large Navy presence there. After that patrol, we flew back to Charleston. I checked out from the boat and bid my farewells. Dee and I began the process of selling our house and getting everything ready to move west.

When you make a permanent change of duty station, Uncle Sam makes all the moving arrangements. An inspector comes to your house to determine if your belongings will be on a separate moving van or combined with another shipment. By then, we had four boys. Our oldest was born August 69. Eighteen months later, Robert made an appearance, and eleven months after that, our identical twins arrived, Rick and Mick. Four perfect little boys in two and one-half years.

I know some of you ladies are calling me bad names and feeling so sorry for my wife. I told her not to get a private room at the hospital. Remember that Pampers had not been invented until the twins came along. Dee used cloth pre-folded diapers and washed a million of them. Dee bought ninety-six jars of baby food at the Commissary each week in addition to other items. Dee was terrific, well organized, and did not hesitate to load the kids in the family truckster and drive to Hamlet, my hometown. I was at sea for six months a year. While in Hamlet, between my mother (Mema), several aunts, and my brother, our boys were well cared for.

The year before we moved, we bought an Apache Pop-up camper that slept six. When I was home, we'd pack up and head to Lake Arrowhead at Myrtle Beach. Family always joined us, and they pitched in to help with the boys. If I was at sea, Dee did not hesitate and loaded everything and everyone and joined the family at Lake Arrowhead. I told you it was a match made in heaven.

Yes, it was a challenge raising four so close in age. As they grew, it became easier. We had four in college at the same time. One by one, they made their career choices, married, and were on their own. The couples who amaze me have one in college and one in diapers. What were they thinking?

Finally, the day arrived for us to head west. Our oldest, Jim, was in kindergarten. He missed his last month. It was the beginning of May when we departed. I took thirty days' leave. That, combined with travel time and proceed time, meant that we didn't have to be in San Diego until mid-June. The first stop was Hamlet. So many came to see us before we went to the other side of the moon. So much crying and hugging the day we left.

One of our twins went to my mother, wrapped his little arms around one leg, looked up at her, and said, "Mema, I want you to come wif me." If that doesn't bring a tear, I don't know what would.

I will not go into our long, slow meander across the country. We camped all the way, and many times, we were the only ones in the campground. We had a magnificent crossing. We saw Mt. Rushmore, Devils Tower, Cody, Wyoming, and on down to San Diego. When we left Charleston, the boys were wearing shorts and tank tops. Dee went shopping in Rapid City for winter clothes. Usually, we stayed no more than two nights at any campground. We stayed longer at Yellowstone and Yosemite. Yellowstone was waist-high in snow.

We could not afford a home in San Diego. After three months of living in a KOA Campground in our pop-up, we moved into brand new Navy housing at Murphy Canyon.

We camped in the mountains and desert during our stay in San Diego, always with other instructors, their wives, and children. It was a very close-knit group.

During my Instructor tour, I taught two Iranian-submarine-sailor classes for two months—wonderful, gracious people who love America. One major problem was that the only way they could pass the course was to cheat—and they *had* to pass. The Iranian students who came before them had memorized our entire test bank. As a result, all the Iranian students passed the course. Another First-Class Sonar Tech, Roger Bolen, and I caught them cheating. They had all given the same answer to a bad question with no correct answer in each test bank. There was a big flap until the CWO4 assigned as the student liaison met with us and the department head. He explained, that if any of his students failed the sonar course, they would be executed shortly after returning to Iran for embarrassing the country. No pressure there.

Dee and I received a gold engraved invitation to the Shah of Iran's birthday party, to be held at the Marine Corps Officers' Club in San Diego. It was the party of all parties. The Shah spared no expense. There was a receiving line, many government officials, and more. The Shah was not present, but all the Iranian officers and civilians brought their wives. I have never seen before or since any women anywhere in the world more beautiful than were these Iranian women. Dee and I were dumbfounded at their beauty. Even to this day, I tell people the most beautiful women in the world are from Iran. No wonder they keep them covered in a Hajib.

It was the most fantastic party we have ever attended. Part of it was American and part was Iranian. Just a fantastic night for us.

During our time in California, we discovered that if you do not like the state, people who live there think you are insane. Dee and I found it overcrowded, overpriced, overrated, and their schools were horrible. If you wanted to go to a state park and have a picnic, you had to reserve a table through Ticketmaster. They would not allow anyone to pull off the side of the road, spread a ground cover, and have a picnic. The Park Rangers would write you a ticket for illegal picnicking. You had to go to traffic court, of all places, and the judge dismissed the charge. If you set your mind to it, you could engage in some felonious and mischievous behavior in the woods.

To hike the Pacific Crest Trail, you had to have a permit. They had rangers sitting in small trailside booths checking your papers.

I took the Sonar Chief's test while there. You have three hours to complete the exam. I was out of there in 45 minutes. I knew the answer to every question. I made Chief first time up. Considering my struggle to make First-Class, this was such a relief.

We drove from San Diego to the beltway around DC in forty-eight hours and five minutes on our trip back east to visit relatives. *Gumball Rally* didn't have anything on us.

I received orders back to *Von Steuben*, same crew. Totally unheard of. My transfer time was in December 77. There are exceptions made for families who will make a permanent station change. I was allowed to send Dee and the boys back east to start school at the end of August. The Navy paid for their tickets and they flew from San Diego to Raleigh on a Lockheed L1011. The boys attended Fairview Heights, and they lived with my mother.

I arrived in the middle of December. Dee and I drove to Goose Creek and bought a house.

It was good to be out of California.

Navy mugs—used throughout the Navy.

CHAPTER TWENTY-THREE

The Great Cup Caper

HOW MANY CUPS DOES A SUBMARINE CARRY?

I had received orders to the Antisubmarine Warfare Training Center in San Diego to teach Sonar School. Under a misguided impression that I would never return to the *Von Steuben*, Bergy and I set about during turnover thinking of something that could be done to the entire crew that would go down in the history of submarine pranks as number one.

We decided that slowly, we would steal almost every coffee cup aboard the boat. It had to be carried out, with Bergy and me being the only two who knew what was happening and how it was done.

We began the first day of my last patrol on *Von Steuben*.

As some know, Sonar goes through thousands of blank magnetic tapes while on patrol. With recordings shifting automatically between an upper and lower tape deck, we recorded everything the sonar equipment picked up. Of course, after patrol, any tapes classified Secret due to content were sent, along with charts and logs, for further analysis.

During load-out, we received many large boxes full of tapes from 3M. Our stowage space was above the CO's stateroom. Our visits to the CO's stateroom were frequent but not so much as to be annoying.

We decided Bergy would put the cups in the waterways outboard the sonar equipment. He was short and slim and could fit through a small space just aft of our BQQ-3 and a set of lockers. I was way too big, so he had to do it. While on watch as Sonar Supervisor, we would cut Kimwipes into squares. We used Kimwipes often to remove grease pencil markings. It is a totally innocent procedure for the Supervisor to be sitting in the back of Sonar cutting them. We needed them to place one square between each cup, so they made no sound.

Whenever there was a coffee or bug juice run, not all our cups were returned to the galley for reuse. Sometimes we'd swing by the QM and ask if he had any cups to go back and take an order for a refill. Later, we would knock on the Radio door and do likewise. That way, no one in the galley noticed that the dirty rotten scoundrels in Sonar were picking up filled cups but not returning any. Believe me, as days went by, small things like that would have been noticed.

We couldn't very well walk down to the CO's stateroom with a stack of cups and put them in our tape boxes in his overhead. So, when we went down, we would only pick up tapes and not drop any off. We had to coordinate our visits when the CO was somewhere else. If he returned while we were standing in a chair with our head and shoulders in his overhead, it was no big deal. He knew we were getting tapes.

You would be surprised just how fast cups could disappear when two devious sonarmen put their minds to it. It was not long before the cooks brought a case of cups up to replace the missing cups. There is always breakage during a patrol, and at first, they did not think otherwise.

Eventually, the first large recording tape box was empty. Bergy brought it back to Sonar and refilled the entire box with sound silenced coffee cups. As I was six feet four at 225 pounds and very strong, it was my job to take the tape case full of cups back to the CO's stateroom, which I did many times. For the life of me, I do not know why none of the other two STS on watch ever saw Bergy pulling cups from outboard. I guess they thought he was getting the old used tapes and putting them in the box.

Over the next few weeks, the cooks picked up their last coffee cup case from Supply. There was a lot of head-scratching going on.

Bergy and I had decided we would not interfere with mealtimes. Every person would have a cup for that. All cups had to be turned in to the mess cook to wash them and be ready for the following meal setting. That meant if you did not have your own mug, you had to use a bowl to take coffee or bug juice with you to your watch station. As every submariner knows, there are no bowl holders, just cup holders. Bowls were sitting in laps, on the deck, all over the place. Bergy and I were no exceptions. We did the bowl thing too.

By this time of patrol, we had about two weeks to go, and there were some people upset about this missing cup crap. There were all-hands field days with an emphasis on finding cups. Just like the missing doors, all of a sudden, the Sonar door would fly open, and the CO or XO would look in to see if we were knee-deep in cups. They never said a word, just looked.

"Hi, Captain (or XO)," we said as we drank out of our bowls. We never received a reply. I guess they knew somehow we were involved.

Then, one day, the prankster god shined his light upon us. A mess cook found an oily, greasy cup in a bag of trash in the trash compactor room. The reaction was historical. You would have thought the corpsman was walking through the boat telling everyone not to eat. Everything was contaminated with E-coli.

Every piece of trash in the bag was examined until they found something that identified the bag as belonging to the M Division. Ah, ha, we caught the cup thieves. Back aft, the CO, XO, ENG, COB, and the third butter cutter on the right went. It turned out it was a cup they had been using for many patrols to dip out a bilge pocket until it broke.

Oh, drat! I was looking forward to a firing squad to break up the monotony of patrol.

The entire time, hundreds and hundreds of cups were resting comfortably above the CO's stateroom. When we finally pulled into Holy Loch, the first person across the brow was the storekeeper with a

Priority One supply chit for two cases of coffee cups. Right behind him were two mess cooks. That had to be a first in FBM history, a pri-one 1348 for cups.

Of course, since the Gold Crew was coming on board to commence turnover, extra cups were an absolute must.

As usual, we went to the CO's stateroom and retrieved all our tapes (cups) cases so we could pack and be ready to head back to Charleston. You will never guess who had made arrangements to have the 04-08 below decks watch; me.

One of the duties of the 0400-0800 watch is to return all cups to the galley that were scattered around the Operations Compartment. What a watch that was; Bergy pulled tapes out from behind all the sonar gear. I made my rounds gathering cups and, at the same time, returning cups from Sonar as fast as I could. I still had to take readings and log them in between. All the cups had to be back in the galley before 0530. That is when the breakfast cook and mess cooks began showing up.

By the time they arrived, the entire galley and mess hall tabletops were completely covered in coffee cups four deep. The cook and mess cooks were blown away. So was everyone else who saw it. I casually walked by the galley and said to the cook, "Man, you would not believe all the cups I have been bringing back from all over."

No one was ever the wiser. In Chapter 17, I mentioned that I confessed to all the other pranks during my check-out interview with the XO, but I did not say a word about the cups. I left for San Diego, and one year later, Bergy transferred. Unfortunately for me, Bergy was a chief and told the Goat Locker we had taken all the cups. Boy, did they want some of me!

Little did I know, and maybe the detailer had a request from about ten chiefs; I received orders back to the *Von Steuben* Blue Crew at the end of my shore duty.

I was not aware that Bergy had spilled the beans. I was headed for a deep benjo ditch and didn't know it.

U.S. Navy Chief Petty Officer's Hat

CHAPTER TWENTY-FOUR

I Make Chief

A CHIEF IS...WELL...A CHIEF!

After completing my tour of duty as an instructor at Sonar A-school in San Diego, I checked in at *Von Steuben's* off-crew office as a First-Class Petty Officer on January 3, 1978. My promotion date to Chief was January 15. Most of the chiefs on the boat were so glad to see me. They had been informed I was ordered back and couldn't wait to get hold of me. Bergy had been transferred somewhere, and these bloodthirsty chiefs wanted revenge for my previous antics.

Now I was back, and vengeance is mine saith the Goat Locker. I believe Bergy spilled the beans after I left town. The Chiefs did not recognize my talent as humorous.

That was fine with me. How else would I get my name etched in perpetuity?

The long-time tradition of initiating a Navy Chief had been in place since Moby Dick was a minnow. When the Navy was established, there wasn't a Chief. Many years later, the rank of Chief was established. These people were far and few between. No ship had more than one. They were the ones who had survived the longest and had the most experience. At some point, the Navy was reorganized, and crew members were divided into specialty groups or ratings. Since sailing days, your specialty was the job you performed—sails and rigging, cook, cannon gunners, and so forth.

As ship types changed, newer weapon systems and the radio, radar, and sonar were invented, the structure continued to evolve.

I retired in August 94. Since then, even more changes to the enlisted and officer structure have come to be. An excellent example is Aviation. We have come a long way since Orville and Wilbur's days. We have planes whose wingspans are longer than the Wright brothers' first flight.

None of the other branches acknowledge the promotion to E-7 like the Navy. Before I made chief, I had never been to a chief's initiation or had heard anything about what took place, and neither will you. In the new Navy, if you do not desire to be initiated, that is your choice. Not a single Chief, Senior Chief, or Master Chief, however, will acknowledge your presence outside of performing your duties. This includes no conversation. You can sleep and eat in the Chief's quarters, but they isolate you. When you are to be transferred, the next command is notified of your status, via one chief to another. You will serve a long, lonely time. You can complain all you want to higher authority, even write a letter to anyone in government, but you will receive no reply. It was your choice not to participate, and you knew the consequences. I only know of one person who did not get initiated.

I survived and had a wonderful time. I will never forget that day. My initiation was videoed and given to me; I burned the video. I did not want my wife or kids ever to find it.

Soviet Victor III Class sub surfaced in the Arctic

CHAPTER TWENTY-FIVE

Spy vs. Spy

SOVIET VICTOR CLASS SUB

It was my first patrol as a Chief Sonar Technician. *Von Steuben* was on patrol at patrol depth, minding our own business, and suddenly, I heard cavitation from a submarine that was coming up from a deep transit. I reported it immediately to the Conn. There was no BTR trace, so I happened to hear him as soon as he made his first sounds. We were pointed directly toward the sub, which we quickly identified as a Soviet *Victor Class*. We immediately rigged for ultra-quiet and manned battle stations torpedo using messengers. The *Victor* was too close to sound the general alarm or use our general announcing system, the 1MC. We slowed to one knot, just enough to maneuver slowly. Initially, it appeared we were on a collision course, but as the *Victor* continued toward the surface, it started to draw to the right. Russians come up on odd hours to copy radio traffic. He was close, *really* close. You could hear people talking inside the *Victor* as it went by our bow. Then the *Victor* started a baffle-clearing maneuver consisting

114

of a collapsing circle. The sub did not go active, fortunately, which in most cases, they do. We were so close, even if she had, I'm not sure her active system would have picked us up, or if it had, we were so close the operators would not have believed it was an actual contact. As the *Victor* began her baffle clearing maneuver around us, we placed our rudder hard over to the right. The Conn has speakers and a BTR. Everyone in the Control Room could hear the *Victor* the same as we in Sonar. At one knot, we were not exactly a nimble craft, but it was enough to keep us pointed directly at her as she turned. The quietest spot on a sub is directly off the bow.

Sound patterns radiate out but not there. The *Victor* had to be within 100 to 200 feet of our bow. If I had spoken Russki, I could have understood them. Here we have the top-of-the-line Russian fast attack almost trading paint with us, and she didn't have a clue we were there. After she completed her baffle-clearing maneuver, she proceeded to periscope depth. She was up two minutes before the odd-hour broadcast and was headed deep again two minutes after the broadcast.

The Soviets seemed to have no sense of how to be quiet; just like coming up, she cavitated, and going down and increasing speed, she cavitated for a long time. We tracked her as long as we could as her range opened.

After we secured from battle stations, we had a stream of people coming by Sonar telling us that hearing the *Victor* was the most exciting experience of their life. It definitely will raise your heart rate when an enemy sub is so close.

We sent our tapes and chart package off to the Intel folks. During off-crew, the Captain came in and told me that Intel's analysis indicated at no time did we encounter a *Victor* or any other Russian submarine. Considering that the Captain had spent time in Sonar listening on headphones as we tracked the boat, he just smiled, and I responded, "Aye, aye, sir. Never happened, and if it did, we were never there."

Years later, looking back on this encounter, I believe she had managed to come around Norway and sneak south without being detected by our SOSUS network. That could be an embarrassment to have to admit to.

This encounter is a prime example of why a good sound silencing program is needed aboard every sub.

In the movie *Hunt for Red October*, they talk about a Soviet *Alfa Class* submarine. What a piece of junk they were. They could go very deep, their speeds were amazing, and they were nearly fully automated with a very small crew. You could hear them coming around Norway for miles and miles. Constructed from titanium, it took the Soviets years to get one operational finally.

We use distilled water in our reactors with a dose of anti-corrosive ingredients. The Alfa used liquid lead-bismuth. These reactors generated magnificent power, but to keep lead-bismuth liquid took massive amounts of electricity. All four Alfas were based in Murmansk, a paradise if there ever was one. Find the place on a map. I've seen it through a periscope, do not tell anyone. The design geniuses who thought this up never considered just how cold the water was and the winters.

Finally, the Soviets gave up. Out of the four super expensive boats, only one was able to go to sea. Eventually, they were scrapped. Even their massive *Typhoon Class*, scrapped after four years. When the *Kursk* sank, we could have had a deep submergence rescue sub there in less than twenty-four hours and saved the crew. No, no, said the Russians, and they all died of carbon dioxide asphyxiation.

Soviet Kashin Class *Destroyer.*

CHAPTER TWENTY-SIX

Thunder in the Attic

SOVIET *KASHIN CLASS* DESTROYER

Thunder in the attic is what WWII submarine crews called exploding depth charges. The attic was the several hundred feet of water above them. Conventional depth charges are nasty drums of high explosive that detonate based upon the preselected depth. A sub tries its best to have them explode above—the further away, the better. If they detonate alongside or just below the keel, a sub suffers damage. Submariners try their best to keep the *people tank* dry.

Von Steuben was on patrol above the Arctic Circle in our assigned area, putting along at patrol depth and not in any hurry to go anywhere. Always rigged for patrol quiet, we were nearly undetectable. When we shifted from patrol quiet to ultra-quiet, we disappeared. We were doing our thing to remain undetected and avoid all surface shipping

117

and submarine areas. You'd be surprised just how crowded it can get underwater if you stray off into specific areas.

Moreover, there is always some country's submarine running at max speed, totally blind, and making enough noise for all of us to get out of the way. They sound like the 9:05 express freight with a highball signal. He is in number eight, the last notch on a locomotive's throttle, and running wide open. You usually could pick these idiots up at least 100 miles away. Rattling and banging like an empty coal train coming through town wide open.

Submarines carry several different types of sonar equipment. One is active, which means it transmits a high-energy pulse into the water, as you hear in the old war movies. We NEVER use it. In fact, the active section is turned off when on patrol to prevent someone from accidentally sending a ping into the ocean. Except for our underwater telephone, all the remaining equipment is passive, designed for incoming sound only. Some of it is specifically for actual listening by a sonar operator. Much time and money are spent training all sonarmen to recognize what they hear and classify the sound. If you saw the movie *Hunt for Red October*, you will remember the second-class sonarman, Jones, who was so wonderful. Between him and Seaman Beaumont, they were the sonar gang. In the real world, a fast attack sub would never get underway with only two sonarmen. SSNs carried a bunch, ranging from E-9 to E4, Master Chief to Petty Officer Third-Class. They would have had many years of training. The missile boats usually carried six to eight sonarmen. There are exceptions to those numbers, but overall, they are accurate.

In most cases, other crew members fill in as sonar watchstanders. Most of their training is conducted onboard since they are operators only and not required to maintain the equipment. Some of the main systems need a year of advanced electronics to sustain operation at 100 percent.

There were usually four people on watch on missile boats, sometimes only three—a supervisor and two or three operators. I always took a turn on the gear to keep my ears sharp. There are a lot more whales out there than most people realize. Like alligators, they have learned to hide when a ship is coming. They love submarines, however, and can be a pain when trying to track a bad guy.

Our equipment does not rely on an operator's ears alone. At the same time we are listening, several pieces of electronic equipment are also listening. These pieces are much more sensitive and are not restricted to the human ear frequency range. They can be adjusted to monitor for a specific frequency or a broader band. In most cases, unless a contact pops up in front of you, the electronic ears are the first to indicate there is something out there on a specific bearing.

One piece of sonar equipment's sole function in life is to pick up active sonar echo ranging, the WLR-9. It will give you a bearing, frequency, and other parameters to identify what country and what types of vessels carry this particular sonar. It does all this using magic, smoke, and mirrors.

Our surface ships recognized a long time ago that passive sonar had a distinct advantage over active sonar. Most still run around pinging away but are using passive as well. I will not elaborate on their passive systems or capabilities, but in past years, our subs had an easy time evading echo-ranging surface ships, not so easy anymore.

Back to the north, on patrol, doing our thing, waiting for a message telling us to destroy the world or parts of it. Some beluga whales, pilot whales, and other northern biological noise makers swam around in small and large pods, thinking we were a big brother. Several sperm whales were off in the distance, sounding like they were building a house. For many years, they had been dubbed *carpenter fish*, but we knew they were sperm whales.

Out of nowhere, the WLR-9 emitted a double-tone beee-burp. All heads looked up to see the bearing and frequency. We continued to watch it to see if it was some random frequency from a whale or a real contact. Simultaneously, both operators turned their passive sonar listening equipment in the direction of the frequency and checked the BTR for anything that looked like a constant noise source. Sweeping their sonar back and forth over the indicated bearing, fifteen degrees each side, both operators listened intently. After a few minutes, we relaxed and settled back into our watch routine. Random alerts were not unusual when so many different whales were around. Human-made sounds were more uniform and would reappear more often.

Out on the Conn, the OOD had a smaller version of what we have, more or less a repeater of the video and audio portion. The OOD called, asking if we had anything on that bearing. I responded we had no contacts and believed the sound was from a whale. He agreed and returned to whatever he was doing. He would have noticed a *trace* starting to develop the same as we. About ten minutes later, beee-burp—same general bearing and frequency. Now the OOD and all of the sonarmen were interested in seeing what the heck this was.

Shortly thereafter, I reported to the OOD that the frequency matched a Soviet warship sonar, but it must be a long way off because we had nothing else. Passive sonar is very sensitive, especially the electronic portion. As the BTR needle slides across a slowly moving paper, it electronically burns a small mark on the bearing if it detects any noise. The paper slowly moves down from top to bottom, and the BTR needle moves left to right from bearing 180 degrees to 000 degrees in the center to 180 degrees on the opposite side. It is not interested in anything but sounds in the ocean and doesn't care whether it is a school of haddock, a fishing boat, or aircraft carrier; only sounds and sound level.

Again, we watched, listened, turned on a new piece of gear, and set it up to look for discrete frequencies or a propeller rhythm. This time, I left Sonar and walked out to the Conn to speak to the OOD. I briefed him on what was going on and told him I was going into Radio to check the Top Secret chart. It showed all known Soviet submarine and surface ship locations. Radio received periodic intelligence updates, and they plotted them on the chart. Only those with a need to know could see this chart.

Sonar and Radio were across the passageway from each other. The Conn was located on a raised platform immediately aft in the center of the Control Room. That is where the two periscopes were, and from there, the OOD had an excellent view of the diving station located right in front of him, the Ballast Control Panel (BCP) just to his left, and the weapons fire control tracking system to his right. He was in charge. The BCP was usually operated by a Chief Petty Officer or a senior First-Class Petty Officer. The Diving Officer was generally a chief or a junior officer. He oversaw two junior enlisted men who operated the sailplanes, rudder, and stern planes. They were known as the inboard and outboard stations. Their seats were very comfortable, with seat belts and an angled platform for their feet.

By flipping a few switches, the system will operate automatically, or the function of each station can be transferred to either inboard or outboard. Some of these men are so proficient they can handle all three functions simultaneously. Every crew member, from the most junior enlisted to all officers, must be qualified to *drive and dive*. The device directly in front of the inboard and outboard station is called a yoke. It is almost identical to what airline pilots use. At high speeds underwater, a submarine handles much like an airplane. We can take forty-five-degree down and up angles. That is why the stations have seat belts and an angled floor to brace against.

One of the most significant touted features of the *USS Nautilus* (SSN-571) was the ability to submerge, reach max speed and max depth, and reverse course in one minute. Compared to the new generation, *Nautilus* was the Wright Brothers' plane. The SSNs are unbelievable compared to a missile boat, like comparing a Corvette to an eighteen-wheeler. We were quiet but lumbering. SSN and SSBN are two entirely different platforms. An SSBN is long and heavy, whereas an SSN is shorter and quicker. In this case, we would be looking to remain undetected, whereas an SSN would be driving down the last bearing to investigate and harass to death whoever it was.

I opened the door to Radio, exchanged greetings and harassments, and lifted the cover off the chart. Way down to the south of us were three Russian warships—a *Kynda* and two *Kashins*. I asked when this was last updated and was told since I came on watch. It didn't appear they had any general direction of operation. They were several hundred miles south of us, just milling around.

The *Kynda* was not a concern, but the two *Kashins* were bad to the bone. Twin gas turbines capable of thirty-eight knots. Covering the chart, I went back out to the OOD and let him know the possible source of the acoustic alerts. He looked surprised and said, "That far?"

I said, "Yes, sound in water does some strange things. One time, I tracked a merchant ship that was closing for four days. It was loud and clear, yet we never saw it when it finally reached its closest point of approach (CPA)."

Sonarmen attended many schools on oceanography. Temperature, salinity, currents, thermoclines, refraction, rarefaction, sound channels, and on and on. In my first fifteen years, I attended forty-one schools.

Back in Sonar, I briefed the watchstanders about the three ships off to the south and told them to keep an eye and ear out for them. The next two hours were uneventful.

When our reliefs arrived, I thoroughly briefed them on the two intercepts, and I took the oncoming supervisor over to Radio to look at the Top Secret chart. Radio had not received an update, so we felt reasonably secure. They assumed the watch, and my group and I went down to eat and then hit the sack. I never knew when we would encounter a situation that would put me in Sonar for twenty-four or more hours, so food and sleep were essential. We were standing three six-hour watch rotations, so my guys had twelve hours before returning to Sonar. Some ate and then played cards to unwind before sleeping. Any of them not qualified did not play cards but continued learning every system on the boat. Me, I ate and went straight to bed.

By now, I was Chief-of-the-Boat, but because I was also in charge of Sonar, Sonar needed me more than anywhere else. Typically, the COB was Diving Officer during battle stations, but I was in Sonar. Invariably, sleep was not guaranteed because the CO or XO wanted to see me about something. I grabbed sack time every chance I could.

What seemed like five minutes was six hours when the messenger came to wake me.

"COB, COB, you are needed in Sonar immediately!"

I responded, "Okay, I'll be right up."

I got up, looked at my watch, and my first thought was, *I wonder what piece of equipment broke.* I stepped out of the Goat Locker and grabbed a cup of black and bitter. I climbed the stairs up one level to the main deck where Control, Navigation, Fire Control, Radio, and

Sonar are located. I noticed a lot of activity. It appeared I was not the only person who was awakened.

As I opened the door to Sonar, the first thing I heard was the WLR-9 playing jingle bells. That thing was continually sounding detection alarms. I told the operator to shut the alarm off. The on-watch supervisor explained that we had those three Russian ships closing. Each ship was echo-ranging on a different frequency, and the WLR-9 responded to every ping. I asked the supervisor several questions. At the same time, I looked at the BTR for any traces. I saw three distinct crisscrossing contacts. They were changing course in unison a certain number of degrees on each side of a base course. I could tell immediately that they were heading straight for us, and unless they changed course, they would pass overhead.

Shortly after I arrived in Sonar, the rest of the sonarmen came in and took their tracking stations. Our more experienced men relieved the current operators, and the rest started doing their thing. A classified tape recording was already in progress, and new prepped tapes were staged for use. The fire control tracking party and plotting party were fully manned and doing what they do out in Control. When submerged, they receive all their information from Sonar. Our job was to ensure we stayed on the same contact, so they had useful bearing information. Normally, that is not a problem. Sonar has an automatic tracking feature that allows it to lock on the target. When you have three warship contacts generating similar noise levels, as their tracks cross, one ship can pull sonar off another. Even if a sonarman is tracking just by listening, it isn't easy to stay on the same contact. The way our sonar worked back then, the operator would put his indicator on the target to track and then switch on the Automatic Tracking Feature (ATF). Electronically, it would balance the incoming sounds and keep the bearing indicator always on the contact. If a contact crossed in front of or behind, ATF could very easily follow the other contact as it went by. The operator had to be ready to put it back on the correct target. These changes cause havoc with the fire control tracking system.

The Captain came in and asked what I thought.

The first thing I said was, "I don't believe the position of the contacts on the Top Secret chart in Radio was accurate."

He agreed. Then I briefed him on what we had, their speed and what they appeared to be doing, and the fact they were headed straight for us. We had not made any noise or gone to periscope depth and raised any mast, so it appeared we just happened to be in the wrong place at the right time, or so we thought. I do not know how often Radio received updates on their positions, but they were much closer than plotted at their last position.

I explained the problem of tracking an individual target and how the bearings jumping around might make fire control tracking impossible. At least the paper plot would show when a bad bearing was obtained, and they could draw a line between the good bearings.

By now, the boat was rigged for ultra-quiet, and all hands were at their battle stations. The hours slowly slipped by, and sonar operators rotated every forty-five minutes. We went through a tape every fifteen minutes, so new tapes and used tapes were starting to become a problem and had to be moved to another area. Gallons of coffee and bug juice came and went not only for us in Sonar but also in the Control Room, the heart of the operation.

Periodically, the Captain stuck his head in and asked a few nervous-type questions such as, Are you sure they are closing? Any indication of a course change? Etc. The fire control system was unhappy with input bearings jumping around, even if it was only a degree or two. Until then, we were only receiving direct echo-ranging pings. Sound transmitted underwater generates a straight source, a surface bounce source, and a bottom bounce source. The first two are worthless for determining range, but the bottom bounce ping allows us to use trigonometry and calculate an accurate range to the target. Unfortunately, you do not start receiving a bottom bounce ping until the contact gets closer.

I had already gotten the water depth, a stopwatch, and our little handy-dandy wheel calculator used for bottom bounce ranging. One section of the wheel was lined up on the correct bottom depth. When the direct ping arrived, I'd start the stopwatch, and when the bottom bounce ping arrived, I'd stop it. Adjusting the second wheel to the correct position gave me a range on the outside ring. We maintained a log of these ranges. After a few bottom bounce ranges, I took them out to the Captain and showed him what we had. He looked at them and at the computerized fire control system. They did not match. By now, everyone on board could hear the echo ranging through the hull. In all the hours we had been tracking the ships, they had not altered their maneuvering pattern. Power levels on their sonar had remained the same.

Back in Sonar, I continued to take bottom bounce ranges, and they continued to close. When they got to 10,000 yards, I told the Captain that I had them at 10,000 yards and closing. Back in Sonar, we were doing our thing, and shortly the door opened again. It was the Captain.

He asked, "What do you have them at now?"

"Eight thousand yards," I said, "and if we don't do something soon, they will pick us up."

For whatever reason, the fire control system had them opening, which only confounded the problem. A few seconds after the Captain left, word came over the sound-powered phone system to rig the ship for deep submergence and sonar. We were going deep and changing course. As the phone talker told me this, the boat started taking on a slow but steady down angle. Speed increased slowly, and then we began to bank as we got out of the way of the approaching Russian warships. The down angle continued to increase—20, 25, 30, 35, 40 degrees. As our depth and speed increased, we added more rudder and played like the Blue Angels at an air show. Our speed and depth are classified, but we had completely reversed course and were flying by the time we got to the ordered depth.

The fire control system was excellent, but as I said before, if it gets erratic bearings, it can do strange things. The system had the Russian ships' trackline but indicated they were opening because the system had the ships heading in the opposite direction. A quick manual override corrected that problem.

We reached ordered depth and speed, and were actually behind the warships and off to the side a safe distance when they started dropping depth charges. Holy crap! You have never heard anything so loud in your life! Of course, we were not close enough for them to do any damage, but unofficially, I think the nukes in Maneuvering went past the throttle speed red line, and we got out of Dodge in a hurry.

As the boat passed a certain speed, we, in Sonar, were blind. There was so much water moving by the bow so fast it masked all sounds except for depth charges. We ran for an hour like this. Then the Captain ordered *All stop!* and we glided up a few hundred feet and changed course ninety degrees. As soon as we could hear again, they were still where we left them, echo-ranging away and dropping depth charges. I feel sure they were chasing the water knuckle we left for them when we went deep and turned at the same time.

We slowly returned to patrol depth and normal speed and continued tracking them until they went over the hill. The Captain and Executive Officer stopped by Sonar and gave us all Atta-Boys, and all was well with the earth.

I'm not sure what, if anything, happened to the Captain once we returned to port, and he turned in his patrol report. He wasn't relieved, but you never know what they put in his record. Our primary function in life was to be on patrol, at patrol depth, maintaining communications, and be 100 percent ready to launch some or all of our missiles if we receive a message telling us to do so. Our other requirement is to avoid detection. In this case, to avoid detection, we had to go deep and run for an hour, which meant we could have missed the entire war because we had no radio receiving ability at that depth and speed. No one of higher authority knew that our target package was not covered. The Commanding office of a ship and especially a submarine is God. Unlike any other branch of the military, he has more power than anyone else in Command. I am sure after all factors were reviewed, he may have gotten an Atta-Boy.

Several years later, a traitor named John Walker was arrested for selling classified information to the Russians. Everything he sold pertained to submarines. They knew where our operating areas were.

It was an exciting time for us all, and the best part, after we secured from battle stations and returned to normal underway watches, was that it was my time to be on watch. The Navy is more than a job; it is an adventure at 78 cents an hour.

By the way—depth charges at a distance do sound like Thunder in the Attic.

U.S. Capitol Building, Washington D.C.

CHAPTER TWENTY-SEVEN

Traveling for the Navy & Other Matters

WASHINGTON D.C.

I was COB and a Senior Chief, but I do not remember why I was sent to Washington—much like many up there. When the movie *Planes, Trains, and Automobiles* came out, everyone who has traveled for the government adopted that movie as their Patron Saint, if that is possible.

As you may know, we enlisted folks traveled on a wing and a prayer. We were given just enough travel pay to do two things, sleep inside, or eat. Years later, I learned a trick for traveling to DC. After checking into a very plush Motel 6, I would order an extra-large pizza supreme, deluxe, whatever was the largest. I put the pizza inside the microscopic fridge. Most times, it had to be folded several times. Each evening I would peel off one slice, zap it, and then eat slowly. That was my dinner for that night. By doing so, I had all kinds of extra money for the free coffee and donuts in the lobby for breakfast. At lunch with my fellow professionals, who had expense accounts, some of the best money-saving ideas were lettuce sandwiches, cucumber sandwiches, and bean sprout sandwiches. I was on a diet and paid for the salad bar.

If I could stick with this program, I still owned my home by the time I returned and filed my travel claim. Not to mention, I was slim and trim. Pretty much the same results if I were to stay drunk a week.

One time, I returned from a one-week trip to DC. I filled out my travel claim and turned it in. Around two weeks later, I received a notice from Disbursing; I owed them $1,800. I had one week to pay said amount, or they would begin deducting it from my pay.

I know most of you could reach in your pocket, pull out a wad of Mafioso cash, go over, and bada bing, bada boom. And here is a little something for you, little lady. In my case, married, four boys, house, car, etc. There was no wad in my pocket other than lint.

Those of you who know me, I am a kind, gentle, understanding, very large man. I radiate love as I move around. I knew there was a simple mistake that would be rectified at Disbursing, and afterward, we'd all have a good laugh. Same as in all *Donna Reed TV Shows*.

Paperwork in hand, I walked to Disbursing. This was before they moved it off base so everyone could have an opportunity to rob them. I climbed the stairs to the second deck and into the gauntlet. A very lovely PO3 DK was dutifully sitting at her desk to greet and direct. Being the Southern Gentleman that I was, I said, "Good morning. I received this and need to talk to someone, please."

She looked at the paper and replied to a Senior Chief, "If this is what it says, you need to pay it."

Arrrrr! This was a *much* larger trigger than the mess cook who accidentally spilled corn on my head and said, "Look, everyone, corn on the COB!" as he laughed.

As I sat looking aft while corn dripped off my head, I saw nothing but complete horror on every face; the young lad was the only one laughing. In fact, I saw NO HUMOR in that at all. Being the loving, kind man I am, I slid out and said, don't worry about it, and kissed him on his cheek. Someone throw a shovel and a bag of lime in the caddy.

Back at Disbursing at what was soon to be *ground zero*, it wasn't so much the money that concerned me, as it was a PO3 addressing a Senior Chief as she did. As an STS3, I would never in a million years have talked to a chief or above like she talked to me. So, I immediately went to 1SQ! Ripple fire! Snapshot! Launch the damn missile!

I raised my right arm as fast as I could, made a very large fist, and brought it down on her desk so hard, the entire building shook. Then, I yelled, "Who is in charge here?"

I managed to scare her half to death, and I had people coming out of cubby holes all over, including the Disbursing Officer.

He came over and smiled. "May I help you, COB?" He knew what the Command Badge meant.

I replied, "Indeed!" and we went into his office.

Could you believe it? Disbursing had made a *grievous* error, and they owed me $1,800. The Disbursing Officer said it would be reflected in my paycheck unless I wanted it immediately. I thanked him and said the next paycheck would be acceptable. Before leaving his office, I explained why I tried to destroy his building. He assured me he would take care of it.

As I headed out, I briefly stopped at the PO3's desk, looked over, and told her, "Now, you have a nice day!"

U.S. Navy Officer's Hat

CHAPTER TWENTY-EIGHT

Moving Up

USS VON STEUBEN

The Blue Crew departed Charleston via chartered jet and headed back across the Atlantic for Prestwick, Scotland. I lost the thrill of flying many years before. At first, it was enjoyable. Not anymore. It turned into drudgery. Nothing ever changed except the length of our patrols went from ninety to 105 days.

Near the end of one patrol, Radio received a message informing us we were extended and to remain at sea on patrol, another FBM good deal. When our Captain made the announcement, this is how it felt. You are at the pain merchant (dentist), and he is drilling away, then stops to inform you, "When I finish with this cavity, I'm going to remove that ingrown toenail you have."

It is hard for me to convey how we felt. Not a single person jumped up and saluted, "Thank you, sir! May I have another?"

This patrol was about as dead as they got—no interesting contacts, just biologics, and underwater ambient noise. To break the monotony, I went out to Control and qualified as Diving Officer on my off time. Then, I began working on Officer-of-the-Deck qualifications. I had only known a handful of enlisted men who qualified in that position. My God, you need something to break the monotony. The boat had a library. A case of books would arrive between each patrol, and the oldest in inventory went back in the box. In twelve patrols, I read like a crazy person. Not this patrol, I decided to do something else.

Eventually, we never were called on to destroy the world and our time at sea ended next to the tender in Holy Loch. This routine had become so bad that I never left the boat to go ashore on liberty. I had seen, done, eaten everywhere, had a mug, a T-shirt, a bumper sticker, and a partridge in a pear tree.

Hi-ho, hi-ho, it is back across the Atlantic we go. Sometime in September, I was summoned to the Captain's office. I knocked and entered. There were the Captain, the Executive Officer, and the Chief-of-the-Boat. That is about as bad as it can get.

"Have a seat, Chief. The three of us have decided you will be our next Chief-of-the-Boat."

I believe the Brits call it *gobsmacked*. I said I had been a chief for nine months; there was only one chief onboard junior to me.

The CO noted, "We discussed that, and we do not think you will have a problem with your leadership abilities."

The XO chimed in with a big smile, "You will be the most junior COB in the Submarine Force, and the Gold Crew has the senior COB in the Submarine Force, TMCM (SS) Miller."

Master Chief Miller had made several war patrols. He lived off coffee and cigarettes, and he hardly ever slept.

Okay, I do have tears in my eyes as I type. All I could say was, "I will do the best I can, sir."

"You will relieve the COB one week before he transfers to shore duty," the CO said.

The Master Chief COB was grinning like a Cheshire Cat. I am sure he instigated the entire thing. I drove home and was wondering how Dee would take the news. When we were gone, all the enlisted wives would look to her. Military wives are two types; they can handle it or lose their minds and are not around when the crew returns. Dee was pleased. I guess I had to be also.

COB is a higher-level management position. I was so fortunate to have a Goat Locker that supported my new role. They could have made my life a living hell. As COB, you wear a small brass badge on your uniform—no extra pay, only much more responsibility. I did finish my OOD qualifications during the next patrol.

Whenever I went up on the tender, the enlisted and officers almost broke their necks when they saw a Chief (as opposed to a Senior or Master Chief) wearing a COB badge. On the base in Charleston, it was the same way.

Try to follow this: January 3, 1978, I reported aboard as a First-Class. I advanced to chief twelve days later, on January 15, 1978. I became COB in September 1978, and the following May, I advanced to Senior Chief. My XO said he believed I held the record for going from a First-Class to a Senior Chief. In May 1981, I was commissioned as an Ensign. I was officially a *Mustang*. Anyone in any branch who goes from enlisted straight to commissioned is a Mustang. Promotion into this program is based solely on your record and recommendation from your command and any former commanding officers who write in. I'm guessing my CO contacted as many as possible for their input.

Here we go again; every command in the entire Navy transferred a new Mustang the same day. Not in my case. After being one of the crew for so long, many were my friends, and they still wanted to be my friend. Now I had officers calling me by my first name and telling me to address them by their first names. I did not know any of their first names. To me, they were CO, XO, Nav, Eng, Weps, and Supply. I was Chief Pait, then only COB.

On top of that, I was eating in the Wardroom. Talk about awkward and a significant culture shock. My head was about to burst. That is the reason newly commissioned officers are transferred immediately.

For me—No, Jerry, you will be with us for a few months. While I was there, the crew was about half and half as far as calling me sir or by my first name as before. All the officers called me by my first name, which was so strange for me after fifteen years as an enlisted man.

Then, the Captain's wife called Dee and invited us to a private dinner at their home. Lord, have mercy on my soul! For Dee, little miss New England manners, it was so excellent.

We enjoyed a great evening. The Captain and his wife were wonderful hosts. He was aware of my inner terrors and wanted to ensure me not to worry. I would be fine.

No wonder it is hard to be chosen for command! A CO has to know more than the COB, and the COB knows everything.

The day arrived, and we all bid each other fair winds and following seas, and I began another life, supporting the submarine force.

Von Steuben ordered in two replacements--a Chief Sonar Tech and a new NEC COB. Personally, I would not like to be COB if I couldn't be in Sonar.

PART THREE
Shore

USS Hunley

CHAPTER TWENTY-NINE

Entering a New World

USS HUNLEY

When I departed the *Von Steuben*, I had to attend several required schools to bring new Mustangs up to speed on Military Law, Etiquette, and various other subjects some of us may have needed. The men and women in my class were from all races and almost every corner of the Navy. We were a mixed bunch of different former ratings. One air traffic controller, two from submarines, many from various naval aviation jobs, another small group of administration types, one Seabee, and one musician. The musician was a different creature. He had no sea time, yet he had a master's degree. The most highly educated segment of the Navy are musicians—bachelors, masters, and doctorates. All musicians enter as enlisted. Their officers are Mustangs. Most were former school band, orchestra, or choral teachers.

Of all the schools I attended, this was my first non-pass-or-fail situation. You learned, or you didn't—a completely different training environment. My officer selection was as a Submarine Electronic Specialty. The majority of my class would return to other commands and assume a job as a Division Officer based on their background. We were the fill-in officers.

The Navy was not about to spend a bazillion dollars educating an officer at Annapolis or a four-year University and send them to a submarine or surface repair ship. Heaven forbid one of their *ringknockers* is assigned to overseas administration. Mustangs and Warrant Officers filled a specialty niche. If you watch a documentary about Carrier Operations, other than the Pilots, Air Boss, Landing, Launching, Navigator, XO, and CO, all the other officers are Mustangs or Warrants. They are in the hanger bay and in charge of all weapons, radar, and combat control centers. Their job is to use their experience to make it happen.

I only witnessed two Mustangs fall flat on their faces. Both were able to revert to the highest rank held as an enlisted man. There is a time limit to do this. Once promoted to Lieutenant Commander, there is no going back. You can retire if you have enough time or throw it all away by resigning your commission.

In keeping with my history, everyone but *guess who?* received orders related to their field.

I received orders to a submarine tender based in Charleston. Yee-haw, buck-a-roo! As I continued to read, I would be the R-3 Div Off. R-3, what the heck is R-3? The Submarine Electronics Division is R-4. R stands for the Repair Department. Each division numbered from R-1 to R-9. Tenders are a floating shipyard. If Repair could not fix the problem, the sub went to the shipyard, or a Tiger Team came to the sub from a shipyard. I finally found out R-3 was the Electrical Repair Division—motor rewind, gyros, interior communications, and the world-famous rubber and plastics shop. Well, that is close to electronics.

The USS Hunley was very close to leaving Charleston Shipyard for GITMO Cuba for a trial by fire, Refresher Training (REFTRA). All ships have the honor of going through one of these hellfire and brimstone places located on the East or West coast. The point was to make sure ships and crews were combat-ready by running them through ship-wide exercises and drills.

A tender is NOT a REAL ship. It is a kinder, gentler ship. We mean no harm to anyone. But we were treated the same as a Frigate, Cruiser, or Carrier. Those people at GITMO are very mean and nasty. They tried to sink us every day for one month. We failed miserably. The only way they let us leave was by us hosting a dependents cruise from GITMO to Jamaica and back. Cookouts on the helo deck, lots of things for kids to do. After that, we received a pat on the head and were sent on our way. They knew from day one that we did not stand a chance.

After we returned to Charleston, we made preparations to take the *USS Hunley* to Holy Loch, change ships and crews, and bring the *USS Holland* back to Charleston for an overdue overhaul. That event is known as *Cross-Decking.*

After that, all of us who had been killed in GITMO would return when *Holland* left the shipyard. Then we would head up the Cooper River and relieve the sub tender chained to a wharf, stern first and spend the rest of our lives repairing submarines.

It was a beautiful January day when we left Charleston for Holy Loch. The pier was covered with girlfriends, parents, wives, and children. We backed away from the pier and began our trip.

As the days passed, we continued a parallel course up the east coast into the North Atlantic, with temperatures gradually dropping and barometric pressure falling. I remembered I had been here before on my first diesel boat. On a tender, you will stay dryer, but you still have to deal with the conditions. The weather became terrible. We could hear distress calls over the radio from commercial ships that were breaking up and needed help. Their position was too far away for us to do anything but push our way through the enormous swells at the rip-roaring speed of ten knots. It did not matter if it was stormy or calm seas; ten to eleven knots was our max. At night you could see six feet of flames coming out of the ten diesel exhaust stacks. Stack temps ran around 1,800 to 1,900 degrees.

Hunley and *Holland* were 600 feet long, eighty-three feet at the beam, with 1,190 officers and crew. Their speed is listed as eighteen knots. That must be for a stripped-down version with jet engines.

Eventually, the seas calmed, and we plodded along. January in Charleston is winter, but up north, it got cold in a hurry. Taking the Great Circle route put us north of Scotland before we finally started heading in a more SE direction. Out of the blue, we entered the end of the Gulf Stream, and we had a very nice warming trend. Unfortunately, as soon as we left the Gulf Stream, it immediately became cold again. We received a weather report from *Holland*; they had heavy snow and freezing temperatures. Good ole Scotland, always a surprise.

Finally, the day arrived, and we were transiting north up Firth of Clyde to the Loch. The countryside was always beautiful, even with snow. For some ungodly reason, we were all in dress blues and manning the rails. I thought this was a bit of overkill. I could accept and understand if we did this right before reaching Dunoon and entering Holy Loch. I'm pretty sure if I had a refrigerator handy, I would have been inside it. We were outside way too long, and chattering teeth could be heard around the decks.

All the years I made patrols out of the Loch, I got the impression that it was a big surprise to the tender when our sub showed up. Maybe it was me, but the image I had every time, we were the red-headed stepchild showing up unannounced at a family reunion.

Our arrival alongside *Holland* generated very similar feelings all over again. What a Chinese fire drill.

The *Hunley* had a beautiful pristine ship and helo deck. The *Holland* had converted her helo deck to a covered storage area. Beautiful rusting metal. She looked like she had been ridden hard and put away wet many times. We found out later, she got underway once a year to dump radioactive waste—an overnight trip out and back.

We met our counterparts when they came over to see their new home. OMG, I never heard so much pissing and moaning in my entire life. The R-3 people came over and went ballistic. We didn't have this, we didn't have that, they were going to have to move so much equipment over to do their jobs. All I could say, we meet Naval Sea

System (NAVSEA) requirements. NAVSEA would send a team of inspectors down to ensure you ONLY had what is on their list at the very end of the shipyard. Any tender based overseas has to adapt to the needs of the fleet they are serving. As a result, they had a lot of leeway and fewer restrictions on equipment and materials. It was not unheard of in the early days of *USS George Washington* (SSBN-598) to charter a jet to bring a needed part or even toilet paper so the sub could go on patrol.

You never run out of TP or coffee on patrol. If this should happen, the Supply Officer would be shot out of a torpedo tube. He would be listed as lost at sea, poor fellow.

It wasn't just R-3 but the entire Repair Department and Submarine Supply System. All these guys returned to their ship and raised a big stink that the *Hunley* was not ready for them to move aboard. Of course, our CO got bent out of shape, and fecal matter flows downhill. The Repair Officer called all the division officers in and wanted to know why we weren't ready; why didn't we have this equipment; and on and on. All of us said the same thing, "NAVSEA."

Secondly, how the hell were we supposed to know what *Holland* had done? *USS Hunley* and *USS Holland* were identical ships. No heads were chopped off. All we could do was pitch in and help the other shops transfer the equipment and supplies they needed to operate effectively. A tender stateside had everything she needed at the main supply center. Overseas, she was on her own.

All our decks had brand new synthetic rubber coverings, sealed decks, fresh paint, etc. We were pretty. On the other hand, due to all the rainy weather, the poor *Holland* was just the opposite. Running rust, bare metal on the weather decks. They needed a few weeks in the sun to do maintenance.

After the initial shock wore off, everyone got along great, and when it came time for us to get underway and head back to Charleston, everything was okay.

For some strange reason, the *Holland* CO insisted that his Navigator bring the ship back. Our Navigator had done all our sea trials, gone through GITMO for REFTRA, and brought the ship to Scotland. I'm pretty sure it was to have something to put in her evaluation that involved actual navigation. It would ensure her promotion to Lieutenant Commander. If you are a Navigator, you should *navigate*. One week at sea, she had us arriving one week late. Our experienced Navigator worked with her and showed her how to lay out a great circle track. After that, we were back on schedule.

We didn't have any women on board, but *Holland* did. With a few exceptions, most stayed in Scotland. Later, I would see my Navy going to hell in a handbasket.

USS Holland *in Charleston at Goose Creek*

CHAPTER THIRTY

Welcome Back to Charleston

USS HOLLAND

The *USS Holland* had been in Holy Loch for a long time. The ship's return was much celebrated, advertised on TV, radio, and in print. I do not believe any of these announcements included the small fact that the only thing returning to Charleston was the ship. 99 percent of the crew were from the *Hunley*, who had been away a few months. Many familiar faces were waiting on the pier. There were TV cameras, news people, government officials, and the Charleston Navy Band playing patriotic tunes. I thought it odd none of these yahoos bothered to appear or play for our departure. You have to love Navy Public Affairs.

The ship moored, and one of our cranes lifted the accommodation ladder into position on the pier. As soon as the rigging was clear, the media stormed up the accommodation ladder and began sticking cameras and mics in people's faces. I referred them to a person close to me who had actually been in Scotland for seven months. Probing questions like: What is the first thing you want to eat now that you are back in the states? A cheeseburger was the answer or pizza. They would not have liked my answer.

Finally, back in the wardroom, we all had a great laugh over these press idiots. If you didn't have the duty, you grabbed your bag, went to the pier, kissed your wife and hugged all the kids, and drove home.

Home, the place I had not seen in five years, according to the TV news story. It looked just like it did three months ago. We *had* to watch the news. Better than *Hee Haw*. I had four little boys using me as their private jungle gym. It was great to be home.

Prior to our arrival in Charleston, as we slowly crossed the Atlantic to Charleston, we began throwing as much of the ship overboard as possible. We already knew what had to be removed and trashed before entering the shipyard. With an experienced, abused crew, this time, life in the shipyard and thereafter would be much easier. I finished my Officer's Surface Warfare qualifications on the trip back. As a former sonar tech, I had an advantage over most. I was well versed in true and relative bearings, angle on the bow (AOB), and how to determine a ship's course. For some reason, I also had an excellent feel for my ship's movement and could easily determine how to maneuver in all situations.

The morning after our arrival, all hands not on leave returned to the ship to continue preparations to enter the yards. All the officers assembled in the wardroom for an awards ceremony. The departing Navigator was headed back to Holy Loch via airplane. For her conspicuous duty as the Navigator, she received a Navy Commendation Medal. She was so thrilled, she actually cried. All the Mustangs and Warrants about threw up. We all knew if it hadn't been for our Mustang Navigator, we'd still be wandering in the wilderness looking for manna from heaven. In keeping with Navy tradition, we smiled, wished her well, and have a wonderful life in DC when you go work for a female Senator. I'll talk about *that* female Senator later on.

Before you continue to mumble non-PC words about me, I do not have a problem with women in the Navy. I don't have a problem with men in the Navy. I do expect them to perform their duties to the best of their ability. Those who do not, I have no use for them. You should be able to tell. I was loved by thousands and hated by many more. If your name is not inscribed inside a bathroom stall, you ain't doing your job.

As a Senior Chief and COB, I got down on my knees in the crew's bathroom and showed a young lad the proper way to clean a submarine stainless steel toilet. I was in plain sight of anyone walking by. Some may have experienced a mild heart attack. How else was the young seaman going to learn if someone who started off doing the same thing did not show him? If you are not willing to serve, you will never lead. As an officer, I expected no less from my people or other officers.

Off to the airport, our beaming, wet-eyed naviguesser went with her Navy Commendation Medal flapping in the breeze.

All was well in the world.

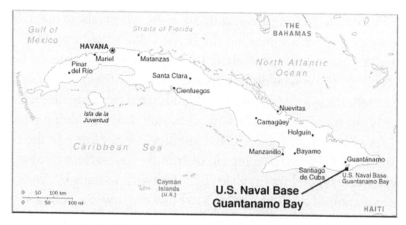

U.S. Naval Base, Guantanamo Bay, Cuba

CHAPTER THIRTY-ONE

Preparing to Survive GITMO

GUANTANAMO BAY, CUBA

Guantanamo Bay (GITMO) is not exactly a garden spot. But for duty, I would take GITMO over Reykjavik any day. With a few exceptions, most only know GITMO as the place where terrorists are imprisoned. That small makeshift prison is only a fraction of GITMO. On the above map of Cuba, you can see Guantanamo Bay on the far east end, down along the flat bottom. This is where the Guantanamo River empties. Cuban civilians enter the base each day to work. They have badges, etc. Frankly, we are still there to be a thorn in Fidel's rear. Now that he is dead, the thorn was moved to another Cuban leader's bottom. If you saw *A Few Good Men*, you know there are many marines there. There are also many spouses and children of the men and women stationed there.

GITMO is where Navy ships on the East Coast undergo Refresher Training (REFTRA). The base has a Navy Commissary and Exchange, which are resupplied once a month. It also has a large swimming pool and a golf course where the only grass to be found is on the greens.

146

Fairways are crushed coral. No matter where your ball lands, it is in the rough. There are Enlisted and Officers' Clubs and K-8 school. All high school kids have to attend in the states. It was the same way in Holy Loch. All high school kids either went back to the states or London. Many duty stations are very hard on parents. On the bright side, all of these kids receive a much better education in government schools than in public schools in the states.

Also at GITMO, on the other side of the bay, is a Naval Air Station. It is reached by ferry. No one lives on that side. Most active-duty men and women are the mean, nasty inspectors who conduct Refresher Training (REFTRA). If I lived at GITMO, I'd be mean and nasty also.

Back to the real world. On our way across the Atlantic for Charleston from Holy Loch, a group of us got together and decided we would not be beaten to death at GITMO. Those who went through REFTRA on the *Hunley* before, saved all paperwork from that little fiasco. We came up with a plan to be 100 percent ready this time. The project was run up the flagpole, and everyone agreed. Our current CO and XO didn't know what we were talking about but liked our proactive approach.

The Charleston Naval Shipyard had its plan for the overhaul. Everyone moved off the ship with all their belongings. Most of the crew lived on base in barracks. All the chiefs and above were already living out in the town. Single officers could stay in BOQ or live in town. The rest of the officers had homes and families.

A very large three-deck crew barge was tied to a pier in the shipyard, and that is where our offices were. The plan I talked about was to include one officer in charge and coordinate everything necessary to ensure the thousands of discrepancies that REFTRA had found were in perfect operating order. In addition to the officer, there were two chiefs, navy personnel from the machine shop, welders, machinist mates, and two people from admin to type all compartment bills. These bills gave directions to the reader on exactly how each compartment was to be prepared for all possible disasters, fire, flooding, biohazard, nuclear attack, and several other toxic situations. Last but not least, two people from the world-famous rubber and plastics shop.

Why am I telling you this? Why does GITMO care?

Over the years, the Russian Navy lost entire ships, submarines, and crews due to a minor fire that got out of control or flooding that could have been stopped, but they were not prepared for any casualties.

The U.S. Navy learned the hard way during WWII, you had best be ready for anything. Onboard our submarines, we drilled like crazy. Our warships did likewise; everyone trained and trained for fighting fires of all types, flooding from any compartment, etc. A submarine tender carried real-live ballistic missiles and real torpedo war shots. Torpedo fuel was very toxic; a missile problem could ruin your entire day. Fire in the engine room was something you never want to hear. Flooding on a submerged submarine is terrible, but flooding can continue for hours on a tender before anyone finds it. Tenders have huge storerooms below the waterline.

There were large double steel doors between each compartment with rubber gaskets that had to be pliable, meet end to end, and completely seal when closed and dogged down. There had to be a piece of pipe dipped in a black plastic coating and hanging on the bulkhead to provide leverage to whoever was dogging the hatches closed on each side of the doors. There were thousands of deck drains inside each compartment throughout the 600-foot-long ship. Every deck drain had to be pulled and repaired as necessary to perfect working order. Close to each deck drain, there had to be a deck drain wrench. It was not like an adjustable wrench for tightening nuts; it was a T-handle with a square end that perfectly fit the deck drain closing fitting that you turned with the T-handle to close the deck drain. Each T-handle wrench had to be dipped in red plastic coating and attached by a special clip mounted to the bulkhead closest to the deck drain. Every deck drain had to have its own T-handle wrench. There were many other items on the list, but I will not drive you crazy.

Instead of telling each Department Head to have all spaces he was responsible for ready for REFTRA, we decided it was better to have a small team to ensure everything was completed correctly. At the end of the yards, every team member received a medal for completing this massive undertaking. Not one person on the ship ever reported finding something they missed.

All the officers called the Officer in Charge Admiral Deck Drain. As a submarine sailor, he would never let on if he didn't like the name.

Naval Investigative Service (NIS)

CHAPTER THIRTY-TWO

Seaman Sams Is Dead

SEAMAN SAMS

During the yard period, my good friend, Bill Hendy, left for Navy Diving Officers' school in Pensacola. I was removed from R-3 Electrical Shop and filled Bill's job as Assistant Repair Officer (ARO)—strictly an admin job. I had nothing to do with repairs—another FBM good deal. One night, I was sitting in the repair office doing my thing, and the 1MC clicked on.

A slow, uneducated voice came over, "Do nots rotitate or radiates from any mats or antennas, dey bees mens workins daloft."

Before he could get it out a second time, you could hear telephones ringing on the Quarterdeck and the Chief on watch screaming for him to stop and hang up the mic. I felt the ship move as the OOD, XO, and CO went aft at warp speed. More screaming and hollering were going on back aft than you can imagine.

Good ole Seamen Sams was standing a qualifying watch as the messenger. I was very familiar with Sams. As drill team coordinator, I walked around the ship during a drill, ensuring everyone was at their stations. As I walked through one male berthing area, I heard a shower running. I walked over, and there, in all his naked glory, was Sams taking a nice long soapy shower. I startled him when I called his name. He jumped a bit and turned around. Then I started with the twenty questions. He didn't know where to go. He didn't this, that, what, who, or what for were his excuses. I told him to rinse off, get fully dressed, and I would take him to his division officer so he could hold a little one-on-one training as to where their Watch, Quarter, and Station Bill was, and where he was to be for any and everything that happened on the ship.

Sams came across as the dumbest person ever to be recruited and make it through boot camp. He made Hogan's goat look like a precision instrument. From then on, every time I saw him, I made it a point to say hello—in a loving way, of course. By the way, he was ordered never to make a ship's announcement again.

Why, you ask, am I devoting so much time to this dumb-ass seamen? Around one month later, I was the Duty Repair Officer, and there was a ship-wide announcement for me to lay to the Quarterdeck. I went aft, and the OOD told me he needed two guys and me to get into a paint punt (small boat) and fish a body out of the water. Here we go again. Am I the only person on this ship? WTF, over? Two guys already have the punt in the water next to a camel (A large wooden spacer to keep vessels away from the pier). I climbed down and got into the boat.

About ten feet from the pier, we could see what looked like a body floating. We paddled out and verified it was a body. I told the guys to take us back to the camel, where I yelled to those on the pier that we needed a stokes stretcher to hold the body. The stokes appeared in a hurry, and we went back out to the body. It was floating face down, and the only thing holding it together was his clothes. We pulled alongside, and I told both men in the punt to move to the outside of the boat since this guy would be heavy. I stood in the middle of the punt and pushed the stokes over to the edge. Fortunately, the dead guy was wearing a wide leather belt. I reached over the stokes and turned him face up. Then I grabbed him by the belt and waistband and, in one sweeping move, picked him up out of the water with my right arm and placed him in the stretcher. I was a strong man, but I believe a bit of adrenalin assisted me.

A Stokes stretcher is not flat like a standard stretcher. It has an iron pipe frame and formed chicken wire. Once a person is placed into the stretcher, the wire cradles the legs, body, arms, and head. It is used for high line transfers or lifting an injured person to a helicopter.

I knew right away that it was Sams. Crabs had eaten part of his ears and nose. He was swollen like a big tick on a hound dog. I told the two guys not to say a word about who it was. They paddled back to the camel. The pier was loaded with Naval Investigative Service (NIS) agents, undercover narcs, ship's company, and others. Two men were on the camel to remove the stretcher. It was all they could do to pick it up and out of the boat. Two more came down to help pass him up to the pier. I told the senior NIS guy who he was, and that Sams had been AWOL for a week. A Navy ambulance arrived. The entire stokes and Sams were placed in a body bag, and they took him to the Navy Hospital morgue.

I instructed the two guys to get out and pull the punt onto the camel. I thanked them. I let them know that when NIS finished with their questions, they were free to go. NIS got down on the camel and, using flashlights that could double as landing lights on a C-5, looked all over the punt for any little thing which might have belonged to Sams. Then, I received the third degree. How did I know it was Sams? Did I remove anything from his pockets, and on and on. You would have thought I killed him and was waiting around for the body to come up. I explained how I knew him and answered the rest of their questions—one of the things I had noticed about Sams when I saw him on the ship, his uniforms were always perfect. His working uniforms were done at an off-base laundry, washed, lightly starched, and pressed. He was a member of the deck force and never had any paint, rust, or grime on his clothes.

When NIS said I could go, I reported to the OOD what transpired so he could put it in the log. He and I briefed the CO and XO that morning.

About a week later, I attended a meeting in the conference room. NIS had the autopsy results. Apparently, Sams had tried to jump from the pier to the living barge and missed. He had a large, bruised area across his forehead where it hit the top railing. That knocked him out and into the water between the barge and pier pilings. He had been on the bottom, under the pier, for a week before enough gases built up to make him float. They also found his new BMW in the parking lot. The trunk was full of stolen goods. Sams was a fraud; it was all an act to reduce his responsibilities. With more digging into his past, NIS found that he had been a gang member, very streetwise, and well-versed in criminal activities. His being dumb was all an act to allow him to get out of work and other duties.

I guess you might say he received his just reward. We didn't send any damn flowers either.

Little did I know, he would be the first of many to come at another duty station.

Official Guantanamo Bay Patch

CHAPTER THIRTY-THREE

Off to GITMO and Far-off Exotic Adventures

GITMO AGAIN

*H*olland finished the yards, and we put to sea. I was the ship's Training Officer. My team and I ran many training drills, motor whaleboat man overboard recovery, man overboard shipboard recovery, fires, flooding, radioactive contamination, torpedo fuel spills, etc.

While the ship was in the yards, our damage control teams attended Prometheus fighting and flooding training. Those are just a joy—especially the flooding trainer during winter. It was great fun inside a mock-up of the inside of a ship while a raging fire comes toward you. The same type of training all fire departments go through. One of the reasons to attend these trainers was to help determine who would be on teams one and two for each damage control station. I was in charge of Damage Control Locker #1. Go figure?

When *Holland* returned from Scotland, except for the *guest* female navigator, we also had a couple more women on board. They were good at their jobs, and we never had any problems.

One day, female officers and enlisted began reporting aboard. They continued to arrive for three days. We added 125 women of all races and rates to our 1,190 men. One Ensign had been a cheerleader at the Naval Academy. Among these ladies were some who played on the other team, but most played on our team. Within two weeks, not all, but many had paired off either with a male of their choosing or a female. It didn't matter if one was married, or both were married, or both single. All outward appearances indicated they were just good friends. I had a few platonic steaming buddies over the years myself. Being from the old Navy, I shook my head, wondering what the hell had happened to my Navy.

After we completed our training time, we headed to GITMO for REFTRA. We were ready for them this time. The big plan in the sky was we'd complete REFTRA, return to Charleston and relieve the tender at the Weapons Station. Little did we know that someone behind the scenes had a much better plan for us—another FBM good deal.

As the ship sailed to GITMO, a previous victim reminded us that one of the favorite tricks of the inspectors was to kill your #1 damage control team, so the DC Locker Officer was forced to send in his #2 team. To counter their trickster-crap, we switched the numbers of each DC team. When they killed what they thought was our #1 team, our actual #1 team went in as #2 and blew their minds. None of the inspectors had ever had any ship come there as prepared as we were, and we were a slug submarine tender. This wasn't our first rodeo; you killed us last year on the *Hunley*. It was not going to happen again. We were supposed to be at GITMO for four weeks, and they kicked us out after two. They didn't even ask for a dependents cruise to Jamaica.

Of course, they didn't remember our faces; they saw thousands of sailors a year. We did not volunteer any information. We did celebrate with a large cookout on the helo deck, steaks, lobster, hot dogs, and cheeseburgers with all the fixings on our way back. Music piped in for listening only. Our helo deck was no longer a large rusting area; it was beautiful. Any helo in the fleet would love to land on it.

Upon arrival to Charleston, we moored opposite the *USS Frank Cable* (AS-40), an SSN tender. That is when we received the fantastic, unexpected news. Congratulations, you have won an all-expense-paid seven-month deployment to Diego Garcia. Such a deal we have for you. The *Cable* was to have made that trip because the only subs who came to Diego Garcia then were SSNs. No, we will send this old FBM tender over there. It will be fun, wait and see.

Those of us who were married did not receive a hearty, well done from our wives. We'd been to GITMO twice, been to Scotland and back, and now we were leaving again. All the wives asked hard questions. "I thought tenders didn't go anywhere?" "Are those women going?" It only got worse from there—something about a rusty knife involved with a sex change.

As all good sailors do, we gave a cheery aye, aye, and carried on. While all this nautical brouhaha was going on, the R-1 Division Officer got fired and sent down to run welfare and recreation. You will never guess who was the new R-1 Division Officer. No, you're mistaken. It was me. For those who do not know, R-1 is the largest division on the entire ship. It was larger than most departments. R-1 consists of Hull Technicians, Rubber and Plastics, Sheet metal, Nuke welders, and High-pressure hose and pipe shop. I had 130 men in my division: one chief and a bunch of first-class running each shop. I was a submarine Electronic LDO (Limited Duty Officer), and now I was totally out of my environment. The fact that I had been restoring cars, and owned a welding machine, helped me immensely.

As impressed as I was with the men who did motor rewind in R-3, these guys were absolute geniuses when it came to doing their jobs.

Before our little honeymoon cruise was over, I'd be so proud of these guys. I watched in awe as they would use various tools to mark curves, angles, make cuts, bend steel plates, and make perfect welds. They could turn a flat piece of steel plate into a thing of beauty. All the other shops were equally impressive, but I must say, the nuke welders were in a class all by themselves—no wonder the Navy can't keep them. I'd go with them on jobs and watch them work. They were hanging upside down, using a mirror to see the pipe's back and weld it. Just unbelievable.

We all did our jobs on the boats, but these people had talent, visible talent, and abilities. Very impressive and something your basic submarine sailor never saw.

Okay, this was the plan. We would depart Charleston in April. At the sea buoy, our ordered course was 089. We would pass just south of Bermuda, then through the Strait of Gibraltar, followed by four-day liberty in Palma de Majorca. Then, through the Suez Ditch, transit the Red Sea, bust out into the Indian Ocean, and head for Diego Garcia. We would anchor in the lagoon for three months providing services for whomever and whatever required them.

Palma de Majorca in the Mediterranean

CHAPTER THIRTY-FOUR

Toward Gibraltar

THE MED

We passed Bermuda a few miles south during the day. About as close as we came was through binoculars. From Bermuda, we continued churning our way to Gibraltar. During that portion of the transit, we had almost no contacts on the radar. As we approached Gibraltar, radar contacts started coming out of the woodwork. Ships were entering and leaving in all directions. As we neared Gibraltar, the best example I can provide is that it was like the entrance to a fire ant nest. Fortunately, the ship separation distance directive by the Captain was revised during this part of the trip. His new rule was not to trade paint with any other ships. The entrance was like a U.S. highway, enter on the right, exit our left. There was a lot of crossing and merging ship traffic. Every vessel out there was much faster than us.

If you were a submarine, there was a maximum depth for entering and a minimum depth for leaving the Med.

If you ever passed near Georges Bank on a sub, you had hundreds of sonar contacts, mostly trawlers, and the BTR was covered in traces. On the *Entemedor*, we navigated through on the surface. As a radar operator, I was up to my knees in hand grenade pins, and they were still coming. I either became very proficient or had a heart attack in the Conning Tower. When on the surface, sonarmen operated the radar. I enjoyed that very much and the busier it was, the more I liked it.

We passed through the Strait during the day, which was a good thing. At a predetermined point on the chart, we hung a left and headed for Palma de Majorca for four days of Cinderella Liberty, a Navy term meaning be back on board by midnight. Because of the ladies on board, the Captain didn't want all-night liberty. I told the Captain that ending liberty at midnight would not stop anything. He agreed. The one good deal, if you were attending a show that wasn't over in time for you to return by midnight, you needed to let the XO know. Our Welfare and Rec Officer (the one fired from R-1) arranged several nightly trips for individuals or groups to attend various culture-type shows in town or up in the hills. We couldn't attend and return by midnight, but the XO blessed those outings.

Majorca was a great liberty port. Europeans flocked to the beaches and pools, and the women were topless. No one paid any attention except for us. At first, we didn't notice they were topless, then all of a sudden, it seemed like it hit everyone at the same time. Hard to believe, but after a while, we stopped gawking. Great food, cold beer, and a garden of breasts. Doesn't get much better than that. The funny thing about liberty there, I never saw any of the paired-off couples in town. They were together when coming down the pier and up the accommodation ladder, however. Officers and enlisted—at least, up to this point, there were no known officer/enlisted matchups. Not publicly. That would be a major no-no.

Everyone was back on board when we got underway for our next stop at Port Said, Egypt. I noticed the Med had all kinds of debris and jetsam floating on or just below the surface. So much plastic and large sheets of plastic. This was 1983, long before people were going nuts to eliminate dumping into oceans. Our engineering personnel noticed some of the engines were starting to overheat and found the main seawater strainers were full of plastic. They began shifting strainers every hour to keep a clean strainer online. I don't know if this was ever a problem with any of our subs.

A few days out from Majorca, an announcement came over the 1MC, "Lieutenant Pait lay to the bridge."

I dreaded those announcements. Everyone I passed wanted to know what was going on. I didn't have a clue. I reported to the bridge, and the Captain said to come with him. We walked across the bridge to the corner where the quartermasters and the Navigator worked. A large chart of the Mediterranean Sea was on the table. The Captain pointed at Sardinia. That is the land over there, and he turned and pointed. The quartermaster placed another smaller chart of the port of Cagliari on top. The Captain slid a finger along the coast, and not far from town, he stopped on a very long supertanker pier.

The Captain said, "We received a Red Cross message." (Not something a married father of four wants to hear!) "Petty Officer so-and-so's father has died."

He almost had my body to offload. "We've contacted the Naval Air Station on Sardinia," he continued, "and they will send a vehicle to pick her up at the land end of the pier. I want you to take a motor whaleboat and deliver her to them."

I thought, *Here we go again. Am I the only person who can do this?* I said, "Yes, sir."

The Navigator jumped in and said, "We will stay out here around three miles offshore and wait for your return."

I headed down to the main deck. The young lady was waiting with her seabag and one of our Chaplains. I did not know her, so she must have been from the ship's company. I introduced myself, "Sorry for your loss, ya da, ya da."

Shortly, the boat crew was lowered to our level, and we climbed aboard and continued to the water. After the engine started and the gauges indicated it was okay, I ordered to let go of the stern line; the coxswain added a few turns to match the ship's speed, and then I ordered cast off the bowline; we pulled away from the ship. I asked the coxswain if he had been briefed, and he nodded in the affirmative. So, there we went over the bounding main, headed for a microscopic pier at our level.

I checked on my passenger, and she was fine. Three miles is a long way to go in a motor whaleboat. Fortunately, we had perfect weather for our transit.

We finally came alongside the pier, but it was way above us. I contacted the ship via handheld radio and informed the OOD we were tied up and were getting ready to climb a ladder to the top. I went up first, followed by the young lady, and then one of the boat crew came up with her seabag. I had him go back to the boat and tell the coxswain to wait.

"I'll be back as soon as I can," I told him.

I started to pick up her seabag, but she would not let me. We began our walk down the longest pier I have ever seen before or since. I could see three men at the end of the pier sitting inside a guard office.

When I opened the door, I said, "*Ban Giorno!*" (That is the Southern version.) They about crapped themselves; scared these brave men to death. They had not seen the ship, our boat, or us walking down the pier. Plus, they were short, and I was a large American.

I pointed at myself and said, "*Mafioso!*" Big eyes all around.

Boy, did I luck out. None of them spoke or understood a word of *Ringrish*. I contacted the ship and asked if there was anyone on board who spoke Italian or Sardine.

"No, no one. You are on your own."

Almost 1,300 crew, many of Italian descent and not *one* Paisano. I tried to get them to understand why we were there. I used all my Italian—lasagna, ravioli, pizza, spaghetti, etc.

One man kept saying, "*Policia!*"

I would say no and shake my head. Finally, I drew a picture of a P-3 ASW airplane with USA insignia. They all went ah, started jibber jabbing, and the Air Station's familiar name was mentioned.

I yelled, "Winner, winner, chicken dinner!" I said yes, pointed to the telephone, held my hand to my ear, and asked if they could call.

One guy got my drift and called the base. He talked a minute and then handed me the telephone. He was beaming from ear to ear. He was da man. I spoke to their duty officer, and he said the time specified in the message was in Zulu, not local. The entire US Military and NATO operates off ZULU time, which is Greenwich Mean Time (GMT).

I told him we could not wait that long, and he replied he would get the driver on the way. I asked him if he thought the young lady would be okay waiting here with these men, and he assured me she would. The driver would be there in an hour. I asked him to tell the head man here to take care of this young lady and why she was flying home.

I asked her if she had any problems waiting there while we returned to the ship, and she said no. Like most women in the Navy, she probably carried a switchblade and knew how to use it. I got the three guys together, looked them in the eyes, and told them they were responsible for her safety. I pointed to the Petty Officer and said, "*Bambino.*" They all nodded, yes.

I shook each man's hand and said, "*Gratsi, ya'll.*"

I left and headed back to the ship. The Chaplain was there to meet me when I got off the boat, and he wanted to know if the Air Force had picked her up, and I told him no. Did I leave her there by herself? I told him I had talked to the Air Force duty officer, and they were on their way. He was beside himself that I had left this child alone with strange men in a foreign country. I told him again, "She is in good hands and will be just fine."

Up to the bridge to brief the CO and XO. They seemed to be okay with my decision, and the fact the Duty Officer said she would be fine anywhere in the country alone was good enough for them. I also told them the Chaplain was about to have a heart attack. I turned in my radio and went to the wardroom. Then it was twenty questions from a gaggle of fellow officers. We had a female dentist with Italian heritage, drop-dead gorgeous, and could not speak a lick of it. If there was one lady on the ship that would make a good dog break his leash, to me, she was it.

When I had a chance, I talked to the XO alone and told him about the time mix-up in the message. Visibly upset, he headed to Radio, and I went back to R-1. I do not know for a fact, but I am sure the XO wanted to see the original message he and the CO had signed. If Radio had not transmitted it verbatim, whoa be unto them. If the CO or XO messed up, no one would ever hear about it.

I had exhausted all the Italian I knew and made it work. I had served with several men on different subs who were fluent because their grandparents were from the old country.

Later, the ship received a message; she had been picked up and was fine. The three men could not do enough for her. She made it home for the funeral and later was flown back to Diego Garcia to meet the ship. The first time she saw me, she gave me a big hug and thanked me for taking care of her. That was the only time in thirty years an enlisted person ever hugged me. I understood and did not object. After all, I am a father, which would get me in trouble later.

AN "I" FOR AN "I" AND HUGGING

As you read my stories, do not think I have an "I" problem. I write about all the different situations I was directly involved in. When I use I, it is me in the first person. I do not plagiarize any events experienced by others.

As an officer at two different commands, I had senior chiefs at both who were selected for Master Chief. One was Jerry Moose on the *Holland*, and as soon as the selection results were read, I immediately went to the Goat Locker, grabbed Moose in a bear hug, lifted him off the ground and congratulated him many times. The Command Master Chief and I always got along great. He told me later, I had no idea the impact I made on the Goat Locker when I hugged Moose. That was a first for them, and it made a lasting impression. As a division officer, you can't help but love wonderful news that involves one of your best people. Moose was sub qualified but had a collapsed lung one time at sea. He retained his SS quals but was medically unqualified for boat duty.

My next hug was when I was a Lt. Cmdr. at Service School Command. I was the head of Surface and Submarine Torpedo School. My #2 was Senior Chief McIntyre. She was the first female Torpedoman to make Chief, and the first to make Senior. I'm telling you guys, she was magnificent in every way. She saved my butt many times when it came to Women-in-the-Navy programs. She didn't take any crap off any male or female in the school. I believe she and Moose could have run the entire Navy. I was able to write only one eval for her. She read it expressionless, signed it, and said, "Thank you, sir." I consider it the finest eval I ever wrote. I walked down to the CO and XO and told them that she had to be ranked as the #1 Senior Chief at service school, and she was. When the selection board results were announced, I was as proud as I could be. I threw both arms around her, squeezed, and congratulated her over and over. By that time in my career, I could have been burned at the stake for that.

When she was up for orders, she went to DC to work in the women's affairs section. We are not called Mustangs for nothing. We are a wild breed.

Ships transiting Suez Canal

CHAPTER THIRTY-FIVE

Onward to Suez, Red Sea, and the Indian Ocean

SUEZ CANAL

Holland continued its quest for Port Said (Sa-eed), Egypt. You have to make reservations; it is not a free-for-all, but close. Nothing of note happened as we transited the last part of our journey in the Med. When we approached Port Said, the radar displayed what looked like a minefield. There were hundreds of commercial vessels anchored on a flat sand bottom.

Another thing we noticed, the land had zero landmarks or navigation aids. There were commercial ships anchored in the channel. Maybe the wind was blowing them away from the channel the day they arrived, but there was no channel upon our arrival.

There we went, literally zigzagging our way to an unknown channel entrance through all the ships. I had the deck. Of course, the CO, XO, and Navigator were up there, and the JOOD was on the radio trying to contact the pilot. Why didn't we pick a spot and anchor? You will love this—we were considered a U.S. Navy warship. It must have been the scary gray paint. Eliminate the Marine detachment, and the only damage we could do was bring up a few thousand pounds of TDU weights and throw them. Seriously, because we were a U.S. Navy ship, we were first in a line of a very long convoy heading south. Our assigned berth was next to the Suez Canal Authority building in downtown Port Said. It was similar to parking a ship across Broadway near Times Square.

Finally, we found the pilot boat, and a pilot climbed up and brought us in. It was early afternoon, but no liberty. We would head south, starting at midnight. We were required to mount a colossal Hollywood-type searchlight on our bow. The deck crew lowered a mooring line down through one of the large hawse holes and then used a capstan to lift it in place. Other smaller lines had to be tied to it, so it pointed dead ahead, and the electricians wired it.

A hawser is a huge mooring line. The average mooring lines are 2½ inches in diameter. A hawser is at least 4 inches or larger. We used these lines to ensure a vessel does not move during a storm. Hawsers were a carry-over from past years. If we needed to make sure the ship would not move, we used wire rope.

Boats of all sizes were running back and forth, carrying people, cars, buses, etc., from one side of the city to the other. Not a bridge in sight. About 2330, a big fat pilot came aboard. He asked for a chair and two cigarette cartons. I believe it was Marlboro, but I don't remember. At least he spoke a little Ringrish, just the nautical parts. As we set the sea and anchor detail, all the lady officers came up and assumed their positions, OOD, JOOD, and of course, Navigator. Tremendous responsibility for their careers, as I mentioned before.

Our pilot stood up for our underway, and once we were in the middle of the channel, he ordered, "Seven knots, stay in the middle," and sat back down.

Looking aft, we could only see the ship directly astern. Every ship in our convoy had a position number and a pilot. Once daylight arrived, you could look aft, and as far as you could see, were ships doing seven knots and staying in the middle.

You may find this a bit strange, but the Canal Authority had manned towers like airports, equally spaced alongside the Ditch. I am sure only relatives of those at the Canal Authority worked in those towers. They timed us to make sure we were not speeding or going too slow.

Around six or seven hours after we got underway, another convoy left Port Suez, headed north in the same channel. Same orders, seven knots, stay in the middle. The timing was critical because once the southbound convoy reached the Great Bitter Lake, we turned right into it and slowed down. Very similar to a railroad pass track. As our last ship entered the lake, the northbound convoy's first ship passed our exit point. We stopped and dropped the anchor to maintain our position and watched a parade of vessels going north. As soon as the last ship came into view, the pilot stood up again. We hoisted our anchor, and we slowly moved forward. As soon as the last vessel went by, back to seven knots, stay in the middle, and the pilot sat back down.

The pilot was a worthless piece of meat. You do not get a discount for using the Ditch, or Panama Canal. It cost the same as if you went around the end of Africa or South America. The only thing you save is time.

We left at midnight, and it was very close to sunset when we reached the end at Port Suez. Then the pissing contest started. The Pilot boat came alongside and picked up the worthless pilot. Another boat matched our speed and pulled right in under our bow, and the crew motioned for the big light to be lowered. Once the light was on their deck, they also wanted the mooring line and would not untie it. So, we started increasing speed; they were screaming and carrying on but would not untie the mooring line. Finally, the Captain told the First Lieutenant to give them the damn line and ahead standard. We just about rolled them over before they got out of the way. Where were TDU weights when we needed them?

OMG, it was like a rolling start at Daytona. We gradually increased speed to ten knots, being a mighty warship and all. Every commercial vessel behind us was cranking on the turns and going by us on both sides like we were backing up. Oncoming traffic was headed to Port Suez to anchor and await their turn. There were scattered oil rigs. What a zoo that was. I felt much safer underwater.

As the sun set, gigantic thunderheads over Africa were backlit, producing a kaleidoscope of colors. It was so beautiful.

It wasn't long before all we could see were stern lights getting smaller. Some of them were doing twenty-seven knots.

All the ladies disappeared, the CO and XO left the bridge, and I was the OOD again as we entered the Red Sea. You know, I was thinking about Moses and the Israelites.

Before entering Port Said, our helo deck was transformed into our little landfill. We had to hold all trash and garbage until we entered the Indian Ocean and were X number of miles from land. Before we reached that spot in the ocean, the helo deck began to come alive. Arrrr, there be monsters a brewing under there.

Egypt has large, red-eyed flies that landed on everything topside. If they land on you, you had to knock them off quickly, or they bite the crap out of you. They loved our landfill.

Finally, the day came to rid the helo deck of this writhing, wretched mess. I don't know how they did it without wearing Oxygen Breathing Apparatus (OBA). After the trash was gone, the deck force was back there with fire hoses, detergent, and scrub brushes for over an hour. They used freshwater for the actual cleaning part, then shifted over to saltwater for a real good rinse. We had all new PRC (rubber) installed on all-weather decks and the helo deck during the yards. Awesome stuff.

When headed north, right before Port Said, the Ditch splits, and all those ships enter the Med away from the ships at anchor. No such good deal going south. It would have been so nice to kick it up to around thirty knots and get out of Dodge.

Another odd thing, the entire east side of the canal was all sand as far as you could see. The west side was green and lush farmland with a small town here and there.

Navy Crossing the Line ceremony

CHAPTER THIRTY-SIX

Crossing the Line

MY STATEROOM ON THE HOLLAND

Before I continue to Shellback Day and entering Diego Garcia, let me tell you about my spacious stateroom on the *Holland*. After years of sleeping in enlisted berthing on a diesel boat and then moving to an FBM with vast amounts of room, and then to the Chief's Quarters with even more space, I moved from Motel 6 to the Ritz. My stateroom on the tender was much larger than the CO's and XO's combined on the FBM. It was a two-person stateroom, but none of ours had more than one occupant. Of course, on many nights, there was more than one occupant in the ladies' staterooms.

When we were in the Yards, the future Squadron Commander's (One Star Admiral) stateroom underwent a major overhaul. R-6 (carpenter shop) was tasked with putting the magnificent carpet down. I talked to the PO1 in charge and asked if I could have any excess for my stateroom. I ended up with wall-to-wall plush dark blue carpet. I had two large lockers, one for hang-up and one for socks, shoes, underwear, etc. A built-in desk, a lavatory with hot and cold running water, and a mirror. Of course, two bunks, but I used the bottom one.

Very large and so comfortable. I also had a small cargo net designed to hang across the bunk's outside edge so I would not get rolled out when the sea was rough. I was in awe.

The CO liked to invite several officers up to share the evening meal with him. Being CO of a ship is a lonely job. Well, if I was in the Ritz, he was in the Penthouse. He rated a personal steward, a separate dining room, a lounge with very comfortable overstuffed couches and chairs, and a large bedroom. All this was behind the door that led to his office. Everyone on the ship ate the same food. Officers had to pay a mess bill each month. The cost was low, but them's the rules.

None of the other officers at my level had a nicer stateroom. Pretty soon, I was giving tours. The Production Assistant (PMA) worked directly for the Repair Officer, and he had had his eyes on that carpet and was very upset that I beat him to it. He had his stateroom completely soundproofed and wanted the carpet to finish the job. Since none of the people in Repair liked him, he lost out. I'll admit, he was a prick with ears.

EQUATORIAL INDIAN OCEAN

One of the heaven's mysteries, when God made stars and planets, he knew navigators would need help. He placed Polaris in the north and made it brighter and easier to see with extra stars behind. As you approach the equator, Polaris gets lower and lower in the nighttime sky. As it is slowly getting lower, however, the Southern Cross is rising and pointing south. After the big bang, it just happened to work out that way. Right?

Our day of reckoning was approaching, Crossing the Line. You had a ship full of slimy wogs and a small number of Shellbacks. Of course, typically, it is all-hands participation for wogs. Because of the nature of the typical ceremony, however, the ladies were given a choice to participate in this long-standing naval tradition or not. I suggested a caveat. If you chose not to participate, you could not change your mind and join in on the return crossing. (Feel free to look up any of the terms I use.)

I had a trunk full of Bluenose Certificates and was looking forward to adding to it. Can you imagine a young lady just out of A-school, going to her first ship, going to sea the first time, becoming a Shellback, and transiting the Ditch and Gibraltar? Many salty guys serve twenty years or more and have nothing. I was a slimy wog, but I made it pretty clear to the Command Master Chief that there had better not be any exceptions made for those who refused to participate. I didn't want them around anywhere to watch. He told me not to worry. They would all be *on* watch. This was their only chance.

All the female officers participated; most of the female enlisted participated, but a handful of ladies chose not to have any part of this demeaning ritual. Good thing we weren't keel hauling anyone. They really would have freaked out. Arrrggg.

I will not go into any details, but it was a fantastic day. Everyone who participated got a good going-over. If you do this on a cruise ship, all wogs have to drink a warm glass of unsweetened tea. Well, maybe not quite so harsh.

Of course, for the next few weeks, those who participated laughed and talked about some of the things they had to do and how much fun it was. Well, the few who did not participate wished they had joined in with everyone else. More about them later. I will say, the Shellbacks did a fantastic job setting up all the trials and punishments. I crawled through some rotten-ass foul garbage for sure. I never will forget that day, and I treasure all my certificates. I do not have an *I love me wall*. Except for my retirement shadow box, everything else is in the garage. I have enough brass out there to open a foundry. Between US and UK submarines, plaques, many certificates, and photos, I need to add a second story to this house to put them all up. I especially like all the UK hand-painted submarine and warship plaques.

My most prized plaque is from *HMS Conqueror* (S-48). Port Canaveral was their first stop after the Falkland War. The Brits love Port Canaveral, and they visited as often as possible. I was assigned to her during her port visit. She looked like crap. I turned contractors loose and sandblasted the hull, and primed and painted her to look fantastic for her arrival back in the UK.

In short, a good time was had by all.

DIEGO GARCIA

If you do not know the location of Diego Garcia, B.I.O.T. (British Indian Ocean Territory), it is one of those *you can't get there from here* places. Look at a world map and draw a straight line down from India's southernmost point and continue 412 miles south of the equator. You will run into a coral atoll about thirty-six miles tip to tip.

Gigantic coconut palms cover most of the atoll. It's long enough for an airbase that easily handles B-52s and SR-71s. It boasts one fueling pier, Officers', Chiefs', Enlisted, and Contractors' Clubs scattered around one end, a small medical clinic, a few administration buildings occupied by the British Military, a giant antenna farm for communications, an Olympic size swimming pool built eleven feet above sea level, an old French copra plantation house, a cemetery, and several lighted softball and sand volleyball fields. Water temperature stayed around eighty-three degrees year-round, with the most magnificent diving and snorkeling in the world, billions of colorful fish, beautiful coral, postcard beaches, and sunsets to die for.

Inside the lagoon at the far end were Military Sealift Command (MSC) and commercial ships loaded with military equipment and supplies. They were part of the prepositioned force. It was not unusual to see ships anchored at night, and they'd all be gone before sunrise. Mass underway drills. They would return later. In the lagoon past the prepositioned ships, in shallow water, I found a large area covered with giant clams. Their mantles varied in a kaleidoscope of colors. Almost every color you can imagine.

On Diego Garcia, you could follow several paths. You could be a complete physical fitness nut, a total drunk, or enjoy the weather and water. I spent most of my time in the water snorkeling. Never saw any sharks in the daytime, but at night, monsters would swim under our lights around the tender, and a fourteen-foot hammerhead would follow every motor whaleboat, just hoping some drunk would fall in. Years before, he had been named Hector.

The water around the atoll had coral extending out on the leeward side, where the reef ended with a wall dropping down to 6,000 fathoms. The wall is where the big boys were during the day. On the atoll's windward side, wind and waves battered the atoll, and some sections were skinny. Tide changes were non-existent.

After a week or so, my preferred hangout was the Contractors' Club. The beaches were the best and you could see magnificent sunsets from there. Many people came each evening with cameras on tripods to get shots of the *green flash* on top of the sun right before it dropped below the horizon. Some people think the *green flash* is a myth, but it has been seen and photographed in tropical waters worldwide.

We entered the lagoon on April 2, 1983. We moored alongside the fuel pier and said, fill'er up. More than 200,000 gallons later, the nozzle clicked shut. The next day, we moved out into the lagoon and dropped one anchor. Backing down slowly, we laid more anchor chain on the bottom, and that was that. There was no boat service for us, but there was for the crews on the prepositioned ships. They used turbine-powered water jet boats that could fly. Our deck force ran our liberty boats back and forth to the base diving locker's small pier.

Having brought our own entertainment, we always had a female dancing partner at the Club. I imagine it was the same at the Enlisted Men's Club. The Chiefs lost out.

I believe, but am not sure, there were either six or nine civilian or military women stationed on the atoll. They all had to have had six-figure bank accounts. Later, after we'd been there a month or so, I found out the island's medical clinic had performed abortions for years, long before it was legal in the States.

Wildlife on the atoll consisted of donkeys, cats, and kittens left over from the French plantation, chickens, and bitties, from the same place. I never saw a seagull or tern. Gigantic coconut crabs eliminated any idea of camping out or sleeping at ground level. Those were some evil critters. Also, the beaches were covered in shells—a shell collector's paradise. And almost every shell had a baby coconut crab in it. You could walk down the beach, and shells were scattered all over. If you got off to the side and sat down for a few minutes, the entire beach started moving. I guess the occupants were looking for food. I found a few extremely nice cone shells and had to evict the occupants.

Next time, let the games begin.

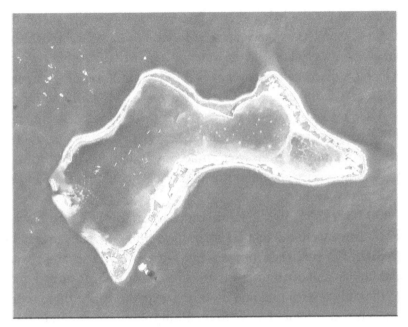

Diego Garcia

CHAPTER THIRTY-SEVEN

What We Did in Diego Garcia

TENDER TO THE FLEET

As I said in the previous chapter, we moored at the fueling pier after entering the lagoon. There was no band, no banners, just lots of diesel fuel, and a group of people returning to the ship or reporting aboard for the first time. I recognized two of the people on the pier. One was the young female petty officer I had taken to the end of the fuel pier in Sardinia so she could fly home. The other was my steaming bud, Bill Hendy.

Bill was the ARO who departed for Dive School to become the ship's Diving Officer. His departure is what got me moved from R-3 to ARO. The real strange thing about Bill and me is that he was born in Jackson Hole, WY, I was from NC, but we resembled each other so much that people kept getting us mixed up or wanting to know if we were related.

Same size, same color hair and eyes, built-in tan, very similar mannerisms. Even the CO and XO would get us confused. We always went to the beach together, spent a lot of time in the water, and enjoyed each other's company. As Diving Officer, he took over as R-6 Division Officer. The carpenters, molders, and diving locker. Before his return, the Master Diver ran R-6.

After refueling, we moved out to our designated anchorage in eighty-five feet of water. A small barge was tied up to our after port side, and one of our cranes set an accommodation ladder on it. The barge was necessary so the motor whaleboats could pick up and drop off the crew members.

On both sides, two gigantic camels were pushed into place and tied off. These were the fenders for surface ships and subs that came in for repairs. I'm sure the word was put out to the fleet that we were in Diego Garcia and open for business. Here is the rub. It turned out, we were the only tender to come there and stay the entire three months. Tenders before us would move to the Philippines or down to Fremantle or other places. Crews on warships were not exactly thrilled to travel to this speck in the middle of nowhere for repairs. In a matter of days, every type of warship, from cruisers on down, was arriving.

As a submarine tender, we knew jack about surface ships, but we did everything we could for them, and in most cases, we wiped out their entire Equipment Deficiency Log (EDL). In other words, the Repair Department fixed everything that was broken. These ships did not have much money for maintenance. The submarine service had almost a bottomless pit of money. One ship was using an outdoor faucet as a valve in part of its steam system. They had some of the most unusual jury rigs you ever saw. We made sheet metal lockers and replaced a lot of steam lagging (insulation). Our foundry cast brand new valves from their blueprints. Then the machine shop milled the castings to required specifications. I told you, the Repair Department was terrific. Every ship was thrilled with the work we did. If there wasn't enough time to finish a repair before leaving, we'd give them the parts to fix it underway. Furthermore, all surface ship crews were in awe of our female sailors.

On one of our times ashore, Bill and I explored where the Seabees construction camp had been set up in the 60s when the US first made a deal with the UK to build a base there. Exploring around the weeds and vines, I found several very large half-inch thick aluminum plates. That was it, no steel or special fittings. Here is a little-known fact. The Chief-of-the-Boat I relieved as COB was a young sailor assigned as part of the supply department when the Seabees were sent to Diego Garcia. It appeared I was following him around. I sent him a coconut crab photo, and he really enjoyed it. He said they were everywhere when the Seabees arrived.

After we had been away from Charleston three months, the 1MC announced for medical and chaplains to lay aft to the aft mast immediately. I thought someone must have fallen from the mast and was near death. Of course, R-1 being almost under the aft mast, I went topside to see what was going on. To my surprise, one of our enlisted married sailors had found out she was two months pregnant. She climbed the mast, threatening to kill herself. Oh, the drama!

Between the Docs and Chaplains, they talked her down, and she was packed up and sent back home to explain to her husband basic math. Whoever the male counterpart was, remained unnamed. Okay, back to work.

You can find *sympathy* in the dictionary between *sh*t* and *syphilis*.

Diego Garcia is not open to the public. Nat-Geo, the Smithsonian, and another vessel with scientists arrived with prior arrangements to study marine life, corals, and the almost pristine jungle life. Then, one day a large ketch sailed into the lagoon. That was a surprise. A man and wife with their children were sailing around the world and ran low on water and food. Later, we found out they had contacted harbor control and received clearance to enter and moor at the fuel pier. When they tied up, a water and supply truck was there to meet them. They were from Australia, and Island Security did not make a fuss. More than likely, they provided their passport numbers over the radio. Once verified, they were permitted to enter the lagoon. In no time, they were ready to depart. I doubt they were charged anything for the water or resupply. They were a refreshing change for us.

We were on a daily grind of not only fixing ships alongside, but aircraft carriers were sending job orders by the dozens for sheet metal lockers and other items. Our sheet metal shop made so many lockers that we spread a cargo net out on the helo deck filled with lockers of various sizes. A helo from the carrier came by, picked up the cargo net, and left for parts unknown.

During our stay, an SSN arrived. All they wanted was a stainless steel grill that would fit through the hatch. My guys had a handle on grills and whipped one out in no time. The CO of the boat was thrilled. They stayed a total of three days and left.

A massive storm hit Fremantle, and several warships nearly beat each other to death until two tugs pulled them apart for the storm's duration. What a mess—one on the port side and the other on the starboard. All my Hull Technicians (HTs) were put into teams to work around the clock removing the damaged superstructure, cutting and welding new pieces, then taking them down to the ships and welding them in place. I contacted Port Ops and told them I needed the large aluminum plates at the old Seabee site. They had them alongside in a large Mike boat in no time. Those plates were a lifesaver because the demand for half-inch aluminum on a sub tender is zero. We used almost every square inch of those plates to fix both destroyers back to practically new condition. Another job well done.

We supported a tiger team sent to replace a jet engine in one of the ships that came alongside. Crane service was all they needed. Once on board a vessel, the jet engines are called gas turbines. From the time the first access plate bolt was unscrewed until the last access plate bolt was tightened was precisely one week. They spun up both gas turbines and left. Probably not their first rodeo.

Getting parts and supplies was not a problem. Regular cargo flights from Charleston and other east coast airbases landed daily loaded with all kinds of stuff. Not only for us but for the Atoll itself.

CASUALTY

Finally, another SSN showed up. Like the first one, it didn't need a thing, only here for a visit for a few days. At some point, while attaching some nuke fitting back aft to send excess liquid to a tank, the nuke technician dropped the *special* nuke wrench over the side. OMG, you would have thought we had a *broken arrow* or something. There was a massive amount of ass-chewing over losing this particular wrench.

Not a problem, we told them. Our divers would go down, find it, and all will be at peace in Camelot. Finally, a real diving job.

Four of our divers, along with Bill Hendy, geared up and went over. They had a rubber Zodiac in the water remaining close to their bubbles. The Zodiac carried a standby diver. All the divers entered the water simultaneously, went to the same depth, found the holy-grail wrench, left the bottom at the same time, made one stop at ten feet for a few minutes, and surfaced at the same time. Everyone was okay, except Bill Hendy. He was bent. A bubble had lodged in his spine, rendering him out of commission below that point. They pulled him into the Zodiac and headed to the chamber on the island. The divers were upset. They reviewed the dive plan, rechecked the tables, and could not figure out how Bill got bent.

Once in the chamber, Bill was taken down to thirty-three feet and put on pure oxygen. The Master Diver ran the show. They followed all the proper procedures and slowly brought him back up again. He still had the bends. The nitrogen bubble didn't move and was not absorbed into his bloodstream. He wasn't in any pain, just messed up by a tiny nitrogen bubble. The Master Diver called Bethesda's diving medical department and discussed everything with them. Bethesda determined that Bill was one of those very few people who did not fall into standard Navy Dive Tables. They thought it was bizarre that he had gone through Diving Officers' School, and this problem never showed up. Bethesda developed a unique re-compression table for the Master Diver to follow. After each session, he called them and reported the results. Then they provided a revised procedure. This went on for a week before they came up with a procedure that worked.

I visited Bill every day I did not have the duty. I was so glad he was not in pain. His biggest problem was a horrible sore throat from breathing pure oxygen every day while he was in the chamber. When the bubble was finally absorbed, he could barely move his toes. In one week of not being able to move his legs, he had lost it all. Me, I'm thinking, *This is BS, all caps. I'm, going to rehab the crap out of this boy.* Bill and I used to jog miles, swim miles, drink all kinds of pitchers of beer. He was my steaming buddy, and I wasn't going to have any of this not-walking crap. As it turned out, his entire body was affected. Before the bends, he could curl 100 pounds; now, he could barely curl an empty bar. I think that is fifteen pounds. I spent as much time as I was legally allowed to be away from the ship, taking him to the gym in a wheelchair, getting him up and on various leg machines. We worked every muscle, and little by little, things started to happen. One day lower body, the next day upper. Finally, he could work out on his own and eventually returned to the ship. He kept tripping over his feet and almost falling, but there was always something to grab to prevent him from hitting the deck. He'd laugh his ass off every time and say, "Honest, I haven't been drinking." Bill was a former west coast submarine A-Ganger MMC SS and, like most, had a great sense of humor.

This little episode disqualified him from ever diving again. He continued to run R-6 and had permission to spend as much time as needed in the gym. He'd go over for a two-hour workout every day, and when he returned, he looked like death warmed over. He was pushing himself.

MORE REPAIRS

In the meantime, life continued, ships kept coming, and then a large Mike boat showed up with two cargo jet engine cowlings with cracks. They wanted to know if R-1 could fix them. I busted out my nuke welders and asked them to check them out. If they thought they could fix them, we'd get a crane and bring them aboard. Usually, you get a flat-out no, order two new ones, but my guys returned and said, yes, we can fix them.

You have to love these men, so damn talented and confident. To me, nuke welders are the only enlisted rate that walks on water. Sure enough, the two cowlings were moved into the large HT shop. The nuke welders got to work checking the type of metal, looking up temperatures, types of filler metal, etc. The other meat and potato HT welders assisted as much as possible. Truthfully, as good as my HTs were, they wanted to watch these guys in action. Nuke Welders require one more year of training than any other HTs.

The two nuke welders adjusted the power setting on their machine, flopped down their helmets, and started laying metal in each crack. This was not stick welding; it was TIG welding in an extremely delicate manner. Leonardo couldn't have done it any better. When they finished, a small amount of light grinding and buffing eliminated all signs of their work. They deserved every dollar of propay they received. I called Port Ops and told them they could pick up their cowlings anytime, and they said tomorrow at 0900. We had them topside and rigged to the crane hook, and the Mike boat didn't even have to tie up. The crane sat them in the center of the craft; the boat crew unhooked the strap, and off they went.

My division's most critical and crucial repair job is next. Then we set a course for home—also, lots of hanky-panky.

Fremantle, Western Australia

CHAPTER THIRTY-EIGHT

Things We Learned After the Fact

THIS AND THAT

On our little seven-month deployment, we took two professors from the University of Maryland. They offered several college courses during the day and at night for the crew interested in starting a degree program. The Navy had hooked up with various accredited colleges around the country. An accreditation group evaluated all military schools and a certain number of credits per course assigned. For example, an Electronics Technician (ET) would only have to take eight to ten subjects to get a double-E degree. Mostly, all electives everyone takes.

We found out later, two undercover NIS agents were on board for the deployment, one RM2 in Radio and one MS1 in the galley. They fit right in with the regular crew; both were officers. Now, that is a hell of a way to make a living. I'm pretty sure their primary focus was drugs. At least, I only knew about two; who knows, there could have been more. Good thing they weren't there for fraternization.

Couples on board got much more innovative about when and where they got together. Once in a while, there would be a Captain's Mast, which reduced ranks and issued fines. Always people of the opposite sex. In an earlier story, I said the selection process would increase in officers' country. All you had to do was look around the wardroom, and you knew right off who was staying up late studying seashells. I never bothered with the enlisted, as long as it wasn't any of my guys. We had one female petty officer meet us in Diego Garcia. She came to my division. She must have been the maximum age allowed to join the Navy. From West by God Virginia and was not a spring chicken. She did her job, which was fine with me.

Of course, the longer we were away from home, the weaker some became, and some women became bolder. I was out at the Contractors' Club one evening for the sunset and enjoying the waves crashing on the coral reef, flow up to the beach, and then all the water was funneled back through clear channels permanently cut into the coral. No one else from the ship was there. Out of nowhere, our married Navigator dragged her body across my back and sat down next to me with her arm and hand slowly coming across my neck and down my right arm. About scared me to death. She was one of the nicer looking out of the group and was abundantly clear as to her intentions. She was also married to an officer on another ship. The first words out of her mouth were, "Fancy meeting you here." ("No joke, Sherlock," said the fly to the spider.)

I asked if I could buy her a drink and the answer was, "Of course."

I went to the bar, picked up her drink, and brought it back. When I sat down, I was on the other side of the table.

She gave me the lower lip pouting thing and slid over next to me. She started running her fingers up and down my arm. If her hand had dropped down in my lap, I would have passed out right there. I'm not using her name on purpose.

I told her, "I'm married, and I'm faithful to my wife."

She replied, "I'm also married, and I don't give a damn."

I said, "Well, then, little girl, join me by the rail." I stood up and leaned against the deck railing. She immediately got up and wrapped her arms and one leg around me. I picked her up and threw her into the ocean. Sharks immediately began eating her. Eventually, her screams stopped.

Sorry, I got carried away.

I know some of you are screaming, "You idiot!" but that is not me. I could never live with myself if I cheated on my wife. I finished my drink and told her I'd see her back on the ship. I got up, excused myself, and walked away.

NUKE REPAIRS

We received a message from the nuclear guided-missile cruiser *USS Texas* (CGN-39). She had a leaking pipe in her nuclear power plant condensate system. At least it was not on the hot or radioactive side. Entering a reactor is at the top of things you never want to do. I had nuclear welders trained to do repairs inside shutdown reactors. We did not do K-19 repairs.

We had a big-time planning meeting to go over what we'd have to do. *Texas* crewman had tried reflowing the joint, but it did not help. Using the info provided, our R-8 Quality Division (QA) people pulled up the specs and determined that R-2 Machine Shop would make a new pipe. R-1 had to have a qualified brazer to do the job, and QA determined what testing was required after the repair to certify the work.

R-8 wrote a detailed work package, and everyone got busy. We did not stock every size or type of metal pipe used on submarines, much less a surface ship. A new pipe of the correct metal had to be machined out of solid stock, and it was going to take time. Unlike wood on a lathe, unique metal mixes do not cut fast. I had an HT already qualified to braze that type and size fitting, but we did another one for practice. It passed QA's testing, so we were good to go. Everything associated with a nuke reactor had to be 100 percent correct. None of this close-enough-for-government-work would do.

Texas arrived before we were completely ready, but they had to shut down their reactor and remove lagging. Then our people removed the existing pipe, and all fittings were prepped before the new pipe could be installed.

I supervised all aspects of the repair from beginning to end to ensure there were no delays. *Texas* had to be somewhere else in a hurry. We worked around the clock to repair it. QA was at the job site waiting to test the repair. It tested *sat*. The Engineer received the certification paperwork. My people gave them the necessary lagging to install themselves. As the ship started the reactor, the crew installed all lagging. The *Texas* engine room mechanics inspected the joint, and the ship departed. I had been up fifty-one straight hours. I told my chief everything was completed satisfactorily, and I went to bed, slept eight hours, and was as good as new.

The next day, the Commanding Officer of *USS Texas* sent a message to everyone he worked for and to us, raving about what we had accomplished in such a short time. That and fifty cents will get you a cup of coffee. Of course, the entire ship's company was congratulated for doing such a fantastic job as well as it should be. I was in my own little world. I had no doubts; many other divisions were helping *Texas* with anything they needed.

FREMANTLE

Finally, our time was up in Diego Garcia. We weighed anchor, moved back to the fuel pier, and topped off our tanks—one last night of liberty for some. I went over with my steaming bud, Bill Hendy,2 and we slowly drank a pitcher of rotgut San Miguel beer—80 cents a pitcher. I returned to the ship early to get some sleep. Bill checked into the BOQ and flew back to the states the day we left.

Up to this point, the *Holland* had been operating off a MOVREP message telling us when to leave Charleston, when to arrive in Diego Garcia, and when to leave Diego Garcia. We had received no instructions as to which way to return. The Captain decided we'd be the first tender to go around the world. The following day, we were underway and headed for Fremantle. After two days and still no message, the ship

---

2 Three years ago, Bill died suddenly. He had not been sick; it was his time. Another great man is gone on "Eternal Patrol." He had three kids and a gaggle of grandkids.

sent a message stating we had departed on time headed for Fremantle and to please make berthing arrangements for five days. It is easier to get forgiveness than permission.

R-1 had worked on forty-two ships, two submarines, two aircraft cowlings, and had completed 1,782 jobs as of the day we left. I don't have a clue what any of the other repair divisions did. I wrote all my shop supervisors Navy Achievement Medal recommendations and some for the other men who went above and beyond. All were approved. I put myself in for two purple hearts and a Navy Cross, but I still haven't received them. During all this mess, the R-1 CWO3, who was fired and replaced by me, made CWO4. The damn guy handed out basketballs and arranged three tours and a picnic.

Arriving in Fremantle is a once-in-a-lifetime experience. Ahead of our arrival, information was provided to newspapers, TV, and radio stations. The breakwaters were lined with hundreds of people with big signs reading *Welcome to WA* (Western Australia), *We love America*, *Thank You*, and lots of cheering. To say we were surprised would be an understatement. We found out later that they do this for all American military ships coming in. We had saved them from the Japanese during WWII, and they were still grateful. Unbelievable! Most of us weren't even born.

As soon as the accommodation ladder went down, three men from the telephone company installed a bunch of telephones and a chalkboard. When the telephone installers completed their work, they explained this was for the local people to call the ship and invite crew members to their houses. Also, for women to call seeking a date with an American, sight unseen. Unreal. A lot of the crew took advantage of this service. They all had a great time. It seemed the big thing over there was to have your daughter marry an American. Pretty much all the Australian men were in the outback working, and the women's ratio to men was around seven to one. Our welcome and how we were treated reminded me of my trips to Halifax, NS.

If you were in uniform, all public transportation was free. If you were in uniform, forget about paying for a drink. Fremantle is the Port for Perth. Perth is inland a bit. A spotless city. Not a speck of trash to be seen. I was walking down a downtown sidewalk, and Aboriginals would walk by. That was a strange sight. Older men or women would stop and shake my hand for saving them from Japan. A bizarre situation, indeed. Every type of cuisine in the world was available downtown. There was no crime, no graffiti, no loud music blasting from car windows. No matter what kind of car it was, however, every one had a large, heavy-duty set of bars attached to the front bumper. I asked a man what the purpose of the bars was.

He replied, "Roo bars."

"What is a roo bar?" I asked.

"To keep the bloody kangaroos from destroying your car when you hit one."

I imagine it was similar to hitting a moose up north. Damn things will kill you.

It was an excellent liberty port. I never returned to Western Australia. After I retired, my wife, a granddaughter, and I spent time in Melbourne and Sidney. Then we explored New Zealand from top to bottom and Tasmania. In my opinion, New Zealand was magnificent.

Our five-day visit was cut short by one day. The Port needed our berth, and we had to leave. Radio and TV announcements went out. Local police went everywhere and told any sailors they saw to return to the ship. After all that, as we pulled away, we had over 100 missed movements. I never watched TV or listened to the radio when I was out in town. There was a Navy Liaison Officer on the pier to make transportation arrangements for them back to Charleston.

After we returned, everyone who missed movement went to Captain's Mast. Later, I told the Captain I didn't think that was right, considering they all had to reimburse the government for their flight back. That was a large chunk of change.

Before we docked in Charleston, there was another event that got my dander up. I'll get to that later.

Galapagos Islands

CHAPTER THIRTY-NINE

Homeward Bound Across the Pacific

THE AUSTRALIAN SOUTH COAST

As we departed Fremantle, we received a goodbye from the people of WA equal to their welcome. As we passed them, we yelled, "Fair dinkum!" In return, they shouted and cheered louder. Beautiful people, Down Under. As we passed the end of the buoy line, we turned left and headed south. If we had maintained that course, we eventually would have spotted Antarctica. We were nowhere remotely prepared to go down there. We skirted the Australian coast and gradually changed course until we were running parallel to Australia's south coast. Blue skies, very little wind, and giant rollers coming north from Antarctica. We rocked from side to side like we were in the worst storm ever—smooth, huge swells, continuously day after day.

Remember the cargo net I could place across my bunk to keep me from getting thrown out? I put that sucker up ASAP. I also lifted the outside of my mattress and set it on the lip of my mattress tray. I rolled an extra blanket the long way to fill the hole between the mattress and bulkhead. I slept like a baby every night.

When I was on watch on the bridge as OOD, I was amazed at all the blank spots on our charts. Some depths had small notations, such as depth recorded in 1890. It appeared all the Oceanographic vessels that mapped ocean bottoms had neglected this part of the world. During the day, I constantly scanned forward for changes in watercolor. You never know when you will get a pinnacle or reef named after you. No radar contacts for weeks, just rocking. The only exciting thing to do was go back to the helo deck and watch albatrosses glide back and forth astern, waiting for the scullery to crank up. They seemed never to sleep. Some of us knew they took ten-second power naps. Always back and forth 24/7. They are master fliers, and the first six years after they learn to fly, they roam the seas before returning to land.

INTERNAL RELATIONS

All of a sudden, I had a feeling the blonde lieutenant had told a couple of other ladies that I was untouchable. One night, as I returned to my stateroom, the door to another stateroom opened as I was almost there, and another lady tried her best to drag me into her stateroom. I told her thanks, but no thanks, and continued to my stateroom.

At night, the passageway outside the staterooms was dimly lit. On another occasion, this spider lady was lying in wait for me. As soon as I started passing her stateroom, she opened the door, planted a lip lock on me, and ran a fathom of tongue down my throat. I never responded. I turned and went on to my stateroom.

After that, there were no more attempts to win me over. I used to wonder what the hell is my Navy coming to. Over the years, I've seen news articles about commanding officers doing all kinds of stupid stuff and getting caught. That is a speedy way to destroy a career and retirement.

In the Wardroom, the XO sat at a table with all the department heads. Most weapons folks had their table. The docs, dentist, legal, and chaplains were at another. The last table was where all the uncouth Mustangs and Warrant Officers sat. It was also where most of the females had gravitated very early when our Princess Cruise Line trip began. All except the one female dentist who was smokin' hot. She stayed back with her peers. Not sure if it was for her safety or what. The Marine Captain had to eat at the Department Head table with the XO. When he wasn't there, however, the former Naval Academy cheerleader was attached to his hip. All the other tables were relatively sedate during meals, while our table was a little rowdier. We were the ones with all the sea stories and jokes. I think that is what attracted all the younger female officers our way. Some of my humor brought gasps and red faces. They never left.

The XO had reminded me once that we were no longer in the Chiefs' Quarters, and to hold it down. Then he would ask me to tell him the story or joke I had told that cracked everyone up. I would, and he'd always laugh out loud and shake his head.

The Chief's Quarters were totally under control. The Master Chief didn't put up with any carrying on during meals and had no qualms about slam-dunking another chief if necessary.

I believe we had only one Mustang who had been PO1 when commissioned; everyone else was a Chief or Senior Chief like me. I always thought I should have been commissioned a Lieutenant and not an Ensign, like some dink, non-qual puke out of the Academy. Big deal, he had a ring. Dumber than a box of rocks.

Remember, on the boat, you had a Sea Pup? You acted like a mother hen to guide him on his way. On surface ships, the same thing.

Our Damage Control Assistant (DCA) was a canoe club grad, and I'm telling you, he was a mess. I saw him limping down a passageway one day. I stopped him and asked what his problem was. Did he sprain his ankle or something? He said no, the heel on his left boondocker (steel toe boot) came off. I stood there and looked at him, thinking, *WTF, over?* I wished him good luck and continued. A few days later, I ran across him again, and he was walking normally. I said I see you got your boots fixed. He told me he took the heel off the other boot. I was thinking of a country and western song about then. I told him to go down to supply and get himself a new pair of boondockers. How much are they, he wanted to know. I said they were free, that they were steel toe and, as such, were considered safety gear. Sure enough, ole *No-Heels* showed up with brand new boondockers. I'm surprised my forehead is not flat.

From that day forward, as an occasion arose, I presented the annual Joe P... *No-Heels Award* to someone who had done something stupid. It was one of Joe's old boondockers. I had the foundry make a mold and pour a new one in brass. The recipient had to return it to me when I was ready to present it to another officer.

LDO TO LINE?

Finally, we passed Tasmania and turned a little northeast for a day or two and then headed east. We were bound for the equator and international dateline. Since we departed Charleston, during the day when I was OOD, the Captain would come out and sit in his chair. He called me over to chat. He often asked if I had ever considered converting to a straight line officer. Yes, a Mustang, with the proper recommendation, can apply to be a line officer. He was relentless the entire cruise. I am sure that's why I could give him feedback about certain events I did not like.

A Mustang can only advance to Captain (O-6). You could command dry docks, some shore stations, and a few smaller vessels, but not warships. I was taken aback the first time he said that. I was happy to keep my head above water. I told him I had never given it any thought, that I was comfortable doing what I was doing, and had plenty of career opportunities.

He told me that I had everything they were looking for, and I would have no problem moving up. I thanked him every time. I had a Surface Warfare pin and was the best ship handler he had, but there is a world of difference, getting this on a tender instead of a warship. There was so much I had never done and never seen, like fueling at sea, high line transfers, vert reps, steaming in formation, and all that non-submarine stuff. He said I'd have no problem picking that up. I left it at that.

The main reason I didn't accept his offer was that I did not graduate from the Naval Academy. It is the same with officers in the Army, Air Force, Marines, and Coast Guard. If you do not have a ring, you are never really accepted as one of them. You can have as much sea time and knowledge as Captain Ahab, but a twenty-three-year-old ensign with a ring will trump you every time. Yes, you will have to train the kid, but eventually, he or she will pass you. I am sure corporations are similar.

CROSSING THE LINE—AGAIN

I don't know why we didn't cross the equator at the international dateline. A Golden Dragon Certificate would have been nice to go along with all the other certificates we earned.

During our time in Diego Garcia, personnel were transferred to and from the ship. There were at least 1,000 who had already been initiated for Shellback and around 100 who hadn't. Several of the ladies who turned it down the first time wanted to join in this time. The Master Chief told them no, they would be on watch and not even view the festivities. Oh, the crying, running mascara, red puffy eyes, snot stringing down from their nose, etc. Some even ran special request chits to the Captain begging for permission to participate. All were disapproved—more tears and pleading. A spectacle I could have done without.

GALAPAGOS AND BALBOA & A BIT OF NOSTALGIA

Oh, look, off the port side, through binoculars, the Galapagos Islands. Our next stop was the Panama Canal. We moored at Balboa Naval Station. Considerably hotter and more humid than Diego Garcia. Those not on watch had liberty until midnight. Everyone had to be on board before 2400. I had the duty. It turns out the keyword in that sentence was *on* board. Being on the pier next to the ship talking didn't count. Every person who came across the Quarterdeck after midnight had their name written down. In my former enlisted mind, standing on the pier next to the accommodation ladder is not exactly liberty—another BS flap. Officers, Chiefs, and below all had to go to mast eventually. I also gave the CO my opinion about that. As an enlisted man for fifteen years, I knew the amount of garbage they had to deal with. This was unnecessary.

For all the liberty ports I had been to on the diesel boats, as long as we were back by 0700, we were good to go. I went to quarters topside once as a Second-Class Petty Officer (E-5), barefoot, no socks, dungaree pants, a T-shirt, and no hat. I was semi-standing in my line, slowly rocking back and forth, when the COB came to me and said I had better be able to stand my maneuvering watch. I told him if he didn't move along, I'd throw him into the bay. He left smartly.

I couldn't stand my maneuvering watch, but I was able to lie on the deck in Sonar with the mic in my hand in case anyone needed me. I'd had way too much tequila in Old San Juan. It was my last underway port call with the *Entemedor* and crew before we returned to Groton. I was going on leave to get married, and then three weeks later, I was to be transferred.

A bunch of my shipmates threw one hell of a party. We had the entire bar and all the whores to ourselves. I only drank. We walked back from Old San Juan to the Army pier. I was amazed the local police did not arrest us because we were singing all kinds of submarine songs along with a few *hims*. Crossing the Quarterdeck of the tender was another story. I think if there hadn't been so many of us, many would have been in the brig. As it was, the Duty Officer paid us a compliment by saying we were a disgrace. I'll drink to that.

It almost brought a tear to my eye. He had to ruin perfect liberty with such a sentimental comment.

USS Holland *through the Panama Canal*

CHAPTER FORTY

The Panama Canal and Beyond

THE CANAL

Unlike our experience getting in and out of the Suez Canal, the Panama Canal was a joy. Everything worked like clockwork. If you have never made a complete transit or taken a Cruise ship, which goes in on one side and later departs the same way, I highly recommend adding the Panama Canal to your bucket list. I also suggest reviewing the history of the Canal. It is a mechanical marvel.

Our beam was eighty-four feet. Like most large ships, we could not enter the locks under our own power. A large ship is like a piston pushing through the water. Without enough clearance on each side for water to move from forward to aft, the propeller cannot get water fast enough to develop sufficient force to move a ship forward. The Canal Authority has pusher tugs with a large rubber-coated pushing device that fits flat against the stern. That tug pushes the ships into each lock. After that, small railroad-type engines attach wire rope lines forward and aft. These keep the ship centered in the lock, pull the ship forward into the next lock, and also stop the ship. Larger ships with overhanging decks would destroy the lights, so each light pole is hinged at the bottom and laid down. Water is not pumped in or out; gravity does it all. No saltwater enters the Canal or Lake Gatun.

We entered Balboa from the Pacific, next to Panama City. The Canal runs north/south and is further east than Charleston, SC. We exited on the Caribbean side at the port of Colon. Completely duty-free shopping.

When planners decided on the route across the isthmus, a jungle river and lake crossed the proposed path. They decided to build a large hydroelectric dam downstream of the Canal. The dam would supply power to most of Panama and water for the locks. It also formed the huge Gatun Lake. They flooded a vast valley to do this. The lake is dotted with small jungle-covered islands. Many of these islands have picnic areas and excellent fishing for peacock bass.

We were in a wide channel for about half of the transit, and then we entered the lake. A large deep basin on the Caribbean side is where ships wait their turn to be lowered by the next set of locks. It is a much shorter transit than the Ditch, and vessels can pass in both directions—two locks on the Pacific side and three locks on the Caribbean side. Due to the mountainous Continental Divide, the planners built the lake to get vessels over it. The Divide had been blasted down a good way. Continuing to sea level so locks would not have been needed would have been an even more massive undertaking.

❋

Since our transit in 1983, Panama secretly leased the Canal to a Chinese company to operate and maintain it. The Chinese have built another set of locks to accommodate much larger vessels. The U.S. paid for the Canal, Jimmy Carter gave it to Panama along with all the former military housing, and the Panamanians could not handle the job, so they leased it to the Chinese. Very similar to Puerto Rico selling its international airport to Mexican businessmen.

I must say, this trip through a tropical jungle was much more exciting to me than most of the journey, one of the best parts of the entire seven-month trip. There were no problems with the lock system when we left the other side. There was no great rush of cargo ships passing us; everyone was spaced a distance apart due to the locks. Ships were going in every direction possible, not being funneled by the Red Sea.

CHARLESTON (AT LAST)

Our plan was to return to Charleston as soon as possible. We passed east of Jamaica, went between Haiti and Cuba, and picked our way through the Bahamas. Yes, you are correct, no liberty ports.

Finally, we arrived back in Charleston. It was Saturday before Columbus Day. Everyone was gone on a long weekend, except for the wives, husbands, and dependents. There was no fanfare to acknowledge we were the first and only submarine tender to circumnavigate the earth—no fanfare when we started, no fanfare when we returned.

We moored across the pier from the *Cable*, the tender that was to have made the trip. Before turning the corner from the river to the pier, you would think there was a nuclear spill all over the ship. All former Love Boat couples, joined at the hip, were now practicing time, distance, and shielding. Husbands were going down, hugging and kissing wives and kids as their cruise lovers watched, same with the married women.

I got on the bow with a bullhorn and pointed out all the men and women who cheated. Just kidding, I didn't do that.

After seven months, everyone not on duty was given off until Tuesday morning. They were so liberal with time off because Monday was a national holiday. We had to head upriver to relieve the tender that was chained to the pier taking care of FBMs. Her crew was ready to be relieved, and we had not done anything but sail around the world, visiting one liberty port after the other.

Everyone who made the complete around the world cruise received a Magellan Certificate. In all truthfulness, there are no Magellan

Certificates. Circumnavigating the world on a Navy ship is very rare; therefore, the companies who print all the other certificates do not have one for Magellan. I've always thought that was strange because Magellan did not travel around the world. His ship did, but he died in the Philippines.

As ordered, everyone showed up Tuesday morning, ready for work. Refueling, stores load-out, meetings to discuss other future discussions, and the plan to take over at the Weapon's Station. All the boomers alongside the current tender had to leave. The current tender left the moor, and we were pushed into place and chained to the pier. By the end of the first day, we had three boomers on each side and one at wharf Alpha.

Every division in repair and weapons were assholes and elbows from day one. Some had a hard time getting up to speed fast enough. In a matter of days, we went from a cruise ship to a working FBM tender. I had told my men and one lady that we would run R-1 like a business. Minimal waste and provide everything asked. I never will forget one particular job order we received. Oven door handle loose, repair, or replace as necessary. One of my guys from the sheet metal shop went down to check it out. He returned in about 15 minutes stating the job was completed. What was the problem?

"Loose screws," he said. "I took a Phillips and tightened the four screws, and that was it." He said he showed the cook what to do if it happened again.

✳

We stopped making lockers for boats. Before a boat left on patrol, she would drop off a stack of job orders in the repair office. We learned in a hurry that very few men on a sub knew how to measure. If they needed a twelve-inch by twenty-inch locker with a shelf in the middle, that is what we would get. Even with a depth measurement, they forgot to mention that the locker would not fit because there was a pipe in the way, or the top right back corner needed to be three inches shorter due to a cable run. I saw the sheet metal shop make and then throw away so many lockers. Finally, I told the LPO not to make a locker unless one of our guys verified the measurements. We saved a lot of materials and time doing that.

We never ran across any jobs as screwed up as those surface ships in Diego Garcia had. All boats were reasonably standard, with very little need for large steel plate pieces to be rolled or bent. The men who had worked miracles were almost entirely relegated to replacing zincs. It was an essential part of a sub, but these guys were wasting their talents. Even the nuke welders never had to use their special talents one single time after repairing the jet engine cowlings. They did their time, got out, and went to big bucks' jobs. The pipe shop and high-pressure hose shop stayed pretty busy. So did rubber and plastic, making composite plaques and dolphins—more wasted talent. The amount of money thrown in the river during a submarine refit was amazing.

Every week, all Division Officers had a meeting with the PMA. He went over every job on a thick computer printout and wanted a status. I usually had to report on 1,000 to 1,200 active or pending jobs—parts, material, qualified brazers, or welders. Was the job completed, in progress, or waiting for the boat to arrive, etc.? The Div Off of R-4, the Electronics Division, never had a clue about anything. He had a Senior Chief running things, and I had a feeling he and the Senior Chief did not get along. Minimal communications.

After one of our meetings where the PMA chewed him a new one, he asked how I remembered all my jobs. I showed him the same computer printout that only listed R-1 jobs and my notes. I told him that before these meetings, I met with all my shop Leading Petty Officers (LPO) and my Chief, and I received an update on every current and future job. My guys already knew what info I was after. When I asked if he did that with R-4, he said no. I knew he was in trouble. I told him to go back and talk to his Senior Chief and get up to speed on his jobs. No division in repair had as many jobs as R-1. R-4 was so easy to run. I'm thinking, *How the hell did he get commissioned?* Years later, he converted back to enlisted status. He never could get out of the hole.

I also heard the PMA had been arrested for DUI. There really is a God. Usually, I couldn't have cared less, but he was such a micromanaging control freak who thought his poop didn't stink.

Divorces on Holland

CHAPTER FORTY-ONE

Consequences & R-1 Div Officer to Cape Canaveral

LOVE BOAT CONSEQUENCES

We had moved upriver to the Weapons Station with six FBMs alongside, and one moored at Pier Alpha. Almost immediately, rumors of divorce made the rounds. The blonde lieutenant who had made the run on me and was married to another officer divorced her husband and eventually married an older Senior Chief who divorced his wife and left six children with her.

Here is a little fact you more than likely do not know. If you are on active duty and are married to the same woman or man for ten years or more, fifty percent of your retired pay goes to the spouse when you retire. It does not matter if your spouse was servicing the fleet and you were squeaky clean. This law protects wives and children when the sailor decides to retire in the Philippines or another country and leaves spouse and children high and dry.

I have seen some disturbing situations. A wife and kids waiting on the pier for the husband and father to return, who retired the day he entered home port. The XO has to inform the wife and kids that husband and father retired and stayed in the Philippine Islands (PI), and is not returning. Just heartbreaking.

I never told my wife what went on aboard the ship—who was sleeping with whom. On every vessel, one crew member cannot wait to expose their wife to every little detail. He is as guilty as the rest in many cases but doesn't bother to confess his guilt. Wives love to tell other wives what someone's husband did. This led to all divorces on *Holland*. They could have lived happily ever after without a divorce, but once that happened, one or both parties were transferred.

R-1 DIVISION

I stayed with my division and continued to make submarine crews happy. It was not uncommon for me to run across someone I'd served with either on *Entemedor* or *Von Steuben*. It was always good to catch up. The rumor mills churned, and divorces continued with both officers and enlisted. The former schoolteacher married the CWO4, who divorced his wife and kids to marry her. I have never seen such stupidity in my life. I don't care if you are married to Attila the Hun. How can you drop your kids like that?

I continued as the Drill Team Leader and Training Officer and something else; I cannot remember now. I make no apologies for giving my Chief and Leading Petty Officers all the credit for my success. As close as I was with former shipmates on subs, I'll always have a soft spot for R-1. One of the significant differences between male and female officers is that once a male officer was assigned a division, he stayed with that division for his entire onboard tour unless something unusual happened. With female officers, every six months, they changed divisions. That looked good in their record for promotion. Let me back up a bit. We had many outstanding female officers who were well educated and well trained, but nobody tampered with the Washington DC system set up specifically for women. Our female Navigator was an exception to the rule. She did not jump from place to place like the others. She was a Department Head and remained as such.

I specifically remember two enlisted ladies in admin who were magnificent. Later on, both went commissioned, and they deserved it. Out of all of them, however, only a few were noteworthy. I know I'm swimming up Niagara Falls, and all my complaining is not getting me anywhere. Of course, I never voiced my opinion openly to anyone. That would be certain death for me.

Our beautiful, full of energy former Naval Academy cheerleader was the senior Ensign in the entire Navy for a while. She was such a dingbat and kept screwing up so much that her promotion to Lieutenant (junior grade) was delayed. Let me tell you something, not to advance to Lieutenant (junior grade), you have to mess up big time. Very similar to not passing mess cooking. You stay here until you get it right. When she had a division, she was not the Division Officer. She was one of the boys. If they went out partying, she went also. She got into a world of fecal matter many times for fraternization. Finally, after three years, she was promoted to Lieutenant (junior grade). Unbelievable.

I do not know what happened to her Marine Captain. He must have been transferred, and they parted as friends and lovers.

My time at home was minimal. I was always getting called in to put out fires. It seemed like flaming ducks were crashing all over the place. Typically, overreactions by a duty repair officer. But still, driving in at 2 AM to resolve a problem a second-class on a submarine would typically take care of was a bit of overkill.

Very seldom did I get an entire Saturday or Sunday off. I guess it was because R-1 was involved with so many jobs on all the different boats. One boat would leave. The next day, another boomer would arrive looking for the world. I never wanted the sub guys to experience what I had on the *Von Steuben*. It was like it was a big surprise we were back from patrol. There didn't appear to be as much enthusiasm as I had hoped.

I went topside on every single boomer as soon as the accommodation ladder was over. I talked to the CO, XO, and COB, welcomed them back, and assured them we'd do as much as possible for them. It was excellent PR for me and my future job at the Naval Ordnance Test Unit (NOTU), plus it gave the key people on the sub a warm and fuzzy.

In case you missed it, I never forgot my enlisted roots or the traits of those I admired—Chiefs or Officers. I always placed the crew first.

As an officer, you have to get your ticket punched if you expect to continue to advance. That was why the female officers were getting their tickets punched twice as often. Each time we transited the Canal or Ditch, only female officers and enlisted were on the bridge. Those little nuggets in their evaluations were worth their weight in gold.

At some point, Sonar became part of Weapons and not Operations. Not exactly sure how they figured that one out. As a result, when it was time for me to talk to my detailer, he offered me duty at NOTU, Port Operations, Port Canaveral.

"You will be the first."

I asked, "First what?"

He said, "Non-weapons person to go to Port Ops to be a Test Engineer."

"What does a Test Engineer do?"

"He gets the submarine ready to launch a DASO missile and coordinates everything with the Range."

"What is a Range?"

"Where they launch a missile."

"So, no more welding or building sheet metal lockers?"

"No," he said. "This is nothing like you have ever done before. Essentially, you are our guinea pig."

"So, if I fail, that will be it for non-weapons types doing this job?"

"Right. You report in August 84. You will have to come up to speed pretty quickly."

This sounded like the story of my Navy life.

NOTU

I went home and told my wife that we were moving to Florida.

"Fine," She said. "When do we leave?"

"I go in August, and you and the kids come down over Christmas break. I should have found a place for us to live by then."

Orders soon came down the line, and my relief was ordered in. He was a CWO3 who was a former HT. The perfect person for the job. Before leaving, the Command gave all my collateral duties to five other officers. We had a hail and farewell event, and I went home. It took two entire days for me to unwind and return to being a normal human. I crashed and burned, and finally, after years, I slept. After my leave, I drove to Port Canaveral and checked in.

The CO was Captain Bill Bancroft, Port Ops was Commander Tom Clark. Assistant Port Ops was Lieutenant Commander Buck Taylor. There were three other Lieutenants besides me. They all came from Missile Tech or Fire Control Tech ballistic missile backgrounds, however, and served as Weapons Officer (Buck Taylor) or Assistant Weapons Officers. All were submarine qualified, and the Lieutenants were, like me, submarine and surface qualified. Cmdr. Clark, a line officer, had turned down command of a submarine because his wife had a brain tumor and needed surgery. SubLant did not take his refusal well. If I had to choose between my wife and a command, my wife and kids would win every time. I was there for a two-year tour—get that ticket punched and move on to the next place on the ticket.

Cmdr. Clark and his wife, Helen, loved our family. All their kids were grown and gone. I learned so much from him.

I was behind the power curve and had to learn a ton of weapons materials in addition to qualifying as a Test Engineer and all it entails. Port Ops was a small group; every ship or submarine had someone assigned to it. We handled the Poseidon and Trident piers. The *Range Sentinel's* permanent berth was in front of Port Ops. She was initially a *Liberty Ship* during WWII. Later, she was recommissioned and modified to be the Range Ship for submarine launches. There were also two all-white-painted range ships—yes, that is my story, and I'm sticking to it.

The *Vanguard* and the *Redstone* were WWII tankers and converted to be tracking ships, among other things. It is the other things I will not address about either *Vanguard* or *Redstone*. I could get into a lot of trouble. They are artificial reefs now but had one heck of a career. Don't bother searching for more info; none of it is public info. Everything written about them pertains to tracking NASA launches.

You can find underwater photos of them as artificial reefs.

Two of my fellow lieutenants were Ron Lubatti and Braxton Stanley. Both had been enlisted and were sent to college by the Navy. Ron Lubatti got me turned on to buying gold in 1985. The best thing I have ever done. The third lieutenant left soon after I arrived.

One day, our Port Ops secretary came out and told me the XO wanted to see me. NOTU headquarters is on the Cape. Also up there is 50 Shop where all the MTs, ETs, and other weapons types worked out of a large hangar. We all worked together during DASOs but remained in our little world otherwise. SP-205 (Strategic Systems Project Office) was out of Crystal City just outside DC. All those guys were former Weapons Officers, and the man in charge was the senior Captain in the Navy. When it came to submerged submarine-launched missiles, he was God, very similar to Rickover and nuclear power. You did not mess with these two men. For each DASO, SP-205 would send a team down to supervise and spend time getting the submarine weapons people ready to be certified.

I went to headquarters to see the XO, and he said, "You will be our Top Secret Control Officer and the Command Security Manager."

Why don't you just run over me with a few semis and put me out of my misery?

"Your assistant will be Ms. Lila so-and-so. She can explain everything to you."

"Not a problem, sir."

The lady was a civil servant and a Southern Belle from Mississippi, Alabama, Georgia—somewhere South. She was married to an engineer with NASA. I imagine in her day, she was very nice looking. She was still slim, but she was getting close to retirement. She had that honey-dripping Southern accent that added extra syllables to every word. I had time, so we sat in her office, and she reviewed the process of how classified documents arrived, were logged in, a control sheet was typed with the necessary blocks filled in, placed in the appropriate folder, Confidential or Secret, with a routing sheet on the outside. First to see it would be the CO, then XO. They would list which department head it went to, or in some cases, multiple department heads were checked.

A pretty straightforward system, laid out as the book said. She maintained one colored copy of the form for inventory purposes, and so she knew which department held the classified document or manual.

As I was getting up to leave for the port, she said, "Lieutenant," (the extra-long version), "we have a problem." Not the words a new Security Manager ever wants to hear.

"What do you mean?" I asked.

"We have so much classified information here, I will need half a day to show you all of it."

I assured her I would find the time and return.

I borrowed her Security-R-US manual and went back to the port.

A Trident II D-5 being launched at NOTU

CHAPTER FORTY-TWO

How My Two-Year Tour Turned Into Five Years at NOTU

NOTU

The Naval Ordnance Test Unit (NOTU) is not what it always appears to be. We worked with US and UK SSNs and SSBNs, SEALs, high-speed patrol boats that support SPECOPS, research vessels with manned and unmanned deep-sea vehicles, MK-48 Advanced Capability (ADCAP) torpedoes, Chief of Naval Operations (CNO) special projects, and hosted various types of surface ships looking for an excellent liberty port, even had a retired admiral call and wanted to park his yacht overnight. During the Space Shuttle Program, the day before a launch, we provided dock space for the two solid rocket booster retrieval vessels.

Years ago, before Trident subs, all Demonstration and Operation Shakedown Operation (DASO) preps were conducted at the Poseidon pier, next to the main channel. This pier is where the *George Washington* conducted the first Polaris DASO.

Due to the beast's nature, companies that started with the *George Washington* Polaris program pretty much stayed through the Trident II D-5 program. Not soliciting bids each time a contract is up for renewal is unheard of in DOD. Sole source is a bad word. The Submarine-Launched Ballistic Missile program, however, was too significant (national security) to reinvent the wheel continually.

Foreign spies, oh, yes! Known agents sat in condo windows taking photos and videos regularly. We had many undercover operatives keeping tabs on them. I even had a Soviet agent move across the street from me with his family. (See Chapter 45.)

I went through the qualification process, observed one DASO on board a sub, and then conducted an observed DASO. After that, I qualified as a Test Engineer. Then I shifted to the operations side of what we did on the launch support ship, *Range Sentinel.* After that, I was up in the big control room on the Cape, learning that part. Working with Range Safety, communicating, and everything required for our launches. Unlike the space program or other rocket programs, we didn't care what the weather was. None of that mattered. Their systems are fragile; weather, upper atmosphere wind speeds, and especially lightning would always cancel their launch, and they rescheduled. In the submarine ballistic missile business, you can't delay the war because the weather is bad. When we went out on launch day, it didn't matter if there were state nine seas and a thunderstorm overhead. When it came time for missile away, it may exit the water on its side, but after ignition, it straightened up and got out of Dodge in a hurry.

I was on the *Von Steuben* when we conducted our Polaris IIA DASO in January 71. Years later, when I returned for duty, the Trident basin had been dredged, a massive wharf constructed, and a much larger crane placed on rails. The Trident basin is where everything DASO-related took place. As soon as a sub passed the breakwater entering Port Canaveral (PCAN), they hung a right into the Trident Basin. Other than the security boats, no other vessel was allowed, whether a sub was tied up or not. Years later, a floating gate was installed, and it was closed when a sub was in.

After everything was secure, dolphins were released to patrol underwater to make sure no one came in. Even if you were military, you were not allowed in there if you were not on the access list.

Before I move on, let me tell you about the Trident Basin's security plan's most crucial part—FISHING. At fifty feet, it was a giant aquarium full of large, edible, magnificent fish. I would SCUBA dive there. I'd let security know where I would be, and they didn't care because I would share my fish with them. I got so many mangrove snappers, sheepshead, flounder, snook, and a few grouper. It was terrific. The water was clear because there was no vessel traffic, making it pleasant. Of course, while I was down there, I conducted a piling inspection. I found a few problems over the years that required repairs. You could say I was providing a service.

One night, a 14.5-pound flounder was caught off the north end of the wharf. The white underside filet was one inch thick. It was almost a world record for that flounder species. I cannot claim it as mine. One of the chiefs I worked with caught it using a bottom rig specially designed for flounder. It was lying on the bottom, looking up under a light at the end of the pier. Catching flounder in May was amazing. Eight to ten-pounders were the norm.

The place was full of redfish, black drum, and plenty of baitfish such as mullet. Giant schools of jack crevalle doing their mating swarms. Fun to catch but not any good for eating, at least for me.

All the men at Port Operations were top of the line. All were submarine qualified and very professional. A CWO 4 ran the dockside, and four quartermasters worked for him. They did ship or sub placement next to the pier and supervised arrival and departure. They monitored all comms and talked to the vessels coming to us when they checked in. They also talked to the port pilots. All the security camera monitors and controls were on their side also. Their side was manned 24/7. We could watch everything day or night. Each camera was movable and could zoom in close.

I was surprised at the number of people who would swim across the main channel at night with fishing gear to fish in the Trident Basin.

None of them ever wet a hook in our water. Port security was notified, and they'd drive up with lights off and arrest them. They were processed at the front gate security office, and a County Sheriff's deputy would pick them up and take them to jail. Trespassing on government land and trying to steal my fish. Our Captain loved to fish, which is the only way we could go over there ourselves. His relief, Captain John Byron (former enlisted), loved fishing even more. He was, by far, the best Commanding Officer I served under during my thirty years.

SECURITY MANAGER

After finishing all my required qualifications, I finally had time to go to headquarters and meet with my civil service security assistant. She started again by telling me how much classified information we had. Just in her office, she had seven four-drawer file cabinets jammed full of Confidential and Secret letters and small publications. We took a tour of headquarters. Every department had walls of the same packed file cabinets. Then we got in my truck and drove over to the big hanger where 50 Shop was. Off one of the halls was a giant, super heavy-duty, walk-in vault. This thing was massive. She dialed in the combination and opened the heavy door. You could not enter the vault. It was stacked floor to ceiling with classified materials.

In submarines, we did not keep classified material very long. It was destroyed after it had served its purpose. Plus, every crew turnover had to conduct an inventory. I asked Ms. Lila where all this stuff came from. She said we had classified information from *George Washington's* DASO forward. I asked when was the last time there was an inventory. Heart attack city—NEVER, she answered. From my background, never inventorying classified material was unheard of. Hell, they were lining sailors up against adobe walls over one piece of missing Confidential. I told Lila I would take care of it. We closed and locked the door.

Back down at Port Ops, I got my Security Manager's manual and started looking for Shore Facilities-R-Us. This is a no-sh*tter—inventories of classified material are not required due to the large volume. I started talking aloud to myself, and Lt. Stanley stuck his head in and asked what I was talking about. I gave a once-over-lightly brief, and then read the line out of the book again. Stan agreed with me. This was a major disaster waiting to happen.

I fitted all this security business between DASOs, loading thousands of ADCAP torpedoes, and more. I made an appointment to talk to the XO about this mess. I didn't take him on tour. He sat there and listened and was more in shock than anything else. He stuck his head in the CO's office and asked if he had a minute; he needed to hear this.

"Sure, come on in and have a seat."

So, I started again, and there was no indication I had struck a nerve.

"Are you sure about this?" he asked.

I said, "Yes, sir. I read the book twice and even talked to Lt. Stanley about it, and he was just as blown away as I."

He asked his secretary to contact the head engineer and have him come down to his office. The head engineer was over all the civil service departments and should shed some light on this. His office was on the second deck, and he was there shortly. The Captain repeated what I had told him.

He said, "Yes, we keep all that information."

I asked, "For whom?"

"In case someone needs a copy," he answered.

I responded it would never be found if they did.

Here is what they were doing. After every DASO, a report was compiled and printed for distribution. Just for the heck of it, they always asked for ten more copies than were required for distribution in case someone, a decade down the road, would like a copy.

His final comment was, "We can't get rid of any of it."

The Captain said okay, and the Engineer left. The Captain told the XO and me that he would talk to 205, as in the Admiral in Crystal City.

"I'll get back to you."

I told the Captain to keep in mind, Confidential is declassified after two years, and most Secret is downgraded to Confidential after seven years.

The Classified Material burn pit

CHAPTER FORTY-THREE

At Some Point in Your Career, Large Quantities of Fecal Matter Will Hit the Fan

SECURITY MANAGER

Before heading back to the port, I stopped by Lila's office and told her what transpired—the Chief Engineer seemed to have won the day, and all the documents were staying. She was not too thrilled, but our hands were tied.

The following week, our secretary told me the XO wanted to talk to me. So, back up to headquarters I went. He took me to the Captain's office and shut the door, not a good sign, usually. The Captain said he talked to the Admiral about our situation, and the Admiral was surprised by what he heard. It was one of those calls where the Admiral said, "I'll call you back."

I guess he didn't realize there was a difference in how subs and shore stations handled classified information. I told you, submarine sailors lived in a small community.

It wasn't too long before the Admiral called the CO and said, "Your Security Manager is correct." He did not know why shore stations never inventoried their classified materials or why NOTU had so much of it. He named the place with a contract to be the repository of DASO and other open-ocean-launch-documents. NOTU was not required to hang on to everything forever.

The Captain wanted to tell me that he would have a meeting with the Chief Engineer and several civil service Department Heads to find out if there was a valid excuse for keeping thousands of classified documents. He said he would let me know the results. I had inadvertently lit a fuse, and not only was our CO asking questions, but the Admiral started asking questions.

On my way out, I stopped by to see Ms Lila and brought her up to date. She let me know that she was looking into getting a job with NASA and met all the qualifications. The position would be opening soon. I wished her good luck and headed back to the port.

Later, the CO's meeting with the Chief Engineer and Department heads at headquarters did not go well. It was like the Captain was going around removing all the pacifiers from kindergarten kids. It turned out that every contractor who had anything to do with submerged submarine launches was hoarding documents from day one, week one of the program. More calls to the Admiral, and a date was set for all the major players, military, and civilians to meet at Crystal City in 205 headquarters.

I started this in January 86, and by the beginning of April, the Admiral sent out a letter telling everyone in his command how it was going to be. There would be no exceptions.

Essentially, properly log and destroy everything over two years old. If you ever need a copy, contact the company under contract to be the custodian of all the documents.

I was no longer welcomed in certain offices on the second deck. Like I cared.

In the meantime, Ms Lila departed for NASA, and her replacement was Ms Marty. It was an *I had it, and you got it* turnover. The XO gave me marching orders to start culling the crop. I was in the middle of a DASO but could sneak off and talk to Ms Marty and get her started filling out as many destruction forms as possible and emptying her safes of all documents over two years old.

As Security Manager, I could not walk in and sign the destruction forms. I had to verify numbers with documents, etc. They were then placed into burn bags. Every chance I could, I'd head up there, go through the newest forms and documents and then head back to the DASO boat. I told her to stop when she ran out of room for burn bags in her office.

DASO OPS

The DASO was successful, like all the others. Then we had several days of round-the-clock work to get the Test Instrumentation Mast off, remove equipment from inside the boat, get the missile tube cleaned and inspected, and load ballast into the empty tube to compensate for the missing missile. After everything was completed, the boat would leave and head back to Charleston or Kings Bay to load real missiles. After that, we didn't care because, eventually, another boat would be arriving. Some arrived the day after the current one left.

Once in a great while, we did not have a sub there for DASO. That didn't matter. NOTU was like a revolving door for US and Brit submarines and warships. Plus, we continued to load ADCAP torpedoes.

BURN BAG OPS

Finally, I had time to devote to hauling burn bags.

On the tender, the burn room was a room that allowed access to a diesel exhaust stack. The stack had a small door. When opened, there was a heavy mesh metal cage inside which could withstand the more than 1,000-degree temps. That is where the burn bags went. Everything instantly burst into flames and was gone in a matter of seconds. Cape Canaveral, Air Force Station, didn't have such a system. You drove up the main paved road from headquarters and turned left on a small, paved road with a big sign, BURN SITE.

When I got to headquarters, I backed the truck up to the front doors and entered Ms Marty's office. I was blown away. We were going to need a bigger truck. She had been a busy little beaver. There were burn bags stacked to the ceiling. I asked her if she was ready to go to the woods. She blushed. We loaded the back of that full-size pickup with as many burn bags as it would hold without losing any over the side as we drove. She locked her office, and we headed to the woods. Neither of us had ever been to the burn site.

The Air Force had used a bulldozer to clear a large area of all vegetation. A sand berm was pushed up about five to six feet high in a 360-degree circle around 100 feet across. I did not know how deep it was, but gray ashes covered it. A man in a truck was there, and it was his job to operate the burn pit. He motioned us to come around and back up to a conveyor feeder belt. He then said to remove any metal bindings from the bags and toss them into the metal drum. No metal bindings or rings, only things that will burn. Okay, no problem. Then he started a six-cylinder diesel engine and started pulling levers.

One engaged the conveyor system; the other engaged a huge hammer mill and blower. When the air from the blower hit the gray ash surface, it turned into a fiery blue cauldron. It would be like uncovering a volcano and exposing molten lava. The conveyor belt also vibrated, so as papers headed up, they automatically separated. The hammer mill turned paper into dust, and blue flames erupted from the pit and consumed it all in a microsecond. I have never seen a system like that. It ensured no one would ever read what came out of the hammer mill, even if there were no fire. As we emptied each bag, we threw it in also. We emptied the back of the pickup in no time. To me, that system seemed like overkill, but it surely could destroy paper.

I told the man we had more to bring, and he said he would be there until 1600. Shortly we returned with another truckload. He cranked up the diesel, and we got with the program. I do not remember how many truckloads of burn bags we took over there, but Ms Marty and I made many trips to the woods. We still had the giant safe to empty. Whenever she had enough to take to the burn site, she'd call our secretary and ask her to tell Lt. Pait she was ready to go to the woods. Our secretary was prim and proper, and I am sure she thought we were up to no good. I finally told her one day what going to the woods meant, and she was so embarrassed, and laughed and laughed. Good people.

TORPEDO AND DASO OPS

Somewhere during all that burning, I had to supervise ADCAP torpedo loading. I was on the pier, and the boat handled everything topside. I watched them like a hawk. I often had to halt the operation and point out a cable that was out of position and would cause problems. I am not sure anymore, but I believe that in one day, two SSNs would come and go from us to the range and fire all the ADCAP weapons. Unlike diesel boat days when we recovered our own, AUTEC provided a torpedo retriever. Like the burn bags, I cannot give you the number of torpedoes we loaded for the ADCAP program, but it was a bunch of *fish*, at least 500.

Marty was a good person and a hard worker. She finally ground through all the paperwork, and little by little, the piles of classified documents got smaller and smaller. I sat in the large safe one day and read the reports from *George Washington's* launch. Talk about security, there was no Navy security above water, but four Coast Guard Cutters were there to make sure no other boats got remotely close to *George Washington*. Of course, over the years, all that went away after launches became commonplace. Between the *Range Sentinel* and Air Force helos, security was adequate. If we needed them, we could always call the Coast Guard base at PCAN, and they'd be out in short order. All the years I was there, every launch was conducted during the day except on British DASO. The year before I arrived, there was a night launch, and one of the Air Force helicopters went down, and all hands drowned. No one knew about it. It was not a good operation.

Even after I arrived, all helos were controlled by Patrick Air Force Base.

When it happened, Patrick AFB helo squadron notified Range Control they had lost comms with a helo. Range Control informed the NOTU team onboard *Range Sentinel*. One of our officers informed the Russian intelligence vessel. They never answered us, but I am sure if they had any info, they would have let us know. In the dark, searching for the helo or any survivors was very difficult. Once the Coast Guard was on scene, they took over the search, and NOTU continued the mission. It was successful. It sounds pretty cold-hearted, but the groups at NOTU and Range Control are a small fraction of the people involved, including specialty aircraft, and all the downrange operations; it is a significant production with so much coordination required.

More Air Force air and sea rescue helicopters arrived and lit the place like a Friday night football field. The Russian spy ship left for Havana, the sub returned to port, and the *Range Sentinel* was close behind. It took two days to find the helo. We launch in the Gulf Stream. When the helo crashed, it moved north. I believe the Coast Guard did some fancy plotting, and one of their boats located a jet fuel slick. They were able to follow it back. I wasn't there, so I do not know all the particulars.

USS Yorktown

CHAPTER FORTY-FOUR

How to Get Ahead of the Power Curve

THE INVENTORY

The entire command was conducting an inventory of all things classified. The first one ever. Fortunately, even though I was the Security Manager, Marty handled most of the inventory. She provided each department with a list of control numbers on file for every piece of classified documentation they held. Depending on the department's size, usually, the secretary could conduct the inventory. Two departments used two people because of how much they had. After they completed their list, over 100 classified documents were missing. Those departments had to go through everything again, explicitly looking for the missing items to get to zero or a much lower number.

Mostly, missing documents were one or two pages with a control sheet attached. During the second go-round, most were found stuck inside the front cover of another classified book. They finally got down to seven pieces of missing classified documents. Marty and I researched the missing documents and found they were over fifteen years old, and all were Confidential. I thought that the result was outstanding and a credit to the accountability system.

Marty typed a list for me, and I presented it to the XO and CO. They were delighted. The Commanding Officer has a lot of power when it comes to classified material. The CO wrote a letter to the Admiral at 205 explaining our results and the fact that all the documents were declassified many years ago and did not present a problem or detriment to the program. I talked to the head Admin lady over all the Civil Service people and asked her to write up an Atta-Girl for Marty for all her work. Never under-appreciate those who hold your butt in a sling. When we had our quarterly awards ceremony, Marty was surprised and pleased to receive her award.

Me, I went back to the Port.

WALKER

All of you should remember this:

John Anthony Walker, Jr. (born July 28, 1937, Washington, D.C.—died August 28, 2014, Butner, North Carolina), was a U.S. Navy communications specialist who for almost two decades (1967–85) passed classified documents, including Navy codebooks and reports on movements of submarines and surface ships, to agents of the Soviet Union. At first, he obtained the documents himself while on active duty. Then he recruited a close friend, a brother, and a son into a growing spy ring that he maintained after his military retirement. Some officials described the Walker spy ring's espionage activities as among the gravest security breaches in the history of the U.S. Navy.

What he did was collect classified documents that he sold to the Soviets. Classified document control is vital to our national security.

GETTING THE JUMP

Talk about the luck of the Irish, and I'm not even Irish. We had not completed our destruction and inventory for more than six weeks when the story broke about Walker's arrest and then the additional arrest of his brother and son. Our CO and XO were thrilled to death, because what we had recently completed was mandated to the entire Navy by the head Security Manager in-the-sky. Commands were going nuts trying to meet the deadline, and we sat down at NOTU fat, dumb and happy. The Admiral (205) called our CO and told him to thank me for what I had brought to their attention. All 205 commands were already in compliance.

Remember, in the movie *Patton* when the Generals were looking for any force that could reach Bastogne and relieve/reinforce the men who had been surrounded and were close to being overrun? Patton had anticipated this and already had his staff working on a plan to do just that. All the other commanders looked at him like he was crazy when he said he could do it. That is the way I felt. I cannot foretell the future, but I didn't like what I saw and thought how easy it would be for someone to walk off with all kinds of sensitive information—and no one would ever know. Little did I know, this little event would start the downfall of my career.

You plow the rows straight, plant the correct number of seeds per hole, grow a bountiful crop, and next thing you know, that is your job forever. Sometimes, especially in the Navy, an officer should move from behind the mule and get on a tractor in another field.

Life at NOTU continued after that, and everything settled into a regular rotating routine. Some days I loaded torpedoes. Some days I greeted a visiting submarine or warship. I loved working with the British. Everything we did for them, as a matter of routine, was met with great appreciation. Talk about submarine characters; I don't know who were the wildest, the enlisted or the officers. Every single Brit boat that visited was the same, "Let's party!" The Brit warships were not as wild, but they all hosted a big party on the fantail with many guests invited and free booze and *ors de ovaries*.

The Brits always wanted me to tell them the best place to experience the *real* Florida. I'd send them to a small fish camp with airboats out on the Saint John's River called Lone Cabbage Fish Camp. It was a rustic country and western place where you could eat gator tail, frog legs, and a seafood assortment. That ended up being THE place to go for them, and the word spread throughout the Brit fleet in no time. Every Brit sub or ship always gave me a signed photo and a beautiful hand-painted plaque. I'm sure it was the same for all the guys assigned to them, not just me.

My most prized plaque is from the *HMS Conqueror*. She is the SSN who sank the Argentine warship in the Falklands. Talk about a group of submarine sailors. Many of the crew were still on board several years after the sinking. They steamed down the channel with a large pirate flag and a large Confederate battle flag. Brought back so many memories of my diesel boat days. Everyone had an attitude—We can kick the world's ass. Where is the party?

Fortunately, I never hit the beach with any of these guys. I don't think I stood a chance of keeping up with them. The odd thing, none of the Brits ever got into trouble on the beach. U.S. sailors were always in trouble with bar owners, waitresses, or the local cops. None were put in jail, but they were brought back to the port gate and sent packing.

Getting on toward the end of my two-year tour, I contacted my detailer about where I would go next. He told me I had been extended at the request of SP-205. What could I say, but okay, I guess. I contacted the XO, and his response was, yes, I meant to call you. Oh, well, I liked my duty there, and it wasn't like I wasn't involved in something that wasn't necessary. The alternative for me was to return to another tender, and it could have been anywhere from Guam to Holy Loch.

My wife and kids loved living on Merritt Island, the schools, and being ten minutes from the surf. As they got older, they all got boards and would go whenever they could. Three of our four sons swam competitively in high school and college. Going to NOTU was the best move possible for my family.

USS YORKTOWN (CG-48)

NOTU was notified that the test range where explosive trials for surface ships were held was going to be down. They wanted to know if we could accommodate the *USS Yorktown* for shock trials during a specific time frame. We had space on the south end of the Trident pier, so we said yes. According to the rules governing DASO, no other vessel could be at the same wharf except for another submarine or warship. *Yorktown* fell into the warship category. Essentially, our involvement would be minimal. Provide line handlers for arrivals and underways, a crane to set or remove the brow, and shore power. The team that usually conducted the test would do everything else.

What are explosive trials of a warship? In basic terms, they try to sink it. To test the survivability of a new class warship, small to very large explosives are placed at various distances from the ship. The ship is filled with instrumentation, and as each charge is detonated, all readings are recorded. The entire test takes place over several weeks. The last explosion is the closest to the ship. In *Yorktown's* trial, the large tracking radar antenna broke loose, a fuel tank ruptured, and every electrical breaker on board the vessel tripped. That resulted in a top-of-the-line warship dead in the water, blind, and not one weapon could fire. The Navy conducts these tests because it is better to find out in peacetime than in war. After resetting all the breakers, she made it back to PCAN. The crack in the fuel tank was patched, and she went back to the shipyards for repairs and modifications. Then they went back through shock trials again at the standard test range. Depending upon those results, every *Yorktown Class* cruiser was built to the new specifications.

If I ever had to go to war, my first choice would always be a submarine. My second choice would be an *Aegis Cruiser*. I took a tour, and the Combat Information Center (CIC) was *Star Wars* on steroids. They received Intel from every source we had in real-time. Every known Soviet submarine and warship position in the world was on one or more screens. Like *Hunt for Red October* when the guy asked the Carrier CO, "Who is this over here?" I was amazed at the technology. I already knew a sub tender was not the real surface navy, but to see one up close and personal was extremely impressive. I know we call them targets, but I would not like to tangle with one.

As impressive as the *USS Texas* was in Diego Garcia, the *Yorktown* was light-years ahead.

CHAPTER FORTY-FIVE

The Spy Next Door

MY NEIGHBOR, THE PAINTER

My first tour at NOTU began in August 84. While performing my duties, I also looked for a house to purchase. My wife and four boys came down over Christmas break from Charleston, and we moved into the same place we live in today on Merritt Island, halfway between highways 528 and 520. We are centrally located for schools, post office, several grocery stores, and the library. A ten-minute drive for me to work, a fifteen-minute drive to several places on the ocean. Forty-five minutes to Orlando Airport and a little less than one hour to Disney, Sea World, etc. From my front door to the Gulf of Mexico is two hours and fifteen minutes. A great place to live. As you'd expect, summers are hot and humid, but we always have a breeze and are never as hot as Orlando due to living on an island. Winter is heaven. Doors and windows open for six months. It is almost the perfect location to live. We did not want a house on a canal, but a pool was a must-have.

Most of our neighbors worked at or had retired from the Space Center. Over the years, most of the original neighbors have died or moved away.

At the end of my first tour, I transferred to Service School Command, Orlando. I didn't ask for it, but that is what my detailer offered. It was a Department Head tour. I had just made Lieutenant Commander. There was no reason to move; it was only a 45-minute drive. After almost two years there, I was ordered to immediately return to NOTU and relieve as Port Ops. I don't know who had talked to my CO/XO, but I was out of there. No time for anything; go, paperwork to follow.

I was back at the Port on the job for a few months when the house across the street was listed for sale. I don't think they got the sign in the ground before a man and wife, with one son, purchased it and moved in.

Being a military family and having moved many times, we usually are outgoing and like to meet our neighbors. But the man across the street beat me to it. He was at our front door, introducing himself like a long-lost relative. We submarine guys are always suspicious of strangers and need some time to warm up to them and check them out a little. In our very first meeting, he was telling me his wife was from Syracuse, NY. That was the first red flag.

I responded, "Really? So is my wife. What a coincidence." Now we had something in common, an ice breaker. They had moved down here from up north, supposedly, and he would paint houses for a living—more power to you.

Of course, he wanted to know what I did.

I said, "I'm in the Navy."

"Wow, I bet that is interesting."

I said it could be. I had not invited him in and had no plans to do so. He said he wanted to meet the neighbors and he would see me later. Before he left, I said okay, closed the front door, and went to the living room to watch him not visit the neighbors. He went straight back home—second red flag.

I continued my regular daily routine, going to work in uniform and returning home in uniform at various times. One day, he came zipping over just as I was getting out of the car in uniform and started pop-quizzing me about the different insignia and ribbons on my shirt.

When I said, "Those are submarine dolphins," he became so excited and asked if he could take a tour of a sub? Another red flag.

While in the Navy, I had never accommodated anyone who had explicitly asked for a submarine tour. I always initiated the invitation, and my guests were blown away that they could go aboard a sub.

"When a submarine comes to the Port," I told him, "it is swamped with work and unavailable for tours." I lied.

He said, "Okay, I'll see you later."

He backed off for a while and did not push the point. Sometime later, he met me again as I returned home from work and started name-dropping Commanding Officers of the *Redstone*, *Vanguard*, and *Range Sentinel*. My neighbor was a walking Navy League directory. He said he knew everyone. I only knew one of them. Another red flag, and another request for a sub tour.

The Navy produced a movie, *115 Volts—Deadly Shipmate*. We must have watched it hundreds of times. There was another movie about how to recognize a spy or something to that effect. The movie covered various methods they used to establish friendships and gain trust. I had seen it many times. So far, he was batting a thousand.

One day, I came home, and he had invited himself for a swim in my pool and was still there when I got back. My wife was not a happy camper. I politely uninvited him from arbitrarily coming over for a swim.

All this was coming between my going out on the support ship for launches and traveling to DC for Uncle. Every time I returned home, it was like he expected a brief on my activities. He painted houses for a living. He wore white pants and tops, a painter's hat, had brushes in a used paint bucket, but he NEVER had a drop of paint on his clothes. He had to be the world's best house painter.

Then the final piece of the puzzle from the movie came out. "Hey, would it be possible for you to get me a Cape phone book?"

Gotcha, you commie bastard.

I asked, "Why would you want that?"

"Oh, it would help me get contracts for painting jobs."

I told him all government contracts for the Cape went through Patrick AFB. During our many training sessions about spies, asking for a base phone book was high on the tactics list.

The next day, I called NIS in Orlando and asked to speak to an agent. When I started telling him about my new neighbor, it had been about a year since our first encounter, and the NIS agent was very excited.

"Can you get me a license plate number?"

I said sure. When I got home, I copied down the make and model and license plate number and gave it to him the next day. Three days later, he called and said not to let him get remotely close to a submarine. No problem.

I went up to NOTU headquarters. I asked the XO if I could talk to him and the CO in private. That is always not a good news request. I briefed the CO and XO behind closed doors.

The NIS agent told me not to worry about it, that they would take care of everything. An odd thing happened a few months later, the house two doors down from mine went up for sale, and an FBI agent and his wife moved in. His job was in Melbourne, and he worked white-collar crime. I'm going, yeah, sure.

In about a month, the house painting business took a turn for the worse, and the house went up for sale. My little commie and family were moving back up north. After they left, I had lunch with the NIS agent from Orlando. He filled me in on all kinds of things they had done after I told them about my neighbor. The FBI guy was not with the FBI; he and his wife were NIS. They also put a 24/7 tail on my house painter.

And a good time was had by all.

CHAPTER FORTY-SIX

Security Guards-R-Us

PART-TIME

During my first tour at NOTU as a Test Engineer, an opportunity opened for me to make some extra money. We had four sons, and one of them was almost ready to begin college. At that point in our lives, every little bit of income would help.

The Cape had two security forces—NASA had their formal-looking police force, and Cape Canaveral Air Base used security provided by contract with Pan Am. All their security force wore camouflage army-type clothing.

Pan Am put out a call for additional temporary non-union positions. Certain times required extra security. For example, during Cape Canaveral

AFS launches such as Atlas and Delta. On other occasions, it may be for a few hours when a military cargo plane landed with classified cargo.

I looked into the offering and checked with my Command to see if there would be problems if I worked with them when I was available. They said, go for it. I would never be a security guard for any operations in the port.

I knew many of the Pan Am guards, and they said they disapproved of what Pan Am was doing, but they didn't have any problems with me working as a temporary security guard. It was a union thing for them.

I signed up, attended the training, passed the PT, firing range, and other tests, and was accepted into the program. I was the only NOTU person in the program.

When they needed extra personnel, they would go down their call list until all the slots were filled. I was never required to work if I was not available. In between boats, I was usually available. I started to get calls, and the more times I accepted, I would move up the list. I did parking for launches and stood on a tarmac more than once surrounding a C-5 or C-141. Once, I was assigned a position in the woods for a Delta launch. A wide fire break cut through the woods, and I was in the middle of it. I had a clear view of the rocket around half a mile away.

When the rocket's main engine ignited, the first thing I thought, *I am too close to this launch!* I about messed my pants when all the boosters kicked in, and it started lifting off. I could have lit the fuse. Talk about loud and scary—it was both to the max. I was thinking, *Feets, get moving!* But I didn't run. As it lifted off and climbed higher, bits and pieces started falling back to earth around me. I found out later that a person in a pickup was supposed to pick me up before the launch. He didn't show.

All the guards got a big laugh about my staying put. If I had been in the union, I could have filed a complaint and all that stuff. Being a submarine sailor, I wasn't afeared of no stinking rocket. Of course, if it had exploded, I would not be writing this.

I made a pretty good amount of change before the union forced them to eliminate all the temporary positions.

MY FRIEND, THE OLD GUARD

My absolute favorite Pan Am security guard was an old white-haired man. He was close to retirement. One day I walked over to the portable security gate; he was on one side and I on my side. This evolution required that I be present, but I didn't have to sit on them like a hawk. Frankly, it was one of those evolutions that appeared like we were doing something else. I struck up a conversation with the old-timer, and he immediately became my best-security-guard-friend out there.

During World War II, he was captured at Bataan, survived the death march, and spent a year or two in that horrible POW camp. He and others were marched out and down a long road to a railroad station around the two-year point. All of them were wearing remnants of the clothes they wore when captured.

Many died on the march to the train depot. Eventually, a train with boxcars arrived, and they were packed in. He said they were so tight that no one could sit. If they had to pee or sh*t, they did it in their pants, and it ran down their legs. Tropical heat, humidity, and the most horrible smell caused some men to stand and cry like babies. No one thought any less of them; everyone has a breaking point.

After several days of train travel with no food or water, the train reached the line's end. Guards forced them out with bayonets. Most could not walk. While we talked, sometimes my friend would pause and say, "Horrible, just horrible!" They finally received water to drink and a bowl of rice. They were at a seaport, and to get clean, they got into saltwater.

As I listened to him, I took it all in. He looked so fit and healthy. I couldn't understand how anyone could endure all that and come out healthy. As a kid growing up in and around farm animals and hog pens, I got de-wormed twice a year.

I'd stop him and then ask many questions about everything swirling in my mind. What about this, how'd you do, and so forth. Then he said, "I haven't reached the hard part, yet."

I had to excuse myself and walk down to the boat. After what he had told me, beginning at Bataan, the POW camp, and the train trip, I could not imagine what the hard part could be.

We had a family member who had made that same trip from Bataan, but he didn't make it home.

I went back to my spot, and we continued. He said the hard part began when they were forced into the holds of cargo ships. These ships were later named *Hell Ships*. You should look them up and read the horrific conditions these men had to endure. A metal ship baking in the sun with a cargo of putrid, emaciated skeletons dying of thirst and agony waiting and praying to die is beyond most imaginations. After one month, the ship finally got underway for the Japanese mainland. The only relief they received was all hatch covers were moved to the open position. They felt lucky when a rainstorm passed overhead. The Japanese never marked any cargo ship that was carrying POWS. As a result, some Hell Ships were torpedoed and sunk, killing almost everyone. The Japanese took great pleasure in informing the USA that one of its own subs sank a ship full of American, British, Australian, and other ally compatriots. None of the submarines were informed until one year after the war. I can't imagine.

Years later, I read that when the Hell Ship survivors held a reunion, they invited the submarine crews. They thanked them for doing their job. Not knowing the conditions, our torpedoes killed many who were suffering and slowly dying.

My guard friend continued the story. His ship reached port. Everyone was forced into boxcars again and taken inland to a slave labor factory.

Not too many years ago, a movie based upon a true story was released, *Unbroken*. As I watched, all I could think of was my old guard friend. He could have written parts of the script.

My friend survived the ordeal and returned to a hospital in Pearl to recuperate and gain weight. He said that to this day, he wouldn't touch a grain of rice. I told him he needed to write a book. He smiled. From then on, anytime I saw him, I'd ask him how the book was coming—he always answered with a smile—what a great man.

I attended his retirement, hugged him, and wished him well.

Here I sit with tears in my eyes, again.

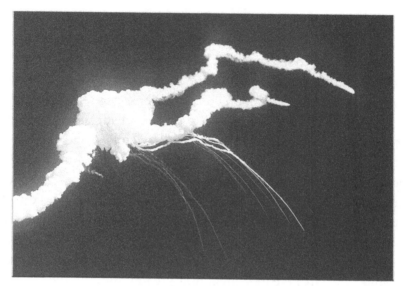

Challenger *exploding in the sky above Cape Canaveral*

CHAPTER FORTY-SEVEN

1986, a Nation Mourns

CHALLENGER DIES

It was a cold January morning as everyone in Port Ops gathered around the TV with cups of hot coffee, engaged in idle chit-chat. *USS Alaska* (SSBN-732) was moored at the north end of the Trident wharf, beginning their DASO. Other than her, the port was tranquil for a change. About fifteen seconds before T-minus 0, we all went outside to watch the shuttle launch.

The sky was crystal clear, and we were expecting a beautiful launch. Sure enough, at T-minus 0, the shuttle's engines and twin boosters ignited, and it was off to space. We watched in silence as she climbed, and soon the initial sounds started hitting our bodies and shaking buildings. Then it happened.

Challenger went to pieces in a gigantic ball of flames. Every one of us was completely quiet. No one said anything, just silence from all of us. My first thoughts were, *I am glad I'm not associated with that launch.* Later, I realized that it was a very selfish thought. Right in front of the entire nation, a shuttle full of astronauts died, and I was glad it was not my problem.

We remained outside, watching as rocket boosters continued to burn and spiral through the air, still trying to reach space. Other pieces fell back to earth, leaving a smoke trail behind. Finally, a parachute emerged from behind the smoke from the fireball. A little heart flutter of hope that this may be the crew compartment. All the Test Engineers immediately realized that it was the nose cone of one of the booster rockets. None of us ever saw the crew capsule falling back to earth.

After we returned inside to watch the TV, the main topic was, where did the crew capsule go? Out of eight people who had witnessed many shuttle launches from that same area beside our building, no one saw the crew capsule. It just disappeared. We had a perfect line of sight from lift-off until the end. It wasn't until later that we saw on TV that one of the NASA cameras had stayed on the crew cabin and followed it down. Even with a big-dollar, fancy telescope camera zoomed in, the capsule blended in so well with the background, it was hard to see. That explained why none of us were able to see it.

The media speculation began. The crew could still be alive. We needed to get a rescue ship out there immediately. I remember going to the North Carolina State Fair every fall and riding some horrendous rides. No one ever died, but on a few, you knew you were close to death. Now, imagine you are nine miles up, traveling over 8,000 miles per hour, and instantly you start twisting, turning, and falling back to earth. No one can tolerate the Gees they experienced. Yes, they may have had a heartbeat, and some might still have been able to breathe up until impact with the concrete-hard ocean surface.

Some of us continued to watch replays over and over; some went back to their desk to plan for their next assignment.

Soon it was lunchtime, and several of us headed up to the Greenhouse to eat. The place was packed with contractors and NOTU sailors, all talking about the same thing. A large TV screen was carrying a network's coverage. Many people had theories about what happened, everything from sabotage to some significant malfunction. I think a significant malfunction was an understatement.

After lunch, we walked back down to Port Ops, and noticed the CO's parking spot had his government vehicle in it. As we entered the Port Ops office, the secretary said, "Lieutenant Pait, Commander Clark would like to see you."

RECOVERY OPS

Instead of turning left, I turned right and went into his office. He was there with the CO and some very senior man from NASA. I do not remember his name. Here we go again.

"Lieutenant Pait, we want you to be in charge of the Challenger's pier-side recovery operations. Everything found at sea will be brought into the Trident Basin and offloaded at the south end. Flatbed trucks will be there to transport the materials. You will have your own Cape Security Team that will block off the pier's entrance and exit points. One CIA agent will be allowed to park on the dock inside the security area. He is authorized to claim and take any item he desires, no questions asked. If anyone says anything to him, you intervene. There is no room for discussion about this. You will also have a shuttle astronaut with you, and except for the riggers for the crane and Lockheed workers, absolutely no one else is allowed inside the security area, and I mean no one. The security guards have the same information. If you have any problems with anyone, call me at home, and I will take care of it."

The man from NASA never said a word. Commander Clark said he would reassign my other upcoming ship/submarine duties, so not to worry about anything but this assignment for the next few weeks or until he told me otherwise.

"Understand?"

"Yes, Sir, I understand completely. What time can I expect to start?"

"You begin tonight and expect to work from sunset until sunrise until further notice."

"Do I report to anyone what I did each night?"

"No. If we need information, either the Captain or I will contact you. Also, do not tell your neighbors and especially the press anything."

The Captain said he didn't think I would be bothered by the media, but you never know. I asked for permission to go home, get some rest, and return with some warmer clothes?

The CO stood up and said, "Absolutely. It is getting very cold at night, especially on the pier."

I looked at Cmdr. Clark, and he nodded in the affirmative. I went back to the Test Engineer area and told the guys what was going on, that I would see them when I could. It was like, good luck, man. Be safe, etc.

I headed home to prepare for a long night and bring some food back to eat. My mother had come down from NC to spend part of the winter with us. She and my wife stood in our backyard and watched the same thing as I did. It bothered her. She had a gentle spirit, and seeing people die was not an easy thing to watch. Of course, our four boys came home after school and had two or three million questions.

One thing about wearing khakis is that there are many uniform variations: shorts, short sleeve shirts, long sleeve shirts, a lightweight jacket, but nothing warm. Who would think anyone in khakis would ever wear them in cold weather on a pier? I had a few choice words about the uniform board. I owned long john tops and bottoms, and I wore that. I had short-sleeve shirts, and I didn't care if the long john sleeves extended below my shirt sleeves or my jacket. You can't wear black gloves with khakis either.

Before I returned, the CO called and said a NASA photographer would be allowed inside the area. When anything was offloaded, NASA wanted a photo.

Initially, the only vessel searching was a Coast Guard Cutter. Search grids had been set up. No coordinated area search had been established, but all those requirements were set up as quickly as possible. The Coast Guard was responsible for setting up the grids and assigning vessels to each grid or series of grids. The Navy was pulling destroyers from here and there to be part of the search team. Our Port civilian divers were contracted to search the bottom in shallow areas where parts were thought to have landed.

Later, with side-scan sonar, more items on the bottom were pinpointed.

When I got to the pier, I introduced myself to the Astronaut and the CIA Agent. He had his trunk lid up and a supply of large, heavy-duty black plastic bags and zip ties. Not a very talkative fellow. I already knew the security guards, crane riggers, and vice versa. We had worked many ops together.

The first night was the only easy night. The one Cutter came in, its helo deck covered with items that had been floating and easy to spot. Plastic bags full of shuttle heat protection tiles. The crew compartment toilet seat (not like ours at home). A few more miscellaneous items from inside the crew compartment showed up, such as female urination devices. Bags for catching poop and other things. So, we knew from night one that the crew compartment was not intact. I checked with the Cutter, and they said they would not be back again that night.

After they got underway, the flatbed truck left for NASA, and we secured for the night. Before I left, I walked the pier to make sure nothing was on the pier that should go to NASA. Finding nothing, I turned the lights off on the south end. As soon as they were turned off, the nighttime circuit kicked in and returned at a lower power level.

We never left the Trident wharf in the dark.

When we were offloading materials from the Cutter, you could see camera flashes across the channel coming from Jetty Park. There wasn't anything to see, but there were several people over there every night taking pictures. Before going home, I stopped by Port Ops to let the duty officer know we had secured for the night. He put it in his log, and I went into my office and wrote down everything we had done and who was there. If there was going to be a reason to pop-quiz me later, I wanted to make sure I had a reference to refresh my memory.

I have many more stories about the Shuttle recovery as it continued for six weeks. The night the astronauts' bodies were brought in was very hard on me. When I returned home, I sat in the dark and cried for a while. It would not be my last time to do so.

Challenger debris offloaded to the pier.
I'm the big fellow on the right with hands in his pockets.

CHAPTER FORTY-EIGHT

The Beginning of the Long Nights

RECOVERY CONTINUES

The second night of recovery would be a long one, and each night thereafter. We began the night with the same Cutter as before. Their helo deck was covered again with all kinds of shuttle debris. Among the search vessels, they decided, the other vessels that had small items would bring them to the Cutter instead of every ship coming in to offload a few things. The ships recovering debris that was too large to transfer at sea would come in one at a time, offload and return to sea.

After the shuttle debris was offloaded, I let our supply people bring their truck onto the pier to transfer mail, spare parts, and fresh food to the Cutter. It was my call.

The first night, several items came from inside the crew compartment. The second night we began receiving personal items from the astronauts. Each person had an assigned seat in the crew cabin. They placed their feet on a hatch that held padded bags of small American flags, patches for that mission, camera gear, and various items to be given to friends and family—a coveted souvenir for anyone who received one. Also, under Christa McAuliffe's feet was an exceptional bag containing a Shuttle model and other models she would use as teaching aids in space. All these bags were buoyant and retrieved from the surface. I do not know what each Command told their crews about pillaging items for souvenirs. But everything recovered was to be treated with respect.

I imagine walking the plank was mentioned.

The Astronaut and I unzipped each bag and looked inside. Nothing was out of place; nothing was mangled or broken; the inside of each bag was as it was when last zipped. Most items were vacuum-sealed inside plastic to maximize space. There would be no reason to open packages of mission patches or flags, etc., in space. The Astronaut took possession of all personal bags. He wasn't about to throw them on the semi's flatbed with parts and pieces of hardware.

That night we brought in the Cutter and five destroyers. I decided there had to be a better way to do this. There was so much downtime as we waited for the pilot to take one ship out and bring in the next one. The next day, I talked to the head port pilot and proposed that once the first vessel was alongside the pier, would they be able to bring the next one in and let it standby in the Trident Basin? Depth was not a problem. They all had twin screws plus bow thrusters, and there were no currents to battle. When the moored ship finished offloading, the pilot could take it out. The vessel sitting in the basin could come alongside, and we'd keep doing that all night, thus maximizing everyone's time. He was all for it mainly because they never had any commercial shipping or cruise ships enter or leave at night.

I will not go through each night because we were on that pier for six weeks straight. Some nights, I about froze. Once NASA began releasing photos to the press, my Captain received a call from some *do-gooder* from the Pentagon, telling him to inform me I was not to put my hands in my khaki coat pockets. I don't know what the Captain said to him, but there were no more phone calls.

As time progressed, we recovered large pieces. The destroyers did not have cranes to haul these items aboard. They had to manhandle them. I imagine they used their rescue swimmers to get in the water and tie ropes around some of the debris.

For a long time, the most significant piece recovered was a section of the external fuel tank, that big orange thing. Part of it had been blown out flat and was twenty by twelve feet. The orange is a type of spray foam insulation about one-eighth inch thick. The metal was one of those classified combinations of unique ingredients that produce strong but very light metal. Four of us could pick up that one large piece without any problem. I was impressed.

When we finally secured, and I arrived home, the weight of what I was doing and seeing hit me. I sat in a chair and cried and cried. You might say it was a form of PTSD. It didn't involve combat or getting shot at but seeing all their stuff was pretty hard on me, and I had to let it out. Everyone was asleep, and no one heard me. I had the feeling my visiting mother knew something was bothering me. Later on, she mentioned the stress I was under.

Let me explain about the External Fuel Tank. First, it was not a fuel tank. It was a streamlined fairing filled with two tanks, one for hydrogen and one for oxygen.

The External Tank, 154 feet long and twenty-seven-point-five feet in diameter, is the largest single piece of the Space Shuttle. During launch, the External Tank also acts as a backbone for the Orbiter and Solid Rocket Boosters to which it is attached. The External Tank holds the liquid hydrogen fuel and liquid oxygen for the Shuttle's three Main Engines in two separate pressurized tanks. During launch, the External Tank feeds fuel under pressure through seventeen-inch-wide lines, then branching off into smaller lines that feed directly into the Main Engines. Some 64,000 gallons of fuel are consumed by the Main Engines each minute. Machined from special alloys, the Space Shuttle's External Tank is the only part of the launch vehicle that is not reused. After its 526,000 gallons of propellants are consumed during the first eight and one-half minutes of flight, it is jettisoned from the Orbiter and breaks up in the upper atmosphere, its pieces falling into remote ocean waters.

THE TRUTH AND NOTHING BUT THE TRUTH

Let me tell you what happened to the Shuttle. Forget everything you have read and heard; this is the straight skinny. Range Control contains a variety of folks monitoring various panels. The Range Safety Officer is an Air Force Officer whose sole purpose in life is to watch two screens; one shows course, and one shows altitude. A computer-generated azimuth (course) is marked in the center of one screen. Range Safety parameters are also on the same screen. When any rocket is on the pad, all three lines converge at the same point. The azimuth line never moves, but a line on each side of the azimuth gradually moves further away from the centerline as the launched rocket gets further away from the surface. If the rocket crosses one of those outside lines for whatever reason, Range Safety Officer flips a switch, and the rocket/shuttle self-destructs. Do not jump to conclusions. Range Safety did not destroy Challenger, but the effect would have been similar to what everyone saw, but more symmetrical. A computer-generated, slightly curved line on the altitude screen represents where the rocket should be on that line at each foot of altitude. Nothing goes straight up, it may seem like it, but it is being guided toward an orbit, hence the curve. Just like the other screen, two lines are together at the pad. As the altitude increases, both these lines follow the same curve and gradually move away. This ensures if there is a failure and the rocket starts coming back toward occupied land, self-destruct is initiated. Having said all that, here is what happened to the Shuttle.

We all have seen after liftoff, almost immediately, the Shuttle does a 180-degree roll. All non-military rockets are like an eggshell and must pass through the atmosphere at a prescribed angle. They do not maneuver around like jet fighters; they must stick to the course and altitude at all times. The steering to keep the Shuttle on course is done by the three Shuttle engines and the solid rocket booster engines, which can all swivel about ten degrees in any direction. Both boosters are identical in all respects. The output of each is the same. We know that one of the sections of the solid rocket failed, allowing hot gasses to blow by two seals due to KNOWN previous cold weather failures. Now you have two boosters that are not putting out equal thrust. The blow-by was placing a small amount of drag on one side. After the Shuttle rotated, Range Safety could see the Shuttle was not following the centerline. Others saw the shuttle engines were working hard to put it back where it should be. As it climbed, it continued to move further away from the centerline, and at the time of the explosion, the Shuttle was no longer streamlined. Even though the atmosphere was getting thinner, speed was increasing. Due to air pressure and flame impingement from blow-by from one SRB, the external fuel tank sheared off, releasing thousands of gallons of fuel and oxidizer that ignited in a giant ball of flame. By the strictest definition, it was not an explosion but a conflagration. The fuels, which usually are metered before combining, were suddenly released into the air. Calling it an explosion is sufficient because the force of the burning fuel did a lot of damage.

In short, before the launch, the Launch Director went down the list asking for a *go* or *no-go*. The Morton Thiokol rep was a *no-go* due to temperatures at that time. His *no-go* was not a gotcha. Every solid rocket booster was recovered after each launch and taken apart segment by segment, and thoroughly inspected. Failure of seals in cold weather had been documented, and the problem was discussed before the launch. NASA decided to go anyway. When the Launch Director got Thiokol's no-go, there was no more discussion. He continued down his checklist, and the rest is history.

I do not care what reports you have read or who put out the info. What I just stated is a fact and the truth. The Launch Control Director for this mission and I attended the same church. His son and daughter were in the same age group as our sons. After *Challenger*, he wasn't the same. NASA gave him another office and let him complete his time until retirement. He continued to attend church but was a very solemn man. Many NASA people attended the same church. When the shuttle program was canceled, 48,000 people plus families left our area. Our membership was reduced to half.

It is incredible how much you can learn from an Astronaut as you both freeze on a pier. The CIA man NEVER mingled with any of us.

NR-1 *searching for* Challenger *debris off Cape Canaveral.*

CHAPTER FORTY-NINE

The Junkyard

RECOVERY CONTINUES

Most of you probably have seen an automobile junkyard on the outskirts of your town. Shadetree mechanics were in paradise for car parts—anything from a hood to a leaf spring and everything in between.

Our search for *Challenger* debris was a tedious examination of the space parts junkyard located in the waters off Cape Canaveral. The bottom was mostly flat sand with a few ridges scattered about as subsurface currents moved sand north to south. By towing a side-scan sonar device, any items from the shuttle and everything else that had been launched from the south area of Cape Canaveral to the northern region of NASA stood out like a sore thumb. Most items were continually being buried or uncovered by moving sand. Picture your local junkyard covering hundreds of square miles, and you are looking for parts for only one particular vehicle. The searchers faced an underwater dilemma. If it was floating, it belonged to the shuttle. If it was not, every target had to be investigated by divers or *NR-1.*

NR-1 arrived. The number of surface ships had increased, and a larger area was being searched. More parts and internal pieces were brought in every night. Surprisingly, some very large items were floating. Air Force Explosive Ordnance Disposal (EOD) said that some of the large floating items had intact exploding bolts. EOD was required to go to sea from that point on. All the search ships' Captains pitched a fit about their crew members dragging unidentified chunks of shuttle aboard with the potential of maiming a member of their crews.

Let's talk a bit about *NR-1*. She and the *ASR Sunbird* showed up about two-three weeks after the recovery began. Outstanding people to work with. At NOTU, we had a very special navigation system that was more accurate than any submarines carried. When you are in the submarine missile-firing business, you have to know the *exact* position where the missile burst through the surface. Several of our ETs from 50-shop went down inside *NR-1* and installed one of those systems.

When *NR-1* went to sea and began her search to identify all the small and large items on the ocean floor, the position of the item was as accurate as possible. Another plus for future use, they took photos of each object.

Deep Submergence Vessel NR-1, was a unique U.S. Navy nuclear-powered ocean engineering and research submarine, built by the Electric Boat Division of General Dynamics at Groton, Connecticut. I was aboard her many times, but I am not saying anything.

Do you remember the early Snark and Shark rockets launched from the deck of some of our older boats? One area off the coast of the Cape's southern end was called *Snark-filled waters*. Many failures in that program before they got the bugs out.

All the item numbers, date, lat/long, right down to inches, and the photos were turned over to NASA, who shared them with the Cape Canaveral Air Force Station (CCAFS). NASA has the north half. CCAFS has the south half, and the US Navy owns the Cape. That has to be the most expensive piece of real estate in the USA.

On the NASA side, a private beach house was built for JFK. He would stay there when he came down for the early NASA launches.

Many times he brought a lady friend with him. Over the decades, the house was expanded so that before a launch, astronauts and their families could stay in private.

Once the larger sections started arriving, the CIA agent became active. Some nights, he had a trunk full of filled black plastic bags, each tagged. I never asked, but I was sure it was communications gear from what I saw. Usually, my attention was focused on whatever was being lifted from the ship to the pier and then to the flatbed. I didn't necessarily realize when the NASA photographer took pictures or videoed what we were doing.

We recovered the part of the shuttle that showed the area of the vehicle where the burn-through had hit. The ordinarily black heat tiles were snow white. The tiles had not failed and had done their job. Thousands of photographs later, the part was loaded onto the flatbed.

One afternoon, I entered the Test Engineer's office, and all the guys were asking for my autograph. They had cut a star out of cardboard, covered it with aluminum foil, and attached it to my cubical. I didn't know what was going on until they told me that I had been on national TV all day. I still didn't know because I was asleep most of the day. NASA had released one of their videos of what we were doing on the pier all or most of each night. There I was, centered, with my hands in my pockets, freezing half to death. Other than my hands in my pockets, you couldn't tell I was cold. What they released had occurred four days earlier.

For whatever reason, NASA never told the truth to the media. There were always some standardized PR statements with blanks filled in to fit the situation.

Meanwhile, *NR-1* was out there every day, steaming across the bottom, checking every object. *NR-1* had several windows, at least one mechanical arm, and the ability to photograph everything she found. NASA made unique tags to attach to every piece of space junk *NR-1* found. Any item that belonged to the shuttle was left on the bottom and salvaged later.

Sometime around the end of the third week, I received word from Cmdr. Clark that our Port civilian divers had found the crew compartment. Nothing was to be put out about this until all relatives and politicians were notified. The Air Force had a temporary morgue set up for the bodies. Special containers were manufactured to bring them up due to the size of their spacesuits.

Two weeks later, a Navy salvage ship, USS Avenger (MCM-1), came down. They did a four-point moor over the cabin, and Navy divers trained to go into tangled wreckage and retrieve bodies went down and got the seven. Later, I talked to several of our civilian divers, and they said the only thing holding the crew cabin together was all the wiring. The outside of the cabin was cracked all over like a hard-boiled egg. There was no way they could go in with scuba gear. From what they could see, everyone was still strapped into their seats.

Finally, President Reagan addressed the country and informed the world. Nothing was mentioned in any official report about the civilian divers or who or how the capsule was located. I was never interviewed by anyone concerning my part. That was fine with me.

That night, an honor guard of NOTU sailors met the salvage ship at the Trident Pier, and, observing all honors, they went aboard. They carried one flag-draped box at a time to a waiting Air Force Ambulance. Two boxes only required four men. After a box was loaded, that ambulance pulled forward to a predetermined position and waited for all to be loaded. As a convoy, they made their way to Cape Canaveral Air Force Station to the morgue. The NOTU honor guard followed them in a van.

NOTU did not have an official honor guard. We did DASOs, and our honor guards were regular everyday submarine sailor volunteers. We had more volunteers than we needed. We had everyone line up, left to right by height, and took a chunk out of the line. Everyone was within an inch of the same height. With a few hours of practice, they could have carried the President. That night, I stayed back and observed that they did an outstanding job. If you didn't know better, you might have thought they flew them down from DC. I was very proud of our men and the job they did.

Let me add a little side note: The Salvage Ship was the USS Avenger. Upon her return to Norfolk, she was greeted by bands, officials, and every kind of press you can imagine. As I read the press release, I almost became ill. The NASA rule of never telling the truth was still in effect. The honor guard was mentioned, but not a word as to where they came from. The next big one was that they made two trips with astronaut bodies, one with four and another with three. Without their spacesuits, fewer men were required. Why, why, why do they do this? All astronauts were returned at the same time.

The Commanding Officer failed to mention that several of his divers were arrested for stealing crew cabin souvenirs. These are highly trained specialty Navy Divers, and three of them collected a few souvenirs and hid them inside their diving suits. One night, they were in a bar downtown Cocoa Beach drinking and showing everyone their plunder. The following day, 10,000 Macedonian Police in full battle array descended to the pier. Those inside Port Ops told me they could hear the CO screaming on the ship's 1MC. Stan told me it was, "All hands lay to the pier in formation!" leaving out a few choice words. The head Macedonians asked a few questions, and the men came forward.

Their CO and XO were ready to bust out the .45s right then and there. The crew members disappeared and returned later. A couple of Macedonians went on board with them to retrieve their bragging rights. I have no doubt the CO and XO had a conversation with the Agents. The trip back to Norfolk was more than likely not a pleasant one for these fine young, stupid men. At a minimum, there would have been a severe Captain's Mast.

Let me back up. When the *Challenger* fell apart, I mentioned, *Alaska* was beginning its DASO at the north berth. One of the things NASA did was freeze all range consoles at the time of the accident. There were many, many people involved with a DASO, spread out over many thousands of miles of air, ocean, and islands. The Captain from SP-205 went to the range people and started prodding them to get NASA to unfreeze the equipment we needed for our launch. He made the significant point that we always launched on time and would not tie up the range any longer than necessary. NASA could take a photo of the screens we needed.

Eventually, 205 prevailed, and *Alaska* went out, launched her missile, returned, got cleaned up, and left. For me, it was nice to have *Alaska* there. She provided line handlers to moor/underway each ship that came in. I always thanked them for helping. If you remember, I began my submarine life as a line handler in the Seamen Gang. It was touch and go for a while. NASA's main problem was the two-range safety screens. Photographs would suffice. It turned out that the equipment could save that screen, return to operations, and then revert to the saved screen. It was a function that had never been needed before or since.

Space Shuttle Columbia was not on any range safety screens when it broke up over Texas.

After six weeks of nights, I was finally relieved by thirty-five people who made up a salvage team from all over. To the best of my knowledge, most of the debris was eventually recovered and arranged in an empty hangar for the investigation (same as NTSB does with air crashes), then disposed of by dumping into two decommissioned missile silos. Once I was relieved, the same rules were still in effect. I had no reason to be on the Trident wharf, and what was taking place was none of my business.

On a good note, *NR-1* identified several lost items from early launches from the space program's beginning. Those items were salvaged later and offloaded at the Poseidon pier with no fanfare. They are located in several museums. I believe the Smithsonian got a GEMINI capsule.

This was a fascinating and sorrowful time. Where else but the Navy could an average young man from Hamlet, NC, be placed in the center of one of America's tragedies.

RETURN TO "NORMAL"

As NOTU returned to normal, a familiar situation from my past slowly started raising its ugly head. We had gone from four Test Engineers to three, then two, then me. Damn, all by myself, I was responsible for doing every DASO for one year. I have no clue how this crap keeps happening to me.

I'd finish one launch, and the Assistant Port Ops would come over and take over the clean-up. The following day, I'd begin the DASO on another boat. Every day, I was there, getting the boat underway, getting it tied up, going on board to see what needed to be repaired under my preview, and returning the following day to start all over again.

As launch day grew closer, I would make sure the pier-side schedule was strictly adhered to, running people off who thought they were so damn important they could park on the pier next to the brow. When people argued with me about how important they were, I'd point to the big forklift and say, "If you go below, you will not be able to find your car when you return."

That usually got someone behind the wheel and the vehicle in the parking lot. If the CO of the sub could not park next to the brow, why did this yahoo think he could? It is hard to be nasty in a loving way.

First submerged launch of the Trident II D-5.

CHAPTER FIFTY

I Can Almost See the Light at the End of the Tunnel

RECOVERY CONTINUES

After almost one year of back-to-back DASOs, new people started to arrive. Capt. Bancroft retired, and Capt. John Byron assumed Command. Cmdr. Clark retired and was replaced by Lt. Cmdr. Reberry. Lt. Mike St. Jean arrived to relieve Lt. Cmdr. Buck Taylor, who retired. Mike Close came in to be a Test Engineer along with Lt. Enos. There was an equal number of retirements and transfers across the hall with the Dock Masters. One of their Senior Chiefs was commissioned under the Warrant Officer program and departed.

＊

While we in the port doing our thing, my two-year tour was extended again. I was never consulted about any extensions. In my mind,

I was accomplishing so much at NOTU, but I knew I needed to get a bunch of tickets punched if I ever expected to ride Space Mountain. Sp-205 informed the XO that he's staying. A significant construction project on the Cape was to build the most technologically advanced (at that time) launch facility on the Cape. Best computers, fiber optics, all the bells and whistles, to conduct test launches of the new Trident II D-5 submarine-launched missile to be used on *Tridents*. I marveled at the irony of that state-of-the-art construction, a short way up the coast from an open-air launch site with a sand berm covered with sandbags left over from the early Snark days.

When you look at a Florida map, that small area known on nautical charts as Cape Canaveral belongs to the U.S. Navy. Early Spanish explorers gave the name Cape Canaveral. It means the Cape of Reeds. I've looked at early Spanish maps of Florida, and there were many natural inlets where you could travel by water across to the Gulf. Over the years, all of those have filled in. Other than the man-made Okeechobee Waterway, that also uses Lake Okeechobee and locks, before continuing to the Caloosahatchee River that leads to the Gulf, there are no other waterways available now.

Once Cape Canaveral was selected to be America's rocket-launching site, the families who lived there had to move. There still is a civilian cemetery there, and relatives can still visit but have to make security arrangements. There is also a substantial Indian shell mound. A fish factory was located near the ocean south of the Cape, and a paved road (eventually) allowed access from Cape Canaveral to the fish factory and lighthouse. Except for the lighthouse and the road, the fish factory and the pier were demolished. When I arrived in August 1984, many crane crewmen were still working. They were the bulldozers and other equipment operators who built the first roads, launch pads, and bunkers. They loved to tell stories about the beginnings of the Cape. Giant rattlesnakes were a daily occurrence. Many deer and herds of wild hogs ran all over the place. Even after all the construction and hundreds of vehicles driving the roads, the area contained so much wildlife. Often, someone would catch a very large diamondback, take photos, and then release it. Florida Fish and Game always had wild hog traps set around the Cape.

In my spare time, I was assigned to the Hubble Space Telescope Project. We had many rehearsals of offloading a mockup of the telescope from a unique ship. When it got down to the nitty-gritty, someone decided to put it on a C-5B and fly it to the Cape. Another example of waste, fraud, and abuse. That specific ship cost a ton of money over the years to be on standby to carry Hubble. At least I was given a Hubble lapel pin. Years later, I gave that pin to a scout with his family we encountered at Grandfather's Mountain. He was beyond thrilled.

One of the most significant benefits of being stationed at NOTU, other than the fishing, is that one could drive a pickup all over the Cape. I checked out every narrow, paved road, saw all kinds of critters cross in front of me, and eventually arrived at an old launch complex. The old launchpad had been reclaimed by nature, and there were some original bunkers that were nothing more than a wall of stacked sandbags with sand pushed against them. No top or thick concrete walls for protection. All launch equipment was sitting next to the bunker wall, exposed to the elements. Other launch complexes had morphed into the realm of sanity and were built with concrete reinforced bunkers and very thick glass viewing ports. Underground tunnels crisscrossed the area, and some of us explored most of them. I was surprised that most still had lighting and a sump pump to keep them dry. Talk about a playground—this place was it. Several years later, when I returned to be Port Ops, I turned it into a Navy Seal playground, and they were in seventh heaven. Nowhere else had what we had.

THE TRIDENT II D-5

After seven successful pad launches of the D-5, the day arrived for the first test-firing of the new D-5. The big difference between a land launch and a submarine launch is that through programming, the land-launched missile thinks it has been jettisoned from the sub, and thus it is time for ignition and flight. Also, the starting point was on land instead of more than thirty miles offshore.

I believe they had planned to launch nine missiles, but after the first seven, Lockheed decided to skip the last two and go directly to the first sea launch. I had trained Mike Close, and he had conducted a couple of DASOs by himself and did well. We decided we'd let Mike do the first Trident II D-5 launch as Test Engineer. It would look good in his record. Along with a few others, I was on the *Range Sentinel* conducting launch ops from there.

Talk about making a list and checking it twice or more. This first submerged launch had to be as perfect as possible. Every VIP in the program was either on the sub, the *Range Sentinel*, or Range Control. I imagine the warhead people were on Ascension Island. Now, *that* place is a garden spot. Besides the excellent fishing, it was a bird-infested, stinking rock and sand sticking out of the ocean in the middle of the South Atlantic. it was the perfect place to set up impact areas in the sea, surround them with sonobuoys, and use the sound a dummy warhead makes hitting the water at a sizzling 18,000 mph to plot the impact point of each warhead in reference to the center of the target. I will not get into the specifics of what was considered a miss even after all these years. I will say that if the warheads were filled with bags of flour and you were standing on the crosshairs, you would be covered in flour. Those of you in the missile business know that there are many capabilities available.

I preferred the Trident warhead filled with M&Ms. Two of them would explode at 1,000 feet and scatter candy all over. When all the kids came out to fill their pockets with candy, then we'd hit them with a thermonuclear warhead airburst. I'm joking!

Launch day arrived. The sub went first, followed by the *Range Sentinel*. I never was informed and never asked, but I always felt that an SSN was out there close, keeping an ear out for everything below water because, between the Air Force and us, we had the surface covered. Like all launches since *George Washington*, a *Notice to Mariners and Aircraft* identifying launch danger zones and restricted air space was transmitted. A Soviet AGI was always present, waiting and using an open marine band frequency. We would give him his position for the launch. They never replied but always went exactly where we told them to go. They had no desire to interfere with the launch. They were there for video and to collect water samples.

The boat submerged, we all manned our positions, and *Range Sentinel* maneuvered to maximize camera tracking. The countdown began. It started way before T-minus 10 seconds and counting. There was a lot of activity on the boat, the *Range Sentinel,* and Range Control. The special aircraft out of Wright Patterson had to be on station, the P-3s had to have set the sonobuoy pattern, the range had to be completely clear of all ships and aircraft except for two helicopters. The two birds and the P-3s downrange had to move out of the way for the launch while staying out and about, making sure no sailboat or wooden fishing boats were in the danger zone.

At thirty seconds to go, the P-3 and the choppers downrange cleared the area. Everything and all parties were ready by the time we got to T-minus 0 and launched. My heart was performing a self-imposed stress test. "Missile away," came in over the radio. This colossal 64,000-pound beast immediately burst from the ocean like a giant sperm whale breaching. The rocket ignited and commenced doing circles directly over the SSBN.

RAT-cheer is what is known as an OH SH*T moment. The *Range Sentinel* was typically almost 2,000 yards away—not far enough! After two turns, the D-5 initiated self-destruct, much faster than anyone at Range Control could have reacted. The massive three-stage explosion did not turn the *Range Sentinel* over, but we were way too close. The dB level, blast heat, and impact of the sonic wave were a bit much. The AGI got the hell out of Dodge, screw the water samples; these people are trying to kill me. Of course, we immediately contacted the sub. They were fine. Nothing falling back into the ocean hit them, and even though they heard the explosion, it did nothing to the boat. I imagine a few sonar techs had eardrums lying on their shoulders.

Back in Hamlet many years ago, on the 4th of July, my first cousin, Tommy Smith (Dahlgren), and I used to swim out into the middle of the City Lake to watch the fireworks. They were great, but nothing like this!

So, the boat surfaced, and the helos looked around to make sure no pieces were floating on the surface. Seeing none, we packed up our picnic lunches and headed back to PCAN. The D-5 program was at *all stop* until the data could be examined.

A submarine-launched missile rarely exits the water perfectly straight. This first sub-launched D-5 exited around seventy degrees to the right. The hydraulic system pushed the nozzle over and held it there to bring this massive beast back to the upright position. This generated much higher pressures than the system was designed to handle. So, the nozzle failed in the hard-over position and commenced the whirligig fireworks show. They thought a redesign of the hydraulic system and beefed-up connections was the fix.

No one from the sub crew wanted to get the hell out of submarines, but they all wanted to see photos and videos of what we witnessed. I don't know how many copies of the picture at the beginning of this chapter were provided to the boat. I imagine enough for every crew member and a few extras. Oh, yes, it made the papers and TV news. I never found out if the explosion sound traveled to shore. As we were over the horizon, I doubt if any windows rattled. Back at NOTU, we were still doing our thing. A few meetings were held to make a few changes to launch publications, one of which moved the range ship back to 4,000 yards—same for the AGI.

Out of all previous D-5 testing, it wasn't until it was launched from a sub that the nozzle hydraulic system got tested. Although the second launch was a success, data showed that the same hydraulic system failed at the end of the first stage flight, so back to the drawing board. For some reason, the computer never got the actual pressures correct. This time, the engineers went way above and beyond, and as far as I know, there hasn't been another failure.

This D-5 Trident system and a few things in space caused the collapse of the Soviet Union. Since then, we have newer and *more-better* stuff to cause them to be very concerned.

Patrick Air Force Base Hospital

CHAPTER FIFTY-ONE

Dead Man Walking

PAIN IN THE GUT

Before the first Trident D-5 UK launch, I had been experiencing severe pain in my lower abdomen. I wasn't sure what it was, but when the pains started, they were terrible. I'd go into NOTU, and maybe about two hours or so later, I'd head home. I had paid several visits to Patrick Air Force Base hospital. Every visit, I had to explain everything to one of their medical types and wait for an hour or two to see a doctor. Usually, by the time I drove down to Patrick, the pains had subsided. SOP at any military hospital, check you out, nothing found, go home, change your T-shirt, take two aspirin and come back in the morning if you are experiencing pain. The strange thing, there wasn't any set pattern or schedule to the pains.

I managed to get through the UK DASO without too many problems. My relief showed up. He was another Submarine Electronics LDO, same as me. It didn't take me long to figure out he would not survive in a Test Engineer's job. I'm not sure how he was selected as an LDO. He was very much like the tender person I had mentioned who didn't know what was going on in his division.

Back to my guts. At our church, we had an Air Force Colonel, a doctor at Patrick AFB. We knew him and his family. I got him aside one Sunday and explained what had been going on with me. He asked many questions and told me to come down and specifically ask for him.

So, armed with that bit of info, the next time I went to Patrick, I had to get past the medic guard dog.

"Send me to Dr. so-and-so."

"Do you have an appointment?"

"No, I don't. He told me to ask you to send me to him."

So began the battle with those in charge of keeping you from seeing a real doctor. Finally, I ended up asking an Air Force E-7 or E-8 to tell the Doctor I was there. It was almost as hard as getting a free ride on a MAC flight.

Once informed, the Doc came down, addressed me by my first name, and took me to his office. They all should have noted that, seeing as how it never happens normally. All it did was spin them up even more. Being Navy at an Air Force hospital wasn't exactly what they wanted to see anyway. An E-5 on subs has more authority than anyone in the Air Force below the rank of colonel.

The Doc gave me a good going over, and for the first time, I had X-rays. Nothing was evident on them, but he gave me a script for pain meds and a referral to a gastroenterologist. What a nightmare that would be. It seems they hire old retired, chain-smoking, alcoholic, former Air Force doctors to do their specialty work. It would be like going to the Chief's Club, telling the bartender your problem, and he has you lying on the bar doing an exam. Pretty damn scary.

Of course, if you have ever had a colonoscopy, you know the joys involved with that; just to get cleaned out is Friday the 13th.

Dee had to come with me so she could drive home. They were supposed to put me in the twilight zone, but the nurse went through the vein, and the sedation was filling up my hand and not doing me any good. So, out comes the garden hose with a flashlight duct-taped to it. It was what is known as a barium contrast with air. They inject barium into your large intestines and then give you a short blast of 4,500 psi air to inflate your large intestines. Then they take an X-ray.

It was bad enough with just the device, but I screamed due to massive, unbelievable pain when the air was applied. The Doc told me to relax. "It doesn't hurt that bad," he said.

After he finished, I was told I could sit up and go home. As soon as the nurse removed the IV needle, she commented to the Doctor, "Look at his hand; it is swollen."

Now that there were two openings in that vessel, all the twilight zone meds started flowing into my blood vessel, and I was out like a light. I endured the entire botched procedure without any pain killer. What incompetent dickheads both of them were. His report on what he found was that everything was normal. On my next visit to my Colonel friend, he had a copy of the barium enema. He showed it to me, and I about crapped my pants.

He asked, "Does that look normal to you?"

I said, "No way." Then I told him what had happened.

He apologized profusely, and I told him it wasn't his fault. (I still have that film.)

The next thing I knew, they wanted to fly me out to Alabama or Mississippi to some big Air Force hospital. I went to see my CO and said, "This is BS. We have plenty of hospitals around here. Why in the world would they send me to Alabama or Mississippi?"

My CO called the Air Force Hospital CO and got things straightened out.

With my inflated intestine test X-ray, I saw an Air Force surgeon at Patrick AFB. He looked it over and poked and prodded, and I responded accordingly. He said he wanted to see an MRI. I told him as long as it was a legitimate place and not located in a back alley. The MRI indicated I had a lot of infection on the outside of my large intestines.

A date for surgery was set, and I was admitted the day before so they could use a fire hose to clean me out. I never knew there was another use for a high-velocity nozzle. Boy, was I cleaned out and disinfected on the inside *many* times. The next morning, I was first. Once the surgeon got me opened and they picked up all my intestines and spread them out on a sterile tray, he sent word to cancel the rest of his surgeries for that day. I was a mess. Plus, there was a benign growth off one of my intestines growing around my bladder. Later, he said I was fortunate it had not adhered to the bladder, or I really would have had some problems. He ended up removing my descending colon. In our conversations after surgery, I asked him what could have caused my problem. He said I was too young to have this problem, and more than likely, it was due to stress. Stress, what a unique concept. The inside of my large intestines was perfect; everything was on the outside.

Now, here is the good part. Back then, when you had this procedure done, you could not have ANY FOOD until you passed gas. Yes, before I could eat anything by mouth, I had to fart. My biggest fear was I would sneeze. Finally, I passed the fart test, and my first meal was clear chicken broth with saltine crackers. My God, it was magnificent!

After two weeks in Patrick AFB Hospital, I was discharged and sent home on thirty days of convalescent leave.

Two weeks later, I got a call from my CO. "We need you to come in and take over this DASO. Are you well enough to do so?"

I said, "Yes, sir," even though I still had two more weeks of recovery time. The person who was my relief broke down and could not handle his first DASO. I took over only two weeks before launch day and completed the launch.

I found out later that the Test Engineer resigned his commission and retired. No significant loss there, from my perspective.

Bales of Key West grouper captured in Cape Canaveral drug bust.

CHAPTER FIFTY-TWO

The British Are Coming, the British Are Coming

KEY WEST GROUPERS

The new Trident II D5 hydraulic redesign was completed and installed, and in no time, we were back in the DASO business. We stuck Mike Close back on board for that DASO. On launch day, it was the same scenario—the Soviet AGI went to his place, twice as far away as before, no arguments from him since we had doubled our distance also. Then we begin the wait for T-minus 0.

Many years earlier, a regular FBM was conducting an OT, an open ocean test. It was before Trident missiles came along. The missile was ejected from the boat in the usual manner, and when it broke the surface, the engine ignited. Instead of heading for the great beyond, the missile flopped back into the water and started running around on the surface, zigzagging all over the place. At one point, it was headed straight for the *Range Sentinel*, and people jumped over the side. I do not remember every detail of the story, and I don't know what happened to the missile. The people who were there said it was the scariest thing they had ever been through.

Everything on this second D-5 launch went as planned, and at T-minus 0, the missile came blasting out of the water, ignited, and took off, heading southeast in a hurry. Lots of cheering as it climbed out of sight. All indications we had, it was perfect. After returning to port, we found out the NEW hydraulic system failed again, and when the second stage kicked in, the first stage was almost out of hydraulic fluid. Test objectives were reached, however. Lockheed went back to the drawing board. The following new fix was almost overkill, but there never was another hydraulic system failure.

Now we were back to our routine of doing what we do at NOTU. An SSN arrived for one of those CNO projects. We didn't talk about those projects, but an exciting development happened one night. It scared the topside watch to death. For this project, the power supply was a large lithium battery designed to fit inside a torpedo tube. Part of the project was loaded aboard the boat during the day, and the battery pack was to go down and be attached the next day. Around 2 AM, the lithium battery exploded on the pier. Not a minor pow-type explosion but a big bam-type explosion. It would have brought down an airplane for sure.

Crap went everywhere, but nothing hit the topside watch. It did scare the bejesus out of him. When he called below to report what happened, no one could understand him, he was so shaken. The below decks watch stuck his head out the hatch and asked him what he had said, and the below decks watch said the guy was shaking badly. He went back down for the Duty Officer, corpsman, and the next guy on the watch list. They took the topside watch down below, and a new guy took over. In the meantime, fire and security arrived, and representatives for the project came. Can you imagine what could have happened if that battery had been loaded and sitting in the torpedo room? I'm not positive, but there would have been more people shaking besides the topside watch. That ended that project before it began.

Soon, a UK *Trident* came for its DASO. The pride and joy of the UK submarine world. I was the Test Engineer for this one. Following the same routine as we had done so many times before, the boat was ready to launch. This test was to be an early night launch. That is how it was scheduled. As I explained before, the last night op resulted in losing a helicopter and crew. After that, no more night launches. So, here we went again, getting underway for a night launch. I usually had very little free time on launch day as Test Engineer. I communicate with all kinds of people, which keeps me at my control station.

I had a few minutes, so I went to the bridge. I hadn't been up there for more than five minutes, and suddenly, there was a large wooden boat off the starboard bow cutting across right in front of us. No lights, no one on deck, but it was underway making way. None of us on the bridge saw it until it was too late. Rig for collision, blowing the horn, backing down like an MF, and we nailed that sucker dead center. The boat slid off the bow and started down the port side. Still, no one topside. The Brit port bow plane cut that thing open from stem to stern. The only reason it didn't sink was the cut was about two feet above the waterline.

Finally, a man stumbled topside and started cussing and raising hell. The helos came over and lit up the area like a football field. The Coast Guard came out ASAP. When the sub stopped, the boat was still stuck on the bow plane. There were two men and one woman on board. The helos spotted a long line of Key West grouper they were towing with a chem-light attached to each bale. The woman had one of her legs broken by the bow plane, but they were all so messed up on dope they didn't have a clue what was going on.

It turned out that the owner of the boat was in prison for smuggling drugs. When the Coast Guard arrived, they boarded the vessel, transferred the woman to another vessel for medical care and transportation to port and then to a hospital. All the Key West grouper was confiscated. The fishing-type wooden boat was taken in tow, and between the Coast Guard and some of the sub's crew, it was freed from the bow plane.

Typically, a collision at sea will ruin your entire day. Between me, the OOD, two lookouts, and a radar operator, no one saw this vessel until it was all over but the shouting. I had been looking forward and around, and so was the OOD. We were not engaged in face-to-face conversation, so all eyes were where they were supposed to be. When you have a situation like this, you have to send a message to everyone and their brother on down to the third butter cutter on the right. The message was drafted, approved, and transmitted. In this case, the odd thing was that just about everyone who was to be notified was already on board.

They cycled the bow planes to ensure they were not damaged, and we continued and conducted a successful launch and returned to port.

Of course, there was a board of inquiry, but it was held at NOTU. As I said, everyone who would usually participate was on board the UK sub. I was a qualified OOD. Their OOD, two look-outs, and the radar operator were the main culprits. Dressed in our finest, we were called in one by one to answer questions and give our testimony. Not as formal as the movies. I stood there and shouted, "You want the truth? You can't handle the truth." Not really; that movie hadn't been released. It was all matter of fact. No one was charged, and the Brit OOD was not chastised.

Service School Command, Orlando, Florida

CHAPTER FIFTY-THREE

Service School Command, Orlando

ONWARD AND UPWARD

So, then the Navy screwed up and selected me for Lieutenant Commander. My two-year tour, which turned into five years, had enough significant high points, that I was promoted. This time remaining at one duty station was not held against me. My detailer called me and asked if I'd like to go all the way to Service School Command, Orlando, to be a department head. I asked if he was pulling my leg, and he said, no, he needed to fill a department head job at Torpedo School. NOTU had a big hail and farewell party, and the following day, I drove fifty miles to Orlando to check in.

Boy, was I in for a rude awakening. Before I could begin the process of checking in as a Department Head, I had to go to legal and sign two documents. I walked over, and the legal beagle politely invited me to sit at a desk while he went back and notified a lawyer. The lawyer came out with two documents. He asked me to read every word and then sign. There was no tiny fine print at the bottom, and the back was blank.

I began reading and could not believe what I was processing. Halfway through the first page, I looked up and asked, "Are you serious about this?"

He said, "Absolutely. It is your choice; either agree and sign or call your detailer."

If I didn't sign them, I would have to call my detailer and arrange orders to somewhere else. I kid you not. I read both and signed. My entire Navy career, past and future, depended on my total compliance.

Have you sat on the planes and received a tap upside the head? Have you, as COW, ever tapped a planesman upside the head? Have you ever yelled at a junior person who was on the verge of doing something foolish?

The two documents I read and signed informed me I was never to do anything to upset a student. I could never use profanity in their presence. I was not allowed to yell, threaten or knock their stupid heads off. I was not to enter their barracks, and on and on. I told the lawyer that this was not doing these kids any favors. When they reach their first ship, and a Master Chief puts a size twelve boondocker up their anal orifice, these kids are in for a rude awakening. He shrugged his shoulders and went back to his office.

After I checked in, I discovered the surface detailer had already ordered in another Lieutenant Commander to be Department Head of Torpedo School. He arrived one week earlier. So, I ended up as the TM A-school Division Officer for both surface and submarines. I didn't make any waves and took the new job in stride.

The main building included all the administration offices, a vast auditorium, a separate area for classrooms and instructors, and a very nice entrance lobby with photos of all who had received the Medal of Honor in the QM, Signalman (SM), and TM rates. An exceptional tribute, I thought.

Outside the primary Admin building were open spaces covered by huge, old oak trees. Under these trees were tables and seats scattered about. The outside area looked more like a college campus than your basic Navy school surrounded by asphalt. Then there were three beautiful five-story barracks equipped with elevators and stairs. Several decks were devoted to female use only, and the rest for the men. I was not allowed to visit the barracks to see how my people lived. Can you imagine? That was the class instructor's job. I never set one single foot inside any of the barracks the entire time I was there.

So, I checked into Club Med for Torpedo persons, Quartermaster persons, Signal persons, and Electronic Technician persons school. Oh, yes, thoroughly mixed young men and women full of hormones. Damn, this was going to be so much fun—or a firing squad. To top it off, my XO was a woman. After my seven-month love boat cruise, this was all I needed—a single female XO.

Our XO was a Commander. She had been the Commanding Officer of the Military Sealift Command (MSCO) in Pusan, Korea. She had recently arrived and was still turning over with the outgoing XO. The outgoing XO was around 200 pounds overweight and refused to do anything to get down to specs. Anyone who said anything, she'd slap a race card on them in a microsecond. I was sorry she was leaving; she would have loved me.

I got along fine with our CO. His wife and my wife grew up in the same Long Island town. His name was Captain Smith, of all things. No relation. The XO was a single mother who had gotten knocked up by a married Captain at some point early in her career.

Our Captain was an ASW P-3 airdale. He had been in PI when the giant volcano erupted, and they had to evacuate and abandon the airfield and hangers. He had many photos of that. What a mess. Then it rained and got worse. Everything covered in ash collapsed. I do not know for sure, but I do not believe the Navy ever reoccupied that Naval Air Station. Captain Smith and I spent many hours talking about the Navy and other subjects. It seems these P-3 guys were very interested in submarines.

I told him my story about when we were off Bermuda with an ocean full of sonobuoys, and we discovered a Soviet *Foxtrot* under the layer. He was almost beside himself. He would have loved to have been there. So, thank God, I became his fair-haired boy. If it hadn't been for him and the XO, I would have been hanged from a yardarm later.

On the other hand, the XO's mindset that all male sailors were dirtbags and females were victims was a problem. We had an officer lounge which was empty most of the time. It had two entrances—one across from the XO's office and the other from the Admin area. Usually, the light was off, and many used it as a cut-through to the CO/XO offices. One day, I entered from the Admin side as the XO entered from her side. As soon as she saw my outline, she froze. Right away, I knew she was scared to enter a dark room with some man.

I said, "Hi XO, it's just me," and continued walking her way. She moved forward, and we passed.

I was thinking, *What the hell is wrong with these people? She views every male as a threat; why, I do not know.* If you haven't figured it out by now, I am not PC and never will be. Get over it! My opinions get worse.

I thanked God my Senior enlisted person in TM School was the first female TMC and TMCS. She was beyond outstanding. She was also the first TMCM. I cannot begin to tell you how many times she saved my butt. Man, talk about a radical change in my Navy life. Every Thursday, she would come into my office with four or five special request chits from female E-2s and E-3s asking for Friday off. The reason was: Personal Business. I asked my Senior Chief, what the heck is this? Just approve them and sign. If you are an officer and your Senior Chief tells you to do something, you best be listening.

I did; she went through the door to her office and around the corner, and passed out the chits. I never saw their faces. Then she returned, closed my door, and asked to sit. I said, "Of course."

Senior Chief McIntyre said, "All these girls are getting abortions on Friday."

It takes a lot to get my attention, like exploding rockets. You could have knocked me over with a feather. In my wildest dreams, I would have never come up with that reason. I was torn between my fatherly instincts and being a Lieutenant Commander. She explained that many of our female students were from the small-town USA and had never been away from home. Plenty of enlisted women were getting laid as much as they wanted, but they were on birth control pills. But the EM Club was full of sweet-talking guys with one goal in mind, so many naive girls ended up pregnant. I was sent back to caveman days almost immediately. I have no words to describe my feelings of disgust. I asked the Senior Chief if we knew who the fathers were. She said the girls never tell.

Guys, I had just condemned four babies to death, is the way I looked at it. Those are my personal views. I about died on the inside. The vast majority of these young girls were away from their small-town USA environment and were not prepared for the street-smart men at the EM Club.

I hope your jaw is open as you read this. I went straight to the CO's office to have a sit-down. He was aware of this problem and, like me, found it revolting. Unless I wanted duty in Tierra del Fuego at a lighthouse, however, I had better not say a word to any of the classes. Over the next few years, I do not remember how many of these I signed, but I never could get used to doing so.

My Senior Chief explained it all in plain English. Like most of us, she began as an E-1 and had seen it all as she moved up. She said she got wise in a hurry and never had an abortion. She had been married several times but was extremely happily married to a Chief Musician. Sometimes you have to try on a few pairs of shoes to find the ones you like.

One of my outstanding SSN TM1 instructors was arrested by housing police for battery on his wife. The XO wanted his head on a platter. I called him into my office and asked him what had happened. I trust submarine sailors with my life. He said his wife was working at a 7/11 store and was having an affair with a member of the sheriff's department. He knew something was up because he was stopped many times by this guy's buddies asking questions and inspecting everything. Way too many times to be a coincidence. He came home one day after work, and his wife started ripping her clothes, screaming for help, threw the widescreen TV out the front picture window, whacked her head against the wall a few times, dragged blood around the room, and sat down. She knew one of the neighbors would call the base police. Sure enough, they come in full battle array. She put her head in her hands and started sobbing (no tears) and yelling, "I can't live like this! I can't live like this!"

My instructor was a big muscular guy. If he had any intentions of ripping her lips off, he could have done so quickly. The base guys arrested him, put him in handcuffs, took him to their headquarters, and filed a report that included his wife was dry crying. He said he was standing there the entire time, watching her throw her fit. He was not sweating, no blood on his whites, and he still had his white hat on when they hauled him off. He told the investigators what happened and his belief that she had been having an affair with a sheriff's deputy.

Having seen more than my share of crazy wives over the years, I could see how she could do all this not only to ruin his career but use it as grounds for a divorce. The XO didn't buy any of his stories and wanted his blood. I stood up to her and told her she did not know what wives of submarine sailors are capable of, and that he was innocent. Set condition 1SQ. Man, did I light her up! She went high, and to the right, so loud the Captain came in to calm everyone down. She explained her side, and I explained his side. The problem was that she was putting herself in the wife's position, and I was taking the submariner's word. Although the CO didn't take anyone's side, I guess P-3 pilots have similar problems.

Based on the XO's own bad experience with a man, no damn wonder she was bitter. She fell for the "I love you baby, no bullsh*t" trick. Kudos to NIS. They not only tracked down the deputy who admitted they were having an affair, but they also located a wife who lived in housing who said the "victim" had told her what she was going to do.

My TM1 was cleared of any wrongdoing. The XO accepted it, but boy, was she pissed. From then on, the XO and I had many discussions about males and females in the service. I could only speak from experience. She had a one-track mind, and her affair had derailed it.

I had witnessed husbands returning from patrol, no wife. When they got home, everything had been sold, from ceiling fans to kitchen cabinets. The sailors had a mailbox full of overdue bills. I have no doubt that it happens in all branches to both male and female active-duty members.

We began having thefts in the barracks, and no one had a clue who was doing it. Remember Sams from one of my stories? We had a streetwise former gang member who was barely doing well enough in school to skim by and had been set back in school several times because we didn't want to upset little Johnny. He was doing this on purpose. He knew how to make an unlocking device out of an aluminum can and would go into a cubicle, slide it down between the pins and the shaft and unlock it. He would open a wallet and only take two tens or a twenty and put the rest back, lock the locker and leave. It usually took a while for the person to realize he was missing money or thought he was. I do not know how much he ended up getting, but someone remembered him in a cubicle where he didn't belong, and that is how he got nailed—a brilliant person. He received a dishonorable discharge and was sent to one of the Navy's finest jails at Portsmouth, NH.

After a year, I was moved over to QM/SM school as Department Head. One day, my QMCM came in with a chit. He gave it to me and said, you will need to sign this and send it over. It was from a young man in QM school who was homesick and wanted to go home. I disapproved it and sent it on to the XO. She and the CO approved it, and in two weeks, he was on his way home. I was so glad I had joined the Navy many years earlier.

Remember Rep. Patricia Schroeder from Colorado? She is the BITCH who started all this crap. I do not wish her any ill will, but would take great joy in reading her obituary.

CHAPTER FIFTY-FOUR

Still at SSC, Orlando

BS BY NIGHT

While I was at the Service School Command, I found out there was a college degree program on base through Columbia College, Missouri. I went over one afternoon and talked to a counselor. They needed to see my record with all my schools listed. I had been to forty-one schools. A few days later, I stopped by and left my record there. About a week later, I returned to get my record and find out the good or the bad news. It turns out; I had received many credit hours from all the classes I had attended. I could go two ways; either EE or BS.

I decided on BS and signed up. Two classes a week after my workday at SSC was completed. I also found I could take a CLEP test for many of the courses. All the years making patrols, I read a lot. Over time, I took twenty-one CLEP tests and passed nineteen. I missed the other two by one point. I passed Western Civ I & II, all the math, biology, geography, and many more. They finally said I could not take any more because I had to sit in class for eight subjects to get a BS in business.

In less than two years, I received a BS in business. I guess when you are a freshman for twenty-six years, you learn a few things. Of course, the Command made a big to-do about my getting a degree, and it went in my evaluations and entered into my record. I knew, unless I wanted to bag groceries or change tires at Allied when I finally hung up my spurs, that I needed a degree in something other than Rain Dancing or Teepee Pitching.

RELATIONSHIPS

My working relationship with my Senior Chief was outstanding. I wrote her the best evals I had ever written anyone and made sure the Command listed her as the #1 E-8 at SSC. Of course, the XO was all for that. Between the two of us, she was a shoo-in. She never saw where she was ranked in the Command, but she was pleased with what she read since she had to sign her evals. I wrote two evals for her before I was transferred across the street to be the Department Head of QM and Signalman school.

Across the street was a different world. My assistant was a QM Master Chief who was well entrenched in the Retired on Active Duty (ROAD) program. On his own, when he left on Thursday afternoon, he went home to Jacksonville and did not return until 1000 Monday morning. He pretty much did whatever the heck he wanted and had been getting away with it for years.

The first Monday after he returned from his long weekend, we had a little one-way chat. I was not going to stop him from leaving on Thursday after work, but he would submit a special request chit to cover his butt and mine if he got into an accident. Like me, he did not move his family from Jax, but it was too far to commute every day. For me, it was relatively easy, less than an hour. I would never try to clamp down on a Master Chief; I would have paid dearly, even as a Lieutenant Commander. He understood my concern and agreed it was the best thing to do.

He also knew I was a former Senior Chief and knew all the tricks.

TELLING TIME & 'RITHMETIC 101

I had an Orange County School Teacher on staff permanently. His job was to teach QM and SM students how to tell time. I kid you not. You would be amazed at the number of young people who cannot tell time unless the watch is digital. He used the same paper plate clocks we had in first or second grade. Each one had a different time, and he'd ask different students the time on this one and give a number. Mickey's big hand is on three, and his little hand is on 12. I was amazed.

He also taught basic math. All incoming students took a test on the first day. Those who did not pass spent the rest of the week in his class, learning to tell time and how to do basic math. They had to pass his class before they began either school. To me, this was almost incomprehensible. They were all high school grads. Before you go apoplectic, the Navy uses digital clocks all over the ship. We have large chronometers all over also. During a casualty or battle, power can be briefly interrupted, or some parts of the ship can become isolated. A time tick is received every day from the great clock in the sky. Then the Quartermaster walks around with his stopwatch, resets each chronometer if needed, and they are wound.

Just like in the movies, all surface ships ring a brass bell every four hours. This is not done on subs; we can't hide going around underwater ringing bells.

SELECTION BOARDS

There has been some discussion in previous years about how selection boards work. One day, the Master Chief came in and dialed a number and told the person on the other end that so-and-so was not ready for Chief. Even though he had met all the requirements, I guess he upset the Master Chief, so he nailed him. That person did not make Chief.

I'll begin with the E-7 selection board. First, you have to pass the test. Then the Command submits a list of all recommendations for Chief. There are people pulled from all over to make up the selection board. Every person recommended has his or her record pulled and sent to the board. Two to three people are given a stack of records, and they go through them one at a time marking a grade sheet and assigning a number based upon the individual's record. There are many of these small teams because the prospective Chief list is long. Before the selection board, every graded sheet is presented. Essentially, these small groups have to sell a candidate to the board based on his or her record. A stack is compiled of those who make the cut. Women have a pile; men have a pile.

I'll stick with submarines. Say there are 100 Chief STS billets to fill. When all is said and done, there is a primary pile of 100 men who made the cut. Then politics raises its ugly head. Out of the 100 STS1s selected, how do they stand as to race? I'm talking White, Black, Hispanic, Filipino, Native American, and anything else you can come up with.

Each race has its stack. Then the demographics for each race are looked at for Sonarmen on Submarines. Whatever the percentage is for each race, that is how many my fictitious stack of 100 has to match to keep Congress at bay. The largest pile is mostly white selectees because there are more whites on submarines. Don't get pissed at me. I'm telling you the way it is and has to be, or Congress will go ballistic.

You have five Black guys who made it on merit, but there needs to be ten. So, five White guys who made it on merit are removed from the bottom of the stack, and from the other pile, they go through and pick five Black guys for advancement and place them in that stack.

No Hispanics made the cut, but three must be added to the pass file. They go down through the stack and pull out the first three Hispanics, and it doesn't matter how deep they have to go to get them.

Then, all the minorities are randomly inserted into the White stack, so it doesn't appear so obvious they were added. The final stack should add up to 100, and the correct percentage represents every ethnicity.

The officers' selections are the same way. You could have walked on water, but when it comes to Commander and above, you can be bumped by someone who is up to his knees in water all the time. Unfortunately, that is how it works, and I'm probably the only person who will tell you this. Everyone who has served on these selection boards has signed their life away. You could talk about a spec op easier than a stint on a selection board.

Frankly, it may all be done by computer in this day and age, but I can guarantee you the program is designed to match current percentages.

The women are selected the same way. All advancement groups have to match ethnicity percentages.

As an officer, I have no idea where I was ranked against my peers at any command. That is a closely guarded secret. It will make or break your career. I would hope that I would at least make the top ten in the Lieutenant listings with all the things I was involved in. None of that matters now anyway.

I do not want anyone to think I am racist or prejudiced in any way. I am a brutally honest person, and that is the way it works. In 2021, the Department of Defense released a directive to all Commands to ensure transgender, LBTGQ, and whatever else is in the military now are not discriminated against, especially for advancement. No comments are necessary. I do not want to get shut down.

Times be-a-changin'; you either go with the flow or get out.

CHAPTER FIFTY-FIVE

Ethics or Why It Matters

THE CHALLENGE

While I was a department head at Service School Command, I was asked by the Commanding Officer to write an ethics course to be presented to all enlisted students passing through Service School Command, Orlando, FL. The course attendees would be Electronics Technicians, Torpedomen, Quartermasters, and Signalmen. We taught both surface and submarine enlisted men and women at our schools. I told him I would start gathering information, write a course, and then present it first to our instructors before implementing the course as part of our new students' training.

I was a Lieutenant Commander and Chairman of Deacons of First Baptist Church, Merritt Island. My Commanding Officer knew this. I also knew I had to leave religion out of the course. As in, no quoting scripture and according to the Bible, etc.

I first contacted the Naval Academy, West Point, the Air Force Academy, and the Coast Guard Academy to see if they taught an

Ethics course. To my surprise, only the Coast Guard Academy taught an Ethics course. I asked if I might have a copy of their course to adapt it for the Navy.

I'm talking basic ethics—no stealing, lying, cheating, etc. I wasn't trying to convert the students to some sort of fanatical religion. I was trying to get them to understand that, in the Navy, you do not steal from your shipmates, and you always tell the truth, something I found out from interviewing new students they knew little about. For most of them, it was getting what you can from others and then bug out. Not exactly the Golden Rule as most of us were taught. For some reason, if a sailor borrowed a CD player from someone and then it was stolen from the borrower, the person who borrowed the player felt he or she had NO obligation to replace the item. It was the owner's bad luck.

In a few weeks, I received the Coast Guard Ethics Course, that was taught to their officers but not enlisted. Their course was much too complicated. It dealt with drug and money confiscations and customs, many things your basic sailor would not be involved in. My course dealt with the thousands of enlisted men and women who came through Service School Command each year. I even queried a few colleges—Harvard, Yale, Columbia University. None of them taught an ethics course. This was very vexing, indeed.

Using the Coast Guard course as a guide, I wrote the entire course tailoring it to enlisted personnel. I had to search for common ground that all enlisted personnel, male and female, could understand as it applied to them.

One would think officers were raised by responsible parents and would know the difference between right and wrong. Was I incorrect about that? Today's parents are not the same as our parents. From what I gathered after interviewing many officers and enlisted men and women, they only knew what their fourteen-year-old babysitter taught them. That is a slight exaggeration but it is about as close to the truth as possible. The truth was that most had never set foot in a church.

If you were stupid enough to leave your $150 Michael Jordan sneakers on the deck under your bunk, then they were fair game.

That was the moral mentality back then. The fact that it was not their property never entered into their thought pattern.

Going back to the mid-60s when I joined, you could leave your wallet full of cash on your bunk, and no one would touch it. You were part of the crew, a shipmate, a fellow sailor, and no one messed with your stuff. Twenty-seven years later, there was a very different philosophy engraved into the brains of the basic nineteen-year-old. I related earlier how we caught one streetwise sailor who would gain access to someone's wallet and only take out some of the money so it would not immediately be recognized that some cash was stolen. He would purposely fail class exams to be set back in a class so he could continue his theft scheme. Eventually, he was caught and tried, dishonorably discharged, and sent to prison.

I finished my course, and the CO/XO set up a training day for all the school staff. I was to present the first training session to all the instructors at the school. I distributed handouts I'd made and then started presenting the course. At the end, I received a standing ovation from all the instructors, except for the Executive Officer. Before I could leave the auditorium, many told me it was about time the Navy got smart and taught these kids the difference between right and wrong.

A school command is a world away from an at-sea command. We were forbidden to do or say so many things to students, things that would not be tolerated at sea. You mouth off to a Master Chief (E-9); you could find yourself flat out on the deck bleeding or, even worse, floating in the ocean. When you were at sea, you had a responsibility to look out for your shipmates and do your job. There are no lone rangers on board a ship or submarine. I am sure it is the same in all branches. You can be a stupid kid in basic training or at a service school. When you report aboard a ship or sub, however, you best have your act together, or you will get a #12 boot up your butt. There is one thing in the Navy you do not mess with, and that is a Master Chief Petty Officer. He may not be God, but he can take His place if God wants a weekend off. Officers may think they are in charge, but it is the Master Chiefs who keep everything on an even keel.

After I presented the initial course, I went back for a discussion with my CO and XO. The CO was impressed; the XO, a female Commander whom I described earlier, was not exactly pleased. She wanted me to remove some of the parts she considered to be religious. I did and resubmitted the lesson plan to her. What I didn't know, the Command sent my lesson plan to the Chief of Naval Education and Training. It was adopted to be taught at all Service School Commands throughout the Navy.

The Ethics course was turned over to several instructors who were responsible for all students beginning school. They taught the indoctrination phase before the students started school.

I didn't do this for any sort of recognition but to "get the student's mind right," as in *Cool Hand Luke*. I ended up receiving another Navy Commendation Medal from The Chief of Naval Education. Whatever, that and fifty cents would buy you a cup of coffee at the Base Exchange.

One of the things that I had absolutely no control over was abortion. It used to drive me nuts how the first time away from home, teenage girls would get pregnant, and on Friday, not pregnant. As I have detailed earlier, I was forbidden to say a word to the young ladies when they first arrived about keeping their pants on. I was not their father, and I was told in no uncertain terms that it was none of my business.

Today, it is still a source of heartache for me. I always knew they were pregnant because I'd receive a special request chit to miss school on a Friday, the abortion day. I was instructed to approve them all.

Navy Court Martial

CHAPTER FIFTY-SIX

Computers and Courts Martial

COMPUTERS

While serving as department head of QM/SM school, I discovered that the ET school, which occupied the largest portion of the same building, had a room full of newer model, working computers. I asked my schoolteacher and head instructor if we could set up a computer lab with general math programs and anything else they thought might benefit the students in the one-week training to tell time and learn basic math. The schoolteacher said right off, yes, and that he had access to all kinds of *floppy disks* (remember those?) for basic math. We had a room and would need twenty computers.

I paid a visit to the ET school department head, and he had no problems letting us borrow the old computers. He said he would have some of his people find twenty computers and make sure they worked properly. To cover all bases, I went across the street and talked to the

CO and XO and cleared it through them to set up a computer lab. They thought it was a great idea. It was fundamental that the students could work at their own pace, and any instruction needed concerning how to use a computer (PC) was provided. It is hard to believe today, but PCs were not available to everyone back then. With the help of a couple of ETs, the teacher and one instructor set up the lab in no time. I wrote up Atta-Boys for them. It worked well, but I do not know if the computers made the trip to Great Lakes when SSC was shut down and moved to old WWII buildings and barracks up there (Politics).

Across the street from the ET school and a little bit down the street, a new state-of-the-art ET school building was under construction. A future ET, beginning school in that building that housed A- and C-schools would be the cat's meow.

E-9 results came out, and my TM Senior Chief was on the list. I congratulated her on a job well down. The first time I ever saw tears in her eyes. It must have been an allergy running around. There was no doubt in my military mind; she deserved it. She transferred before me to DC to work for a congresswoman in charge of the Military Affairs Committee (you know who) or something like that. I never tried to follow up with her to see how things were going.

COURTS MARTIAL

One of the benefits of being a Lieutenant Commander in Orlando, you have many opportunities for Court Martial duty. I was so blessed (*very* sarcastic) to serve on nine of them, one of which I was President of the Board. Members were Lieutenant and above. I could be the lowest rank, middle or highest. It all depended on the rank of the person charged. Military courts martial are all the same, except possibly for the depiction in *A Few Good Men*. You have various military board members sitting in a row, a military judge, the standard two legal officers representing the two individuals, and various people sitting in the audience.

Every court martial I participated in had to do with Sexual Harassment or Sexual Assault. It's the new Navy. No dereliction of duty, no assault and battery, no larceny, just plain man and women issues—some guilty, some not guilty.

Not guilty verdicts brought down the wrath of Rep. Patricia Schroeder (D) CO. Three times, I and the other board members were investigated by Schroeder regarding our decision making. What upset her one time was that she recognized me from two previous times. She claimed I was leading a vicious plot to undermine the entire Women in the Navy program. Remember the Senator in *G.I Jane*. Schroeder was a powerful person who could have had me castrated and sent to Area 51 as a test subject.

I will not bore you with all the details of each of the courts martial. You'd be found hanging in your jail cell with your hands zipped-tied behind you. Fortunately, my CO, XO (surprise), and my former TM Master Chief, now working for her, intervened and made sure she understood that I was not the problem. Feel free to watch some of her YouTube videos. What a piece of work. From what I've seen of them, she tries to come across like a kind, caring grandmother, but she was not.

Being raised in the South, I always said, *yes sir, no sir, yes ma'am, no ma'am*. She DID NOT like the *ma'am* part and would go ballistic.

MOVING ON

As time progressed, rumors started that SSC Orlando was moving to Great Lakes. Soon it was official. It seems there was not enough Naval presence in the upper mid-west to attract people to the Navy. After all, Orlando had Nuke School, Boot Camp, a hospital, exchange, etc. We had the newest, most efficient barracks heating and cooling systems, a brand-new ET building under construction, our full-size torpedo tubes mounted and operational, and everything worked fine, were fail-safe, and drained to the bilges. I was in the process of getting permission to build, across the lake, an upper ship's signal bridge with a mast with every possible light configuration. Signalmen could send and receive semaphore, flashing light, and there were lanyards for pennants, black balls, and triangles—basically a trainer for SM school. We could simulate day or nighttime situations. I had command support; all we needed was Chief of Navy Education and Training (CNET) to approve and bust loose with some funds. There was a large lake out front of SSC, so this would be perfect to have this simulator platform on the other side of the lake.

With the move to Great Lakes, that plan was scrapped. As a nuke, how would you like to go straight from a classroom to a sub or surface ship without any hands-on experience? My goal was to have these guys hit the deck running.

I addressed a class twice, once at inception and once at graduation. I tried to impart information that would help. Open an account at the Credit Union, do not save your money under your pillow or in your locker. Keep your locker locked at all times.

Then the big lead shoe fell. Commander, the XO wants to talk to you.

I went over, and she said, "Your former Commanding Officer at NOTU wants you back immediately. He has already spoken to your detailer and made arrangements for your relief to come in and take your job here, but it is up to you."

My answer was, "If he wants me back ASAP, I should go."

The Navy spent over $100 million setting up the new school. The brand-new ET school building is not finished to this day. The contractor was paid the total amount as if he had completed the project. As far as I know, all the barracks and main SSC buildings are falling apart, if not demolished. It all belongs to the City of Orlando, and I do not know if they ever did anything with the land or facilities.

CHAPTER FIFTY-SEVEN

Welcome (back) to NOTU, PCAN

PORT OPS

Reporting back to NOTU was like a homecoming. With very few exceptions, everyone was the same; everything was the same. Captain John Byron, the best CO I ever had in my career, was still there, and he was the one who asked my detailer to send me back ASAP.

Under President Clinton's watch, changes were happening at an incredible pace. The Pentagon was in high gear, getting rid of personnel in all branches of each service—500,000 over three years. The reason for the sudden request to bring me back to NOTU, Denny Reberry had to report to Sub Base New London to relieve as Weapons Officer. Without a Port Ops Officer, it would put NOTU in a major bind. NOTU needed a Port Ops who was already qualified in all aspects of Submerged Submarine Missile Launches, DASO. I thought that was strange when it did not apply to my relief two years later. I was very happy to be back at a Command that semi-resembled the real Navy.

I would not be conducting launches anymore, but someone was needed who understood everything involved, and the pressure on the Command to release Lt. Cmdr. Reberry was immense. I was the closest and most qualified person for the job.

If you sat down and made a list of all the great things you could get in a Commanding Officer, Captain Byron would be the one. Ex-enlisted, NESEP, eventually CO of a Diesel Boat, and loved to fish. My only complaint, he walked too fast, and I would have to ask him to slow down. One other thing, he backed me and my decisions 100 percent. From where I had been (SSC, Orlando), that was a breath of fresh air.

Reberry and I took about two days to turnover, and he departed to what would be the worst job of his career, while I assumed one of the best jobs of my career. My XO was Barry Mills, who I had worked with when he was at SP-205. Except for the Civil Service Department Heads, I had been at NOTU the longest of any military member. There were very few things I did not know or hadn't experienced. I had the Ops Department bring me up to speed in a hurry, and for my first Department Head meeting, I was ready.

The big job was getting as many UK Tridents certified with US boats sprinkled in. Next was, for me, running an advertisement campaign to get more surface ships in for port visits. How can you make a profit when you have empty pier space?

I hit the road to SubLant and SurfLant. While I was at SubLant, I tracked down the Communications Officer. Once I found him, I did the old pop-quiz routine. Specifically, why did they send NOTU Top Secret messages that pertain to what Lat/Lon a sub is going to after leaving NOTU? When I was at NOTU, I was the Top Secret Control Officer, and we didn't need Top Secret messages.

Here is the explanation. I would receive a phone call at home, usually at 2 AM, from the NOTU Duty Officer informing me there was a Top Secret Flash message at Patrick Air Force Base for me to pick up. I'd get up, get dressed in my uniform, and drive down there to pick up a useless TS message. I would have to return to the Command, log it in, and lock it in the empty TS safe. Go home, go back to sleep, and return at the usual time. The very first thing I had to do was go back to headquarters and attach a routing sheet to the message, put it in a TS folder, and present it to the XO, who would check a box and take it to the CO. He'd read it, check the box and mark destroy, which I did.

I asked the CO at the time, "Do we need this?"

He would say, "No."

So, during my SubLant visit, I asked the Comms Officer why we received TS messages we didn't need. His answer, "A CO must have wanted to see it at some time in the past."

I told him all we needed was their secret move rep to know what time to schedule the Pilot, tugs, and line handlers. Where she went, we could not care less.

"Not a problem." He removed NOTU from the Top Secrets distribution list. That took care of that little problem.

One of the items I received after I checked in was a secure telephone at my house. It replaced our regular phone but could go secure when I received calls from SubLant or DC.

My involvement with arriving and departing ships or subs was minimal. Everything worked as before, someone was assigned to the visiting vessel, and they took care of them, as I did when I was there the first time. If a Brit ship was in, they always threw a big party, and my wife and I would attend. I found the UK subs and ships were so appreciative of everything we did for them. It was like it was above and beyond anything they could have expected. On the other hand, U.S. subs and surface ships always had their hand out. Two different aspects. I never asked, but I guess the Brits had to beg, borrow, or steal back at their home base.

One day, I went over to the Trident Basin on business, and a sub tender was tied up there, enjoying our excellent liberty port. They were making preps to get underway when I arrived. Lo and behold, I spotted my former blonde LT from the *Holland* standing on a weather deck. She was a Lieutenant Commander and looked to be somewhere around six months pregnant. I didn't jump up and down and wave to get her attention, but I did ask one of the ship's crew on the pier if he knew her. He said, yes, she worked in the Supply Department. I thanked him and left it at that. I did not care to know any more about her than I already did.

When I was at NOTU before as a Test Engineer, I never really paid much attention to what the Port Ops Officer did. It turns out he traveled a lot. I was surprised at how much.

FIRST BAPTIST GOES TO SEA

Shortly after moving to Merritt Island, we found a church that fit our needs. Over the next few years, the church grew to around 10-12,000 members, and not one person there ever asked me if they could go aboard a submarine.

Later, I made arrangements with a Trident CO to have about seven of our male church staff ride the boat on one of his daily DASO training trips to sea. He was thrilled. I cleared it with the SP-205 Captain, and he didn't have a problem. All I needed was their full names and SSNs for a quick check. I had to make sure I could get permission before I offered to take these men to sea on one of our newest Tridents for a day. Talk about kids in a candy store; they could not believe it.

The Pastor asked, "You can do this?" I said yes.

During their ministry career, these men get invited to tour local plants, maybe go for an airplane ride around the local area, and things like that. Our ministers had been on many tours of the Space Center and had seen many things, but to go to sea and submerge was something they had never dreamed would be possible. There was a conference that day they were to attend, but the Pastor said to forget that. They would not miss a chance to ride a submarine.

Their wives were not thrilled because they wanted to go. So, I made arrangements for all of them and the older kids to take a pier-side tour.

I had to make sure none of the guests were claustrophobic. It turned out the CO and the Captain from SP-205 rolled out the red carpet for them. Everyone got to look out the periscope, took turns at driving and diving, and all the other usual things such as angles and dangles.

Even today, all these many years later, if I see one of them somewhere, not around here, that day is always at the top of their list of things they have ever done.

CHAPTER FIFTY-EIGHT

SEAL Games

NOW YOU SEE ME—NOW YOU DON'T

When I returned to Port Canaveral, I wanted to expand our horizons. Going through our youngest son, I contacted SEAL Team 8 out of Little Creek and asked them if they would like to come to the Cape and play. Lots of excitement on their end. I told them I would get back to them after checking with all the security people to see if they wanted to allow the SEALS to come down. Of course, times and dates would be coordinated, so no one got carried away.

I informed my Command, and they were happy with that. I called the SEAL Team back and told them the Cape would need times and dates and gave them the phone numbers, so I wasn't the middleman. We would provide them with a building in the Port for staging purposes.

Let the games begin! Keep in mind, SEALS do not play fair. When they arrived at the Port, the team leader, a Senior Chief, came in to get the building keys and introduce himself. I introduced him around, and then we walked down to the building they were to use. It was just fine and suited their needs.

I knew I could not take him up on the Cape for a look around, and I told him. He said it wasn't necessary; they had everything they needed. Even though this was training, they did the same workup for any job they were assigned. That night was their first infiltration, and before sunrise, they were out. When I came to work, their building was locked. They were in town asleep. When they returned around 1400, the Senior Chief came down, and I asked him how it went last night; he said it was great. We had a wonderful playground for them with all the old launch pads, tunnels, tanks, and concrete structures. They didn't see anyone from Air Force Station Security.

The next night, they went in again to a different area and left before sunrise—the same routine as before. The Senior Chief showed up around 1400. Another great night; simulated blowing up many things. They made many videos and photos, etc.

That afternoon, the security guy at the Cape I dealt with called and wanted to know if the SEALS had changed their minds and decided not to come down. I told him they were here and had been in his territory the last two nights. He freaked out. I told him I wasn't sure, but I imagined they would be back tonight. I suggested he come down to the Port and talk to the senior chief.

He came down, and the Senior Chief showed him some of the videos they took. He was rather upset they had been in twice, and none of their sensors or people had seen them. I imagine when he returned, there was a meeting and a one-way conversation with his leadership.

The entire week the SEALS were there, they pretty much owned the Cape.

While all eyes and patrols were on the ocean side, they entered and left from the riverside. I told you they didn't play fair. Unlike all our ASW exercises, you do not put these guys in a box and have them use flashlights.

Before I go any further, the SEALS never intended or tried to gain entry to any active launch areas. I do not know if they could or not, but I would not bet any money against them. As a temporary security guard, I knew there were some places out there that had the most sophisticated security I had ever seen. I will not describe that, either.

So, that began a significant relationship between the Cape and Little Creek. After SEAL Team 8 returned, we started receiving calls for reservations.

I received a call from the Senior Chief one day, and he wanted to know if they could come down and penetrate the Port and ride a cruise ship out underwater? I said, let me make some calls.

Several members of the Port Canaveral Port Authority were ex-NOTU officers. The one I called was my former Commanding Officer. He was all for it, but he had to run it through all those involved. Here again, dates, times, etc. To remove me as the middleman, I provided phone numbers as before.

This event had more participants than before. The SEALS came in submerged on an SSN to some point near the channel. From there, they swam out, removed the submersible underwater craft, and went into the Port completely underwater and undetected. Knowing the cruise ships would have divers swim the hull before departure, they waited near the ship but far enough away not to be seen. As soon as the divers finished, they moved in and somehow attached to the cruise ship.

Just before the ship left, my cell phone rang, and it was my son. He asked me to tell him when the cruise ship left the dock. I thought that was a bit of cheating, but I told him. Later he told me it allowed them to get into position to retrieve the SEALS based on the average transit time to the sea buoy. After the SSN recovered the underwater vehicle, it departed, and the *USS Shamal* (PC-13) came to retrieve the SEALS. Mike was on it when he called. We had no way of seeing that far out, and fishermen never told us when they saw a Navy vessel since they were a common sight offshore anyway. Everything went well, and everyone made the trip out and was recovered by the *USS Shamal*. With everything and everyone secured, they wound up their twin turbines and departed rapidly.

The next exercise with them was at the request of NASA. I was good friends with the #2 man at NASA Security. They had heard about the Cape activity and wanted the SEALS to do some specific things to test their systems. Everything was arranged, and we provided the same building in the Port for them to use. I enjoyed going down and talking to them but did not make a nuisance of myself, like some groupie. After all, they had already told us on SEAL team ops we were insane for riding submarines. So, we had their respect also.

This operation was a more controlled exercise since NASA Security and the team communicated with each other. The team would approach their usual covert way, and NASA Security would ask them for their positions. Things did not go well for NASA. They had paid big bucks for some high-tech devices for security, and not a single one of them indicated the SEALS were there. They ended up asking the SEALS to do some things they would never normally have done. In each rubber raft, three SEALs stood up and held their rain ponchos out like an eagle, and NASA's system finally picked up a small blip.

Realizing they had been paying people to monitor security devices that could not pick up a Semi, they were distraught. NASA terminated the op and told them they would be in touch. Then they called the company that sold and installed the security system and had an unfriendly chat. This was more perimeter security than access to secure sites. Of course, if your first line of protection doesn't work, what is the point of having it?

After the techs came down and checked the system and reset everything, NASA had the SEALS come back and try again. This time, the team was detected. NASA was happy, and so were the SEALS; they learned they needed to do something different to evade these systems. While they were there, they had an exercise to come to the beach, pick up a defecting scientist, and then swim out underwater to an SSN offshore. One second, he was on the beach, then he was gone. They put him on a re-breather and took him out.

I was more of a facilitator and didn't directly participate except for the phone call. But I enjoyed working with them. I do not know if they continued to play at the Cape after I retired. I do know NASA and Cape Canaveral wanted them to come as often as they could.

Rainbow Warrior *before she was sunk in 1985*

CHAPTER FIFTY-NINE

My Last Year in the Navy

NOTU

After one year back at NOTU, the best CO I ever had retired from Active Duty. Capt. John Byron never micromanaged me and always supported my decisions.

He and his wife, who had been with him his entire career, were ready to become civilians, if that were possible. It was a huge event, the largest retirement I ever attended. John knew so many important people out in all the surrounding towns. Many of the top dogs from NASA, the Air Force, and of course, SP-205, were present. It was a great day for the two of them. Two years after he retired, his wife died from cancer. They had no idea at his retirement.

His relief was just the opposite. He was one of those who showed up and wanted to reinvent the wheel. Not that there was a reason to. You have served or worked with them and know what I'm talking about.

Since 1961 when *George Washington* launched the first SLBM, the Navy retained the same companies. There were no bids requested every few years to choose the low bidder. Of course, that is not a standard procedure with all programs.

As submarines changed and SLBMs changed, most of the procedures were changed to keep up. However, they were minor tweaks compared to the comprehensive documents. Like the cigarette commercial, *We've come a long way, baby*—Polaris to Trident D5 II program. You could put *George Washington* inside a Trident sub.

THE RAINBOW WARRIOR

Launch security was also scaled back. *George Washington* was smothered by US Navy, Coast Guard, and Air Force. Once the Trident Basin and wharf were constructed, the Coast Guard was no longer needed. When a boat went to sea, we had a range ship, an Air Force helicopter, and unless we had Intel that the *Rainbow Warrior* was coming down to be a pain in the rear, that was it.

If we knew she was coming, we requested a US Navy Salvage Ship. Those vessels are heavily constructed. No aluminum hull or fragile superstructure for them. They were built to take a beating. The few times I saw them in action, they were like a cowboy on a cow pony and had no fears about making contact. They would get right next to the eco-terrorist vessel and turn the rudder to push her away. While that was going on, two fire hoses were manned up top, sending thousands of gallons of seawater down their stack.

If *Rainbow Warrior* managed to break away, the salvage ship immediately came back alongside and repeated the same maneuver. I believe it was the water down the stack that got their attention. They always departed, and we continued the launch.

A few days before the launch, a very tall Test Instrumentation (TI) Mast was lowered into the center of the submarine's sail and bolted to the pressure hull. When the sub was at 150 feet, we could communicate, and all computer information was transmitted to the Range and the *Range Sentinel*. There was a flashing beacon on top and three curved radar reflection plates welded just below the antenna. The TI mast was metal and reflected radar, but the three curved plates amplified the reflected energy for a much bigger return. When *Rainbow Warrior* arrived, they always tried to tie a rubber raft to the TI mast with people sitting in it. We wouldn't launch a missile and crispy critter them, so we contacted the sub and asked them to increase their depth to 160 feet for one minute. The TI mast slowly disappeared, the raft stood straight up, occupants were in the ocean, slowly the rubber raft submerged, the line used to tie it to the mast snapped, and out popped the rubber raft. Those adrift climbed in and headed for the mother ship.

I will not go into the classified history of the origin of *Rainbow Warrior*. She interfered with every country conducting at-sea missile launches except for Russia.

BACK TO BUSINESS

Only the Civil Service people at NOTU had more experience than I. As far as assigned military people went, I was way ahead in knowledge. When the CO gave his comments and what he wanted to do at department head meetings, I was the lone dissenter. Many times he proposed a plan that had been tried in the past and failed. Fortunately for me, the XO had been at SP205 for a few years before coming to NOTU. The majority of the time, he would back me up.

I have never been a yes man, but I'm not about to let someone waste everyone's time. Besides, I was protecting him from 205. The Admiral in Crystal City was not someone to mess with. But, in my friendly way, I did manage to upset the CO a few times. As I was going down the hall after a meeting, I could hear him screaming at the XO while using my name. I just smiled.

As a former Test Engineer, I knew the hours my Test Engineers were putting in. For many weeks they were on-site working all night.

The standing rule when I got there was to get qualified. Sound familiar? After you became qualified, you were assigned a boat, and you worked that boat until it left. If you worked all night, stop by the office before you go home and see if anything is happening. It was that way before I arrived in 84 and was that way when I retired in 94.

One day in the late morning, the CO dropped by for a visit. Before he let me know he was in the building, he wandered around a bit. When he came in, I stood up and welcomed him.

His first words were, "Where is everyone?"

I told him they were home. OMG, what kind of department are you running here; that was the expression on his face, but he didn't say that. Then he asked if I had permission from the XO to let them go.

I said, "No, Sir. I do not check with the XO when I send my men home."

"Why not?" he asked with a red face.

I responded, "For the same reason, I don't ask permission for them to work all night or all weekend."

Boy, was he hotter than a popcorn fart! He spun around and left the building. I don't know if he talked to the XO or not, but the XO would have told him those guys worked all kinds of weird hours.

Just like when I was a Test Engineer, we were professionals and took our jobs very seriously. It was the same as Port Ops. The subject of working hours was never brought up again. I did receive an outstanding evaluation, so he must not have been *too* upset with me.

THE WHITE HOUSE

About two months before the end of my two-year tour, my detailer called and asked me if I would like to go to the White House and work in the OPS department. It would be a four-year tour with lots of travel. I immediately said, yes, I'll take it.

He said, "Not so fast. You should talk to your wife. You will be on the road a lot."

I repeated, "I'll take it."

He said, "Okay."

Three weeks later, I received a letter from the second-round downsizing board. *Your retirement date is August 1, 1994. Have a nice day.*

I immediately went to see the XO and said, "What the +*&$*&& is this?" I handed him the letter.

He started reading, and his head dropped. The XO said the board never consults the command. It is always a surprise. I had told him what my detailer had offered me, and the XO said the only thing that would save me from this was if the detailer had already written my orders. I called my detailer, and he about crapped when I told him. He had not yet typed my orders. Now he was in a bind to find someone else to take my place. He apologized and said there is a routine they follow, and my orders hadn't made it to that point.

Apparently, all I needed was one more week, and I would have been protected. I was due for Commander the following April. Oh, well, that is the way it goes.

RETIREMENT CEREMONY

We had my retirement in my church's gym. The church staff was thrilled to host it. My Navy retirement was their first. Always thinking of the troops, I didn't want everyone to melt in Florida's August heat. NOTU people decorated the gym with flags, pennants, and bunting. It was very nautical and patriotic. Many of my friends at church attended. I had a large crowd by the time everyone took their seats. I believe about every contractor at NOTU who could get off attended. Many of the men assigned to OTSU-2 came (Operational Test Support Unit, a navy group on the *Range Sentinel*). Their OIC even presented me with a plaque and some other things. Our youngest son, who was with SPECOPS, came and was one of my side boys. I will always have a special memory of his being there.

In my retirement address, I left my Navy's running to Second-Class Petty Officers and Chief Petty Officers. From my experience, they were the ones who made things happen. Both trained the junior guys to be their relief, something I was not fortunate to have received. I did make sure it happened everywhere I was stationed. Even as a Senior Chief and COB, I got down on my knees in the head and showed a young sailor the proper way to clean a submarine toilet. I was never too proud to serve. Everyone plays a part, but those are the two key positions. I know the officers think they are, but we know better.

My Port Ops relief showed up three days before my retirement. I gave him a once-over lightly brief, introduced him to my best Test Engineer, and asked him to make sure my relief was fully briefed and to get him qualified ASAP.

I have been back to NOTU once since I retired, to attend the retirement of a longtime friend from Lockheed. I had attended his Navy retirement years before.

Many Pan Am and Lockheed employees had been a part of the Cape since its beginning and the *George Washington* launch. Over the years, I had listened to some fantastic stories about the early days.

I never considered working for any of the contractors or at NASA. Those were the two primary sources of employment for former NOTU people. Many people got hurt financially when the Space Shuttle program was shut down and NASA's budget was cut. Approximately 48,000 left the area. I had bigger plans, we had three sons in college, and I needed to hit the deck running.

One year after I retired, I received a call from the Port Canaveral Port Authority offering me a position as assistant Port Operations Manager. By that time, I was having a hard time tying my shoes, much less going to work.

Brown & Root

CHAPTER SIXTY

Retirement and OMG!

BROWN & ROOT

I retired on August 1, 1994, with thirty years of active service. I had been selected to go to the White House and work in the Operations Department down in the basement—a four-year tour. Instead, I was snagged by the down-size board so President Clinton could show a budget surplus, and that was that.

Over 500,000 were forced to retire. You usually have to serve Twenty or more years to retire. A special deal was set up so the downsizing board could go down to fifteen years. Those forced to retire between fifteen and nineteen years could not draw a check until they were sixty-five. Those people got the shaft.

As Port Ops, anything happening on the north side interested me. Brown and Root, out of Houston, TX, was building a concrete roll-on, roll-off pier right down from us. I frequently talked to the building supervisor, and sometimes, we'd go to the Greenhouse for lunch. Brown and Root is a giant construction company involved in projects all over the entire world. Tunnels, airports, seaports, Interstate Highways, bridges, refineries, water plants, power plants, just about anything that needs to be built, they can do it. For years, they have had a standing contract with the Pentagon. Several other large companies also have the same arrangement with the Pentagon.

One day the supervisor called me and asked if I could go to lunch at the Greenhouse. His boss was in town and wanted to meet me. So, I did and we met. B&R could build a seaport but had no idea how to run one. The Pentagon had notified them that they would need someone to take over the operations of the port of Port-au-Prince, Haiti, after the invasion. We talked for a while in generalities. I said cleaning up the port and getting it operational wouldn't be a problem if I had the correct equipment and people. Also, I would need to know how much power/authority I would have and the budget. I listed some equipment, personnel, armed bodyguards (at least two), and some other odds and ends. He left, and I went back to see what my guys were doing.

I started getting calls at my house from the Personnel Manager from B&R, who wanted to talk to me about a position as Sea Port Director in Haiti with unlimited power and unlimited budget. I asked if he would like a resume, and he said sure; send it to blah, blah, blah. All this was going on in June 94. So, I tailored my resume toward that type of job and included Navy Diver, electrical repair, heavy metal fabrication, assistant repair officer, port operations, and a BS in business. I received another call from the personnel guy, the Head Project leader, and some Grand Poobah in the company. They had changed their mind, and instead of being hired to work on this temporary project, they wanted to offer me a job with Halliburton's main company.

What that meant was that when the project in Haiti was over, I would still have a job with Halliburton and be shifted to B&R as necessary on another job. I also would have different benefits than the others and a starting salary of twice as much as my Navy pay, plus bonuses. I said, sure, that was fine with me. Dee about went ballistic when I wrote down the starting salary. I didn't ask for more or add all kinds of caveats. All those years we sold blood to buy food were over.

For some reason, it never occurred to me that I could have gone to Jacksonville, attended Railroad Engineers school, and worked for CSX.

THE NAVY FINE PRINT

Due to the Navy's total lack of ability to plan anything, I was unable to use my leave before retiring. We were right in the middle of teaching the Brits how to launch Trident II missiles. My relief was not even named, and I was getting down to less than a month to go. There was no negotiating with the downsizing folks. I was out on August 1 with or without a relief. That ain't no way to run a port. I needed at least a month with my relief to introduce him to the people at NASA, Range Safety and Control, Cape Canaveral Range Officers, all the Washington DC people, the heads of all the contractors who we worked with each day of a DASO, and on down the line.

My relief had a mountain of things to learn. This was not an *I had it, you got it* kind of deal. There were billions of dollars going on here. My relief finally showed on Monday before my Friday retirement.

HAITI

At the end of September, I flew to Haiti, right behind the Army. Two thousand Haitians lived in the port with no potable water and very little light to allow work at night. Five sunken ships rested on the bottom alongside the piers. Thousands of empty shipping containers were everywhere. I was in seventh heaven. I felt like John Wayne down there barking orders to all the grunts and Haitians.

In one day, all the squatters were gone. At gunpoint, I ordered the Haitian Port Captain to leave and not return. Also at gunpoint, I ordered the Director-General of the Port/Customs to leave. When he refused, I had two guys in cammies with M-16s physically throw his butt out of the building. He never returned.

See, all those years of watching westerns while on patrol, I did learn something, Pilgrim.

None of the Army brass had ever worked with an ex-Navy officer, much less a Mustang. The Army guys loved me. I loved the Haitian people. I had been there twice before on mission trips and knew the educated Haitians were dirtbags who took advantage of the uneducated Haitians. Uneducated is relative; I had to laugh. Most of these *uneducated* Haitians spoke at least three languages.

The port at Port-au-Prince was one giant urinal, gross and foul-smelling. We used Army divers and a 240-ton floating crane to lift the sunken vessels until the main deck was about two inches above the waterline. We used gas-powered pumps to de-water each ship. The divers covered holes where water was being sucked in. No one claimed any of the vessels, so I had the tugs take the ships out to a reef and set them high and dry with the crane.

Working with the Army, around the port perimeter, we laid a double layer of containers on the bottom with another double layer on top of those. The Army set up their watch stations and sandbag machine-gun areas on this artificial breakwater. Someone either at the UN or State Department told the Army to be prepared for another Somalia. I knew that was not correct, and at our first combined meeting with all the players, I told them so. The UN Rep did not take kindly to my advice. He wasn't aware how many Brown & Root people had been in Somalia. They agreed with me. Haitian people love Americans and America.

A few weeks later, I learned that each Army diver had become extremely ill and evacuated to Walter Reed for treatment. Something from the water.

The project manager and assistant project manager were both retired Army Colonels. Each day before our evening meeting, I typed a report detailing what we had accomplished that day and what we expected to accomplish the next. I gave them my estimate of when we could bring in the first ships to start offloading equipment.

At the end of the first week, I received a retroactive promotion and pay raise. When I notified them that we would bring in the first ship two days early and invited them down to watch it come in and moor, that was all it took. I received another pay raise. To me, none of this was a big deal. No one else had a clue how to do anything that involved water. I loved that job, the people I worked with, the men who worked for me, and the Haitians. We had former military, like me, take complete control of the international airport.

Then my world came tumbling down.

OMG

One morning at 0530, my assistant and I were up on a barge to oversee unloading. It was a grain barge with shipping containers on top and other materials inside. I don't remember any of this happening but was told later. The crane picked up a container at the opposite end from us. That released all the torque from the cargo that had shifted during transit. By the time it rumbled down to us, I was thrown off the container and did a flip in the air.

I fell eighteen feet, landing on a thick steel-reinforced deck. My long bones survived just fine. How I landed destroyed my lumbar, crushing L-3, 4, and 5. They compressed my spinal cord as hard as possible without severing it. Most of that area has been repaired and fused. I broke my neck from C-3 to C-7; that area has been fused. I also suffered a severe concussion that lasted for two years. When that went away, I was diagnosed with a *closed head injury* on the back left quadrant of my head.

As a result of this *closed head injury*, I have no common sense, lost all math capability, have limited reading comprehension, can't spell, don't drive, and many other things I can't remember. I lost my short-term memory, back to two years before I retired. All my testing shows my vocabulary is college level, and I'm in the fourth grade in the other areas. I worked on the fourth-grade final test for three days, an hour each day, and flunked. I really am not smarter than a fifth-grader. Those two little invisible people who stand on each shoulder and control what you say—the little red one with horns has a louder voice now.

I look the same and talk the same, and most people would not know anything was wrong. You would have to be around me for about a week before you would start noticing things. I am 100 percent disabled and will never work again. The most technical I get is changing the batteries in the remote; I usually mess that up. I take two pills a day to keep me from killing people. The brain is a strange critter.

That was November 1994. During the first ten years, I had eight back surgeries and one neck surgery. I lost the use of my left leg and right arm. I had four and one-half years of one-on-one intensive physical therapy and had to learn to write again. Some of my PT was done at the University of Miami's Comprehensive Pain and Recovery Center. It took me seven months to relearn how to send emails again. I suffer from chronic pain. In church, I sit on the front row to keep my left leg out and not trip people. I sit a lot when others stand because my left leg will go numb if I stand too long.

I have never asked God why, but only, "What do you want me to do?" I traveled with Dr. Bill Darnell and taught people how to share Jesus, but I had to travel with a friend; otherwise, I would get lost in the airports going and coming.

I didn't drive for over sixteen years because there was too much information coming in for me to process. Thank God for spell and grammar checkers. At church, I served as a Deacon where I could, and when I did, I sucked up the pain, put on a smile, and carried on.

It was not an easy life for Dee because she had to listen to my moans and groans and watch me when I began hurting badly. I have my bottle of little blue friends that will knock me on my rear and put me to sleep. I try not to use them unless as a last resort. I get headaches equivalent to getting shot in the head with a nail gun loaded with 20-penny nails. Ye-haa buck-a-roo. Fortunately, most headaches only last five to ten seconds, and I've gotten used to them and hardly flinch now. They used to bring me to my knees but not anymore. They are just one of many minor electrical storms in my body.

So, when I smile and tell you I'm doing fine, don't believe it for one second. I do not request any special attention because of my disabilities, and I enjoy visiting people in the hospital. I know how important it is for those lying in bed wondering if anyone even cares.

God is good, and I love Him more today than ever. He didn't have to kick me off the shipping container, however. A postcard would have done just fine.

Other than that, Mrs. Lincoln, how was the play?

THE AFTERMATH

The previous material was written years ago. I was forced to start driving again in 2010. Dee came down with Limbic Encephalitis (look it up) two weeks after returning from a Russia, Romania, and Hungary Concert tour. She was *my* guardian, and now, I am *hers*. She had an early stage-one spot of cancer on her left kidney. Once her kidney was removed, her memory started returning. As of today, March 30, 2021, her short-term memory is around ten seconds—very similar to Alzheimer's but not terminal.

I'm married but do not have a wife. I am not allowed to touch her, or she goes berserk. Even a hug is out of the question. When I walk into a room where she is, she is startled and lets out a yell. We have been through the *for better* part, and now we are in the *for worse* part. My number one purpose in life is caring for her. For now, my number two is typing my stories.

My pain level finally got the best of me, and I had to stop attending church—just too painful to sit for twenty minutes.

I told the Preacher, "If I get up one Sunday and start shouting and jumping around, don't think it is your sermon. It would be nerves in my lower back going crazy." He thought that was funny.

My neurologist said I need more surgery to lower my pain level, and I said, "No thanks, I've had enough." I force myself to do outside work. What I used to accomplish outside in ninety minutes takes three days now.

I finally downloaded *Grammarly Pro* to correct my stories, spelling, and other things. Otherwise, you would not have been able to read any of my ramblings.

I do the best I can, but it is not easy. Getting old is hard enough, but getting old the way I am, is even more challenging.

That is my story, and I'm sticking to it.

UPDATE

Ninety-nine percent of my pain disappeared around December 1, 2019. After twenty-five years of suffering from chronic pain, I finally have relief. I didn't do anything, and neither did my doctors. I guess God felt I had suffered enough.

This whole project started out as stories I wanted to share with my friends, shipmates, and especially my grandchildren. As you can see, it has evolved into a book of over 300 pages that is much more than just a bunch of sea stories.

You have accompanied me through thirty years of hijinks, shenanigans, triumphs, and even frustrations and failures. I trust I have convinced you that I played the cards I was dealt to the best of my ability. If you think I was dealt a couple of sh*tty hands at the end, I wouldn't disagree with you, but I hope I've been able to show you that adversity presents challenges—the greater the adversity, the greater the challenge.

Some of you have shared part of this journey with me. I will always be grateful for that. Those of you fresh out of the starting gate, learn from my experiences, good and bad. You could do a lot worse. And those of you who never knew me, you sure as hell do now! I hope you got a laugh or two along the way, and that you will carry some of me and my friends with you on your own journey.

✸

Je suis prêt (I am ready).

Please Post A Review For
Sŭbmarine-ĕr

I really appreciate you posting a review on <u>Amazon</u> and <u>Goodreads</u>. Good reviews are a writer's lifeblood. Posting to <u>Amazon.com</u> is intuitive. To post a review on <u>Goodreads.com</u>, click on this link or go to their website, and become a member if you are not already one. Search for *SŬBMARIN-ĔR: 30 Years of Hijinks & Keeping the Fleet Afloat*, and click on the "Want to read" button under the image of the book. Indicate that you have read it, and then you will be able to post a review. Thank you very much for going through this effort!

About Jerry Pait

Lieutenant Commander Gerald L. Pait was born in Hamlet, North Carolina, in May 1946. He was a self-described free-range kid living in a small rural railroad town where everyone knew everyone. He joined the Navy right out of high school and found himself on the open bridge of a diesel submarine in a north Atlantic storm several months later. Before he completed his thirty-year career, Jerry worked his way up to leading sonar technician on his diesel sub and then graduated to nukes where he ultimately became Chief-of-the-Boat before being awarded a commission for his outstanding service. Ashore, he managed test missile launches for the entire east coast submarine fleet and coordinated NASA's down-range space shuttle launch recovery efforts, climbing to the rank of Lieutenant Commander before he finally retired to a civilian position where he continued to serve the Navy's and NASA's needs.

A train wreck took the life of Jerry's father in 1966. Cancer took his younger brother. His mother remained mentally alert for ninety-nine years and six months until she passed away in 2018. His older sister is still doing fine. You know all about Jerry's full life, having absorbed the fascinating volume you hold in your hands. At this stage, Jerry takes care of his wife, Dee, enjoys his grandchildren, and continues to write.

Glossary For *Sŭbmarine-ër*

1348—DD Form 1348-1A—The most important requisition document.

1MC—Ship's announcing system.

1SQ— Condition 1SQ. Short for "One status quo," which means the submarine is ready to launch its missiles. In Navy jargon, 4SQ means the lowest level of alertness for missile launch, essentially, a submarine is back at its base.

A-Gang/A-Ganger—The submarine division that manufactures and stores oxygen, removes carbon dioxide, carbon monoxide, and hydrocarbons from breathable air; maintains and tests emergency diesel engines, watertight doors and hatches, and mast and antenna hoists; repairs and replaces on-board equipment such as valves, filters, pumps, compressors, and hydraulic and pneumatic devices; operates and repairs refrigeration systems and water desalination plants; and maintains air conditioning systems and galley equipment.

AGI—A Soviet "fishing trawler" equipped with sophisticated sensors and communication equipment to observe (spy on) practice firings of modern weapons and record the acoustic and/or electromagnetic signature of the sonar, search radar, fire-control radar, guidance, and/or command electronics of each weapons system. The United States Navy officially designated these trawlers as Auxiliary, General Intelligence or *AGI*, and informally known as "tattletales."

Accommodation ladder—A portable flight of steps down a ship's side. Can be mounted parallel or perpendicular to the ship's board. If the ladder is parallel to the ship, it has an upper platform that is normally turnable. The lower platform (or the ladder itself) hangs on a bail and can be lifted as required. Has handrails on both sides for safety. Are constructed so that the steps are horizontal, whatever the angle of inclination of the ladder.

ADCAP torpedoes—Advanced Capability torpedoes. Heavyweight submarine-launched torpedoes, designed to sink deep-diving nuclear-powered submarines and high-performance surface ships.

Airdale—Any sailor who flies or has anything directly to do with flying. Doesn't have to be a pilot. Aircrew also.

ARO—Assistant Repair Officer.

ASR—Submarine rescue ship (Auxiliary Submarine Rescue)—Ships specially designed to rescue crews from downed submarines. They originally carried McCann Rescue Bells. Later, two catamaran ASRs (the *USS Ortolan* (ASR-22) and *USS Pigeon* (ASR-21)) carried the *DSRVs*.

ASW—Anti-submarine warfare.

ATF—Automatic Tracking Feature. Allows sonar tracking equipment to lock onto a target.

AUTEC—Atlantic Undersea Test and Evaluation Center. A laboratory that performs integrated three-dimensional hydrospace trajectory measurements covering the entire spectrum of undersea simulated warfare—calibration, classifications, detection, and destruction.

Baffles—The area in the water directly behind a submarine or ship through which a hull-mounted sonar cannot hear. This blind spot is caused by the noise of the vessel's machinery, propulsion system, and propellers.

Ballast Control/Ballast Control Panel (BCP)—The station from which water is pumped into and out of a sub, and distributed fore and aft in the sub. The *Chief-of-the-Watch* occupies this position, under the control of the *Diving Officer* or the *OOD*.

Beam—The width of a ship at its widest point.

Benjo ditch—An Oriental toilet. Little more than a ditch in which you deposit your waste.

Bluenose Certificate—Commemorates crossing into the Arctic Circle (66-32 north latitude).

Boat—Slang term for submarine. Officially, all modern nuclear subs are called *ships*, but in practice, most submariners call them *boats*.

Boomer— Fleet Ballistic Missile Submarine.

BOQ—Bachelor Officers' Quarters.

Bottom—Bottom of the ocean, the seafloor. As a verb as in *to bottom*, putting the submarine on the seafloor.

BQC—The emergency underwater telephone, usually called the *Gertrude*.

BQH—Bathythermograph recorder—measures water temperature against depth.

BQR-2—Passive sonar system.

BQS-4—Active sonar system.

Bow—Front of a ship or sub.

Bridge—The place on a ship from which it is driven. On a sub, it is the conning station at the top of the sail. (See *Conn.*)

Broken arrow—An accident involving a nuclear weapon, warhead, or nuclear component.

Brow—Gangway onto a vessel from the pier or another vessel.

BTR—Bearing Time Recorder.

Capstan—A revolving cylinder with a vertical axis used for hauling in a rope or cable.

Captain—The officer in command of the ship or sub. He is an absolute dictator, subject only to the Uniform Code of Military Justice and the orders of his superiors in the chain of command.

Captain's Mast—A procedure whereby the *CO* inquires into the facts surrounding minor offenses, gives the accused a hearing as to such offenses, and then dismisses the charges, imposes punishment, or refers the case to a court-martial.

CCAFS—Cape Canaveral Air Force Station.

Chain fall (on rollers)—A chain fall is a block and tackle (set of pulleys) using chain instead of rope or line. The "chain fall on rollers" in Chapter 4 was a 1-ton block and tackle hanging from an overhead track, swinging heavy chain around while unsecured during heavy seas.

Chief-of-the-Boat—COB; the senior enlisted man on a submarine who serves as advisor to the commanding officer and executive officer. When a new enlisted sailor joins a *boat's* crew, the *COB* is usually one of the first people the new sailor will meet.

Chief-of-the-Watch—COW; the enlisted *watchstander* (usually a chief petty officer) who sits at the *BCP* and controls the ship's load of ballast water and its distribution throughout the submarine. The *COW* is also the senior *watchstander* for all the non-engineering spaces.

CIC—Combat Information Center. The tactical command center for most U.S. Navy ships.

CINCLANTFLT—Commander-in-Chief, Naval Fleet Atlantic; the commander of all naval forces in the Atlantic.

Clear the baffles—A submarine tracking another submarine can take advantage of its quarry's *baffles* to follow at a close distance without being detected. Periodically, a submarine will perform a maneuver called clearing the *baffles*. The *boat* will turn left or right far enough to listen with the sonar for a few minutes in the area that was previously blocked by the *baffles*.

Cleat—A T-shaped piece of metal or wood, especially on a *boat* or ship, to which ropes are attached.

CNO—Chief of Naval Operations.

CO—Commanding Officer.

Coastwatchers—Also known as the Coast Watch Organization, Combined Field Intelligence Service, or Section C of the Allied

Intelligence Bureau, were Allied military intelligence operatives stationed on remote Pacific islands during World War II to observe enemy movements and rescue stranded Allied personnel.

COB—see *Chief-of-the-Boat*.

Column—(water column) All the water above and below.

COMSUBLANT—Commander, Submarine Force Atlantic; the commander of all submarine forces in the Atlantic.

COMSURFLANT—Commander, Surface Force Atlantic; the commander of all surface forces in the Atlantic.

Conn—(1) The *Conning Tower*, the location from which the sub is controlled by the *OOD* (Officer-of-the-Deck). (2) The Conning Officer (Conn), the watch position for the person who controls the sub's direction, speed, and depth. The *OOD* usually has both the Deck and Conn, but can pass off the Conn to another qualified officer. Sometimes the *Captain* will assume the Deck, leaving the Conn with the officer *watchstander*.

Conning Tower—A small watertight compartment located in the sail of a diesel submarine above the *Control Room*. This is where the *Conning Officer* uses periscopes for navigation and directing the sub in battle, and where the *helmsman* steers the sub.

Control Room—The operating center of a submarine where the *dive planes* are controlled and the sub's *ballast control* is managed.

COW—see *Chief-of-the-Watch*.

DASO—Demonstration and Shakedown Operation, actually, a submerged *SLBM* launch.

Deck—The watch position of *OOD* (*Officer-of-the-Deck*); the person-in-charge of the sub when the *Captain* is not in the *Control Room* or has not assumed the *Deck* while in the *Control Room*.

Ditch, The—The Suez Canal.

Dive Planes—Horizontal control surfaces near the *bow* and *stern* that allow the sub's depth and angle to be controlled. They are operated from the *Control Room*.

Diving Officer—The officer or specially qualified Chief Petty Officer controlling the submarine depth. Works directly under the *OOD*. The *COW* works directly for the Diving Officer.

DIW—Dead in the water; a ship that is not moving through the water.

Dolphins—The insignia worn by qualified submariners, silver for enlisted, and gold for officers. It represents about a year of hard study to gain complete, detailed knowledge of the submarine.

DSRV—Deep Submergence Rescue Vehicle, carried by the catamaran *ASRs* or specially designated mother subs. They could attach to a downed submarine in salvageable waters and rescue survivors.

EB—Electric Boat Division of General Dynamics.

EM Club—Enlisted Men's Club.

Emergency surface—Dumping high pressure into the *main ballast tanks* at a high rate, causing the submarine to surface very quickly.

Eng—Engineering Officer.

Engineering-Officer-of-the-Watch—*EOW*; the individual on watch who operates the powerplant.

EOW—See *Engineering-Officer-of-the-Watch*.

ESL—Equipment status log.

Executive Officer (XO)—Second in command of a ship or sub. Responsible for ship's administration and personnel.

Fallboard—An annual anti-submarine warfare exercise

Fast-attack—See *Nuke fast-attack*.

FBM—*Fleet Ballistic Missile Submarine—SSBN*.

FBM good deal—A sarcastic comment on the things that often happen on *FBMs*.

Fish—A torpedo.

Fleet Ballistic Missile Submarine—*SSBN*.

Floe—See *Ice floe*.

GMV-16 diesels—Diesel engines used on diesel subs.

Goat Locker—A berthing area on the sub which is reserved for the exclusive use of chief petty officers.

Hawser—Heavy line used to moor subs and other vessels.

Head valve, head valve cycling—The large diesel air intake valve in the snorkel. When washed over by a wave, it shuts temporarily to keep water out of the ship.

Heaving line—Also *messenger line*. A light line, often with a *monkey fist* at one end, used to haul or support a larger cable.

Hell Ships—Ships used by the Imperial Japanese Navy and Imperial Japanese Army to transport Allied prisoners of war (POWs) and romushas (Asian forced slave laborers) out of the Dutch East Indies, the Philippines, Hong Kong and Singapore in World War II. These POWs were taken to the Japanese Islands, Formosa, Manchukuo, Korea, the Moluccas, Sumatra, Burma, or Siam to be used as forced labor.

Helm/Helmsman—Ship's wheel and steering mechanisms. The person manning the helm.

HT—Hull Technician.

Ice floe—A floating piece of consolidated sea ice typically at least 20 yards across and often miles long.

JOOD—Junior-Officer-of-the-Deck; the individual (usually an *OOD* in training) who works directly for the *OOD*. The JOOD is responsible only to the *OOD*.

K-19—The submarine K-19 was one of the first two Soviet *SSNs* containing missiles with nuclear warheads. K-19 suffered from poor workmanship and was accident-prone. On its initial voyage on 4 July 1961, she suffered a complete loss of coolant to one of its two reactors. A backup system included in the design was not installed, so the *Captain* ordered members of the engineering crew to find a solution to avoid a nuclear meltdown. Sacrificing their own lives, the engineering crew jury-rigged a secondary coolant system while working in a high radiation area, and kept the reactor from a meltdown.

Key West grouper—Also known as "square grouper." Slang terms for illegal drugs packaged into waterproof blocks and towed behind contraband speed boats.

Lie to—A ship comes almost to a stop with its head into the wind.

Line officer—A Navy officer who exercises general command authority and is eligible for operational command positions.

LDO—Limited duty officer. A Navy officer who is selected for commissioning based on skill and expertise. They are the primary manpower source for technically specific billets. They are experts and leaders in the technical specialty enlisted rates from which they came.

Liberty Ship—A class of cargo ship built in the United States during World War II. Though British in concept, the design was adopted by the United States for its simple, low-cost construction. Mass-produced on an unprecedented scale, the *Liberty Ship* came to symbolize U.S. wartime industrial output.

LPH—Landing Platform Helicopter, an amphibious warfare ship designed primarily to operate as a launch and recovery platform for helicopters and other *VTOL* aircraft.

LPO—Leading Petty Officer.

Main ballast tanks—Saddle-shaped tanks that fit around a submarine's hull near the *bow* and *stern*. They are open to the sea at the bottom and have large valves at the top. When the valves are opened, water quickly fills the ballast tanks causing the submarine to submerge. Air entering the tanks forces water out through the bottom openings, bringing the submarine to the surface. Dumping high pressure into the main ballast tanks at a high rate causes the submarine to *emergency surface*.

Maneuvering Room—That part of a sub where the engines are directly controlled.

Maneuvering Watch—The special set of watch assignments for a sub or ship that is getting underway.

Messenger line—A light line, often with a *monkey fist* at one end, used to haul or support a larger cable.

Mike boat—(Landing Craft Mechanized, Mark 8 or LCM-8). Refers to the military phonetic alphabet, LCM being "Lima Charlie Mike."

Missed movement—When a service member misses the movement of a ship, aircraft, or unit.

Momsen lungs—An early type of submarine escape hood.

Monkey fist—A type of knot, so named because it looks somewhat like a small, bunched fist/paw (also called *monkey paw*). It is tied to the end of a rope to serve as a weight, making it easier to throw. Also, an ornamental knot.

MOVREP—Ship's Movement Report.

Nav—Depending on context, the ship's/sub's Navigator; or the navigation stand—typically near the *Conn*.

NESEP—Navy Enlisted Scientific Education Program.

North Sail—A diesel submarine sail with the *Bridge* at the top of the sail instead of at an intermediate level as in the *Step Sail*.

NOTU—Naval Ordnance Test Unit.

NR-1—Deep Submergence Vessel *NR-1*, a Navy engineering and research submarine, was the smallest nuclear submarine ever put into operation. Her missions included search, object recovery, geological survey, oceanographic research, and installation and maintenance of underwater equipment. *NR-1* had the unique capability to remain at one site and completely map or search an area with a high degree of accuracy.

Nuke—(1) A nuclear-powered submarine. (2) A nuclear-qualified sub-crew member who works with the nuclear reactor and associated equipment.

Nuke fast-attack—A nuclear *fast-attack* submarine—*SSN*; a hunter-killer submarine.

OOD—Officer-of-the-Deck; the individual in charge of the ship or submarine at any given moment. The OOD is responsible only to the *Captain.*

Ops—Operations Officer.

P3—The Lockheed P-3 Orion, a four-engine turboprop, anti-submarine and maritime surveillance aircraft developed for the United States Navy and introduced in the 1960s.

PCAN—Port Canaveral.

PCS—Permanent Change of Station.

PI—Philippine Islands.

Planesman—A sailor who operates the planes on a submarine.

PMA—Production Management Assistant

PMS—Planned maintenance system.

Port—Left.

Prairie Masker—A two-part system of small bubbles generated by warships and some diesel subs. The Masker consisted of perforated strips alongside the machinery spaces that emitted small bubbles to minimize sound from transmitting away from the vessel. The Prairie consisted of small holes in the trailing edges of the propeller blades that emitted small bubbles to mask propeller noise.

Propay—Proficiency pay.

Radio Shack—That part of a sub or surface ship that houses the radio equipment, where the Radiomen stand their watches. Usually close to the *Bridge/Conn.* Often abbreviated as *Radio.*

Range ship—A tracking ship, also called a missile range instrumentation ship. Is equipped with antennas and electronics to support the launching and tracking of missiles and rockets. Since many missile ranges launch over ocean areas for safety reasons, range ships are used to extend the range of shore-based tracking facilities.

Ratings—General Navy enlisted occupations since the 18th century, which denote the specific skills and abilities of the sailor.

R-C-H—Slang for a very small measurement.

REFTRA—Refresher training.

Ripple fire—A mode of firing missiles in rapid succession.

S&G—Sh*ts and giggles.

Sea Daddy—A senior enlisted man who acts as a guide to a junior, showing him the ropes and guiding his early career.

Sea Pup—A junior officer who is guided by an experienced Chief.

Seamen Gang—The non-rated E-2s and E-3s under control of the *COB*. They handle lines, maintain topside, and stand topside watches in port and stand lookout, plans, and helm watches underway.

Secure—Stop or finish a process, such as "Secure from *Maneuvering Watch*," or when used as a verb, to make something safe, as in "secure the lines in the locker."

Shellback—A person who "crosses the line" of the equator and who has participated in a line-crossing ceremony. A Golden Shellback has crossed the equator at the International Date Line. The Order of the Emerald Shellback is for crossing the equator at the Prime Meridian. The Ebony Shellback is for crossing the equator on Lake Victoria, and a Top Secret Shellback is a submariner who crossed the equator at a "classified" degree of longitude.

Skimmer—A surface ship, or officers/crew of same. Frequently modified with the adjective "f*cking" by members of the submarine community. Also referred to as a "target" by submariners.

SLBM—Submarine-Launched Ballistic Missile.

Sonar Shack—That part of a sub or surface ship that houses the sonar display equipment, where the sonar techs stand their watches. Usually close to the *Bridge/Conn*. Often abbreviated as *Sonar*.

Sound-powered phone—A shipboard communication system powered only by the sound of the speaker's voice.

SP-205—Strategic Systems Project Office.

Springboard—An annual anti-submarine warfare exercise.

SSBN—*Fleet Ballistic Missile Submarine* (*Boomer*).

SSN—Nuclear *Fast Attack* Submarine.

Starboard—Right.

Steinke hoods—An early type of submarine escape hood.

Step Sail—A diesel submarine sail where the *Bridge* is located between the *deck* and top of the sail.

Stern—Back of a ship or sub.

SUBDEVGRU—Submarine Development Group. A special organization in the Navy that conducts submarine experimental work and carries out intelligence gathering activities.

SubLant—Short form of *COMSUBLANT*.

Submarine Escape Training Tower—A facility used for training submariners in methods of emergency escape from a disabled submarine underwater. It is a deep tank filled with water with at least one underwater entrance at depth simulating an airlock in a submarine.

Sub tender—Submarine tender. A ship that enables repairs for ships and submarines docked alongside the tender. It carries parts, equipment, and staff to conduct those repairs in specialized shops such as welding, carpentry, fabrication, sheet metal work, and machining.

SurfLant— Short form of *COMSURFLANT.*

T-boat—Training submarine.

TDU—Trash Disposal Unit.

Thermocline—A thin but distinct layer in a large body of fluid in which temperature changes more drastically with depth than it does in the layers above or below. In the ocean, the thermocline divides the upper mixed layer from the calm deep water below. In the open ocean, the thermocline can be important in submarine warfare because it can reflect active sonar and other acoustic signals.

TM—Torpedoman.

Topside—The outside *deck* of a submarine. Can also refer to the watch station at the top of the sail when a sub is underway.

UDT—Underwater Demolition Teams, predecessors of the Navy's current SEAL teams.

VTOL—Vertical Take-Off and Landing aircraft.

Watchbill—A list of a ship's company divided into watches.

Watchstander—A person assigned to a specific role for a period of time to ensure that responsibility is covered at all times.

Weps—Weapons Officer.

Wog—Short for "pollywog," as in "wog ceremony." A wog refers to someone who has not crossed the equator.

WTF—What the f*ck? Also WTF, over?

XO—*Executive Officer* (See *Executive Officer*).

Acknowledgments

Mrs. Lina Bauersfeld, my 12th grade English teacher. As the rest of the class stuck to the curriculum, she allowed me to write stories about my adventures. She introduced me to creative writing.

To all the men in the Submarine Service, especially the chiefs, COBs, and officers whom I admired for their leadership and ability not to waste time while teaching and training others.

To my father, who, by his actions, taught me everything not to do to be a good husband and father.

To retired Navy Capt. George Jackson for his insightful comments and delightful foreword, and to Prof. John Rosenman and SciFi author Alastair Mayer for their thoughtful pointers.

To family and friends who laughed at my stories and made helpful suggestions.

And finally, to my story compiler and editor, my old shipmate Robert Williscroft and his patient wife, Jill, who corrected countless typos and grammar errors, fixed my punctuation, and turned my meanderings into the beautiful book you hold in your hands.

Of course, any remaining shortcomings are entirely my own. That's my story, and I'm sticking to it!

Jerry Pait
Merritt Island, Florida
June 2022

Fresh Ink Group

Independent Multi-media Publisher

Fresh Ink Group / Push Pull Press
Voice of Indie / GeezWriter

❧

Hardcovers
Softcovers
All Ebook Formats
Audiobooks
Podcasts
Worldwide Distribution

❧

Indie Author Services
Book Development, Editing, Proofing
Graphic/Cover Design
Video/Trailer Production
Website Creation
Social Media Marketing
Writing Contests
Writers' Blogs

❧

Authors
Editors
Artists
Experts
Professionals

❧

FreshInkGroup.com
info@FreshInkGroup.com
Twitter: @FreshInkGroup
Facebook.com/FreshInkGroup
LinkedIn: Fresh Ink Group

Fresh Ink Group
Guntersville

Saturation Dive Team Officer-in-Charge (OIC) Mac McDowell faces his greatest challenge yet, leading the team into a critical Cold War mission. With a security clearance above Top Secret, Mac and his off-the-books deep-water espionage group must gather Russian intel to avert world war. Join nuclear-submariner Mac as he extreme-dives to a thousand feet, battles giant squids, and proves what brave men can achieve under real pressure, the kind that will steal your air and crush the life out of you. *Operation Ivy Bells: A Mac McDowell Mission* updates the popular bestseller by Robert G. Williscroft, a lifelong adventurer who blends his own experiences with real events to craft a military thriller that will take your breath away.

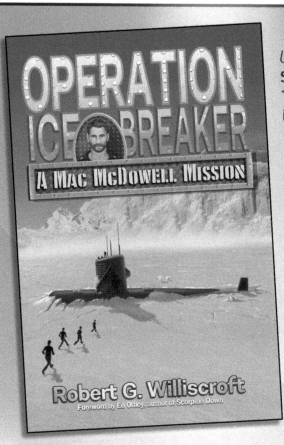

As *USS Teuthis* Saturation Dive Team Officer-in-Charge (OIC) Mac McDowell leads his submarine team laying SOSUS arrays under the Arctic ice, they capture an abandoned fully automated Alfa-class Soviet sub. Piloting their prize through the ice pack to the U.S. East Coast, they must evade or confront other Soviet subs trying to recover the sub—or sink it. Breathtaking deep-sea clashes erupt, including hand-to-hand combat with Soviet Morskoy Spetsnaz divers under the ice. Too far from *Teuthis* to escape, the Americans are accosted by a 5-ton orca. Will Mac's ship survive long enough to reach friendly waters, or will the men become just another meal for a deadly whale?

Hardcover, Softcover,

All Ebooks, Audiobook

Fresh Ink Group
FreshInkGroup.com

Ingram Content Group UK Ltd.
Milton Keynes UK
UKHW021823130423
420127UK00013B/1008